THE BEST OF
FRENCH COOKING

THE BEST OF
FRENCH COOKING

THE EDITORS OF MARIE CLAIRE

McGraw-Hill Book Company
New York   St. Louis   San Francisco
Hamburg   Mexico   Toronto

The publishers would like to thank Vicky Hayward for her work on the recipe
introductions and Ralph Hancock for his work on The French Larder,
Stephen Hayward, Susie Durbidge and Jeremy Round for their help with the
manuscript, The Covent Garden Fishmongers, Endell Street, for their advice
on fish, Odile Charbonneau for her organizational skill, and all the many
willing hands who helped at the books' various stages of production, especially
Emma Callery. Last and by no means least, we would like to thank all the
chefs who have generously allowed to use their original, and often previously
unpublished, recipes.

First published in 1988 by Conran Octopus Limited,
37 Shelton Street, Covent Garden, London, WC2H 9HN.

Copyright © Marie Claire 1987, 1986, 1985, 1984, 1983,
1982, 1981, 1980, 1979, 1978.

Copyright © English translation Marie Claire and Conran Octopus Limited 1988.

Translated by Ros Schwarz

First McGraw-Hill edition 1988

1 2 3 4 5 6 7 8 9   87

ISBN 0-07-011110-3

Compiled, researched and edited by Vicky Hayward
Cookery consultant for Marie Claire: Jacqueline Saulnier
Further research and editing by Ralph Hancock and Norma MacMillan
Editorial assistants: Jane Harcus and Lucy Russell
Designed by Caroline Langton and Pam Drewitt-Smith
Production controller: Michel Blake

Library of Congress Cataloging-in-Publication Data
The Best of French Cooking / by editors of Marie Claire.
    p.   cm.
    ISBN 0-07-011110-3
    1. Cookery, French.   I. Marie Claire.
TX719.B423 1988
641.5944—dc19   87-26064
                                             CIP

Printed in Hong Kong

CONTENTS

INTRODUCTION

French cooking, despite its very traditional basis, is constantly changing. Sometimes these new approaches win all our attention; at other times conservatism blinkers us. *Marie Claire* tries to strike a balance; while welcoming and reflecting innovation, we do not ignore the charms of the past. It is this sense of balance which has given our cooking its reputation and distinctive personality.

The themes that have run through the monthly articles of the last ten years stand out clearly in this book. One is the work of our dedicated chefs, some of them young – among them the Bocuses, Guérards and Chapels of the future – and others well-established, although they may never have won great fame or fortune. Meeting these chefs, watching them work, and talking to them at length about technique, sources of inspiration, and ideas for home cooking has been one of the greatest pleasures and privileges of my work.

Another theme has been the promotion of good quality produce (such as free-range chickens) and ingredients that have been neglected (such as freshwater fish) or are making their appearance in the stores and markets for the first time. Some of these, especially herbs and spices, reflect the impact of colonial cooking. We are also, of course, aware that the gourmet of the late twentieth century, the working man and woman, increasingly wants to enjoy the pleasures of eating without the constraints of too much tedious preparation or the consequences of badly controlled nutrition.

Food photography, too, can reflect an innovative attitude. *Marie Claire* has always been a *creuset* – a crucible – of talent, where countless great photographers and designers have trained and worked. In the late seventies we wanted to move beyond showing the presentation of a finished dish and began to introduce a new style developed with one particular photographer, Jean-Louis Bloch-Lainé. So we zoomed in very close on the colors and shapes of the food, showing the ingredients cooked to perfection and exactly as they should look. The visual impact of the first photographs, printed over full pages to accentuate the effect, was quite a shock – as it was intended to be. Soon they won acclaim; critics said they were *extraordinaire*, and captured the taste, smell and texture of the food.

These reflections of new influences and attitudes have been balanced by an appreciation of tradition. When I first joined *Marie Claire* in 1970, I was sent to the provinces to do a series on the cooking of *"la France profonde"*, translated in culinary terms, "this is everyday food as it is cooked and eaten in French homes." Ideas came from every possible source: village cooks, *petits* and *grands* restaurants, old cookbooks, conversations with farmers and the like. These articles, which were published with their original photographs by Robert Freson in *A Taste of France*, introduced an approach that still threads its way through *Marie Claire*'s cookery pages: authentic recipes and traditional preparation methods – simplified and made with less fat and flour, but taking few short cuts and preserving all the essential flavors.

Moderation between old and new, past and future, has become central to post-nouvelle French cooking. Today there is a dual trend: on the one hand, a return to the roots of culinary art – a respect for, and return to, traditional methods and dishes – and on the other, an increasing reliance on food processors, ready-prepared ingredients of higher quality than ever before and new forms of cooking – steam, *sous-vide* and microwave. Happily, there is also a far wider acceptance of the idea that the quality of a dish can never rise above that of its ingredients.

I hope that this book proves that *Marie Claire*'s sense of balance between innovation and tradition can be as exciting and satisfying as the best French food.

Jacqueline Saulnier.

THE FRENCH LARDER

Asterisks * in the recipes refer readers to this section

apples The French grow many excellent varieties of apple for the domestic market. Several recipes in this book originally specified Reinette or Boscop, both of which are solid, sharp apples similar to Newtown Pippin or Rhode Island Greening. The French never use the type of apples which disintegrate when cooked.

aspic Savory jelly made from meat, poultry or fish in gelatin stock rich enough to set when cold. You can use canned consommé set with unflavored gelatin for dishes in which the flavor is not too prominent.

bacon This is always very fatty, whether smoked (*lard fumé*) or salted (*lard salé*), and mainly used as a source of fat in recipes. American sliced or slab bacon may be used in recipes calling for smoked bacon; salt pork should be used where salted, unsmoked bacon is required. See also **lardons** and *couenne*.

beer There are both pale and dark French and Belgian beers. Unless stated in the recipe, use a pale lager. For a *carbonnade de boeuf* a dark brown beer is needed; the nearest equivalent is a dark ale.

biscottes Toast-like rusks, eaten at breakfast and for snacks and useful as a bread-based thickener. Available in some specialty food stores. You can substitute white bread dried in a slow oven until golden or Melba toast.

bouquet garni A classic version consists of a few parsley stems, a sprig of thyme and a bay leaf, tied together with string or in a cheesecloth bag and removed after cooking. Celery or fennel leaves, garlic or a little tarragon are sometimes added. For other, more particular *bouquets garnis* see pages 62, 125 and 130.

brioche Rich, semi-sweet yeast cake sold by bakers specializing in Continental items. Substitute light, semi-sweet bread.

butter French cooks use both unsalted and slightly salted butter; recipes state which to use if it is important. Avoid heavily salted, strong tasting butter for all recipes.

cane sugar syrup (*sirop de sucre de canne*) This syrup, which comes from the first boiling when sugar is extracted from sugar cane, is commonly called light molasses in the US.

Cantal See cheeses.

cendré See cheeses.

cèpes See mushrooms.

chanterelles See mushrooms.

cheeses Some of the cheeses used as ingredients in the recipes are easy to find, others only at specialist shops. These substitutes are suggested for the particular recipes in this book only. Cantal is a hardish pale cheese, mild and slightly sour when young, becoming more nutty with age; substitute a good Cheddar. *Cendré* is a generic name for cheeses coated in wood ash. There are various types, mostly of cow's milk; no exact substitute but any sharp-flavored cheese will do at a pinch. Chaource is a mild, soft cheese, high in fat; substitute a similar creamy cheese like Neufchâtel. Comté resembles Gruyère, which may be used as a substitute. Coulommiers is of the same type as Chaource. *Fromage blanc*, a fresh white cheese, is widely used in French cooking; substitute any mild white cheese, such as farmer's or pot cheese but not cottage cheese, which is too lumpy. In France *fromage blanc* is available with different fat contents, expressed as a percentage. Laguiole is hard, similar to Cantal but stronger and flavored with herbs; substitute Gruyère or a herbed Cheddar-type cheese. Mimolette is a cheese close to Gouda; use this (preferably a mature one) as a substitute. Pont l'Evêque is quite widely available, but blander semi-soft cheeses such as Port-Salut can be substituted if it is not available. Tomme is a semi-soft, mild cheese which comes in various forms. White Tomme is fairly easy to find; substitute Cantal.

chestnut purée The widely available canned purées, unsweetened or sweetened (choose the appropriate kind), are a good substitute for a fresh purée. This is laborious; cook by boiling gently until soft, then peel and purée.

Comté See cheeses.

confit d'oie Preserved goose, made by cutting

up the goose, poaching it in goose fat and sealing it in jars, protected by a top layer of fat. There is no substitute, but if it is unavailable when preparing cassoulet, make up the deficit with a piece of roast duck or pork.

couenne Pork skin with the underlying fat. In France, salted *couenne* can be bought, but fresh is always preferable. It can be taken from a pork roast, or obtained from a good butcher.

Coulommiers See cheeses.

crème fleurette Slightly sweetened *crème fraîche*, used in both sweet and savory recipes. Add 3 tablespoons sugar to 2½ cups *crème fraîche*.

crème fraîche French slightly cultured cream; obtainable in some specialty food stores. Make by heating until lukewarm 2 parts heavy cream with 1 part buttermilk, sour cream or plain yogurt (which must contain

the active bacteria culture to cause the fermentation). Half cover and leave at room temperature for about 6 hours, or until it thickens, then cover well and keep chilled. The flavor will slowly become more acidic over a period of days.

crépine Caul – or *crépine* – is the thin, fatty membrane with a network of thicker strands, which encases pigs' intestines and is used as a wrapping for ground meat dishes, charcuterie etc. Available from some butchers. French *crépine* is often salted and has to be blanched in boiling water before use. There is no real substitute, but in certain recipes you can use very thinly sliced unsmoked bacon. Foil or lettuce leaves may also be substituted in baked dishes. In the recipe for white sausage (*boudin blanc*), wide sausage casing is perfectly satisfactory.

dandelion leaves See salad greens.

eau-de-vie General French term for various white alcohols, often rather rough; some are flavored with fruit or herbs. Large liquor stores will probably have a few kinds of *eau-de-vie*. To some extent, one fruit flavored spirit can be substituted for another.

Framboise – raspberry *eau-de-vie*, not the same as *crème de framboise*, which is a sweet raspberry liqueur – is one of the most delicate, as is Poire Williams, made from pears. *Alcohol au genièvre* (juniper alcohol) is a coarser product; substitute Dutch (not English) gin, or vodka with a few juniper berries. Kirsch, made from cherry pits (and quite different from cherry brandy), is widely used in French cooking. Since it is very expensive to buy use kirsch *de cuisine* (cooking kirsch), it is of good quality but lower alcoholic strength. Marc is a rough spirit made from grape skins and seeds left over from wine making. Italian *grappa* is similar and may be used instead; many liquor stores sell this. Otherwise, substitute cheap brandy which has had raisins soaked in it.

escarole See salad greens.

feuille de chêne See salad greens.

fines herbes Mixture of parsley, chervil, chives and tarragon (go easy on the tarragon).

flour Use ordinary all-purpose flour for pie pastry, pâtisserie and cakes. French cooks sometimes lighten these by replacing some of the flour with a more delicate product such as potato flour. This is mentioned in appropriate recipes. Use strong bread flour for breads.

foie gras Fatty goose liver made by force-feeding geese; its very expensive products, mainly specialties of Strasbourg and Périgord, may be found in specialty food stores. Pâté de foie gras is not a substitute for the fresh liver.

fromage blanc See cheeses.

garlic Fresh young garlic has a milder taste than dry old garlic, so use more. The flavor of garlic is strengthened and changed by exposure to air before cooking, which is why some recipes specify that it should not be peeled, or should be cooked whole.

gelatin French gelatin comes in leaves (*feuilles*) weighing ⅕ oz. Powdered unflavored gelatin is slightly stronger, weight for weight.

goose fat In France *graisse d'oie* is sold in cans. It may also be taken from the top of a jar of *confit d'oie* (seen above). It may be prepared simply by rendering (boiling down) the fat of a fresh goose. Pull out the loose fat from inside the goose, chop it roughly, simmer with a little water in a covered pan for 20 minutes, uncover and boil slowly to evaporate the water. When the fat stops spluttering, strain it into a sterilized jar. It will keep for at least a month in the refrigerator. Any fat can be used as a substitute but real goose fat does have a unique flavor.

harissa North African hot paste, made from chili and sweet peppers, peppercorns, garlic and tomatoes. Available from Middle Eastern grocers. It can be made from powdered chili,

paprika, tomato paste etc.; or just use a little powdered chili.

hazelnut oil Excellent flavor. Cans of *huile de noisettes grillées* are available from specialty food stores, but are expensive. Substitute

olive, or other vegetable oil, but you will miss the flavor.

jambon cru Raw ham. There are many kinds, smoked and unsmoked; the mildly smoked kind from Bayonne is well known and quite easy to find. Substitute Italian *prosciutto crudo*. Cooked ham is not a good substitute, even in cooked dishes.

juniper alcohol See *eau-de-vie*.

Laguiole See cheeses.

lardons Strips of fatty bacon threaded into meat with a special larding needle to prevent the dryness.

9

lemon grass *(citronelle)* A grass with a lemony flavor; sold fresh, dried or powdered (careful with the powder, it is very strong) at Southeast Asian and some Indian food shops. Substitute a strip of fresh lemon zest.

lemons These are normally sold sprayed with a chemical to suppress mold. Where the rind is to be grated, the French recipes specify untreated lemons. These are hard to get elsewhere, but you can remove at least some of the chemical by washing the lemon in soapy water.

lemons, pickled Much used in Middle

Eastern cooking, but not difficult to make. See the recipe on page 174.

liqueurs Apart from well-known brands, recipes in this book specify black currant *(crème de cassis)*, raspberry *(crème de framboise)* and strawberry *(crème de fraise)*. Good liquor stores will have these. If unavailable, substitute another sweet liqueur. Walnut liqueur *(liqueur de noix)* is hard to find and very expensive, but you can make your own by steeping green walnuts in brandy with sugar for several months, shaking occasionally; or substitute a brown, round-flavored liqueur such as Bénédictine or Drambuie.

marc See *eau-de-vie.*

Mimolette See cheeses.

morels See mushrooms.

mushrooms Many recipes use ordinary cultivated mushrooms, but where more flavor is needed, wild or dried mushrooms, or a mixture of kinds are often called for. You may be able to buy fresh oyster mushrooms, *pleurotes,* which have a meaty flavor, or fresh *shiitake,* very full flavored and expensive, in

bigger supermarkets. Chanterelles, *girolles,* attractive yellow, trumpet shaped funghi, tasty but rather tough, are also sometimes on sale. Morels, *morilles,* which have a fine flavor grow under oak and apple trees all over the US, and can be bought dried in cans. You may also be able to find canned *cèpes* (strong flavor), but these are more widely available dried, often under their Italian name, *funghi porcini,* or their German one, *Steinpilze.* Some recipes call for "horn-of-plenty" mushrooms, *trompettes des morts,* hard to buy but common in woodlands in fall and easy to identify because they are black and trumpet shaped; in France they are often used for faking

truffles. Ordinary cultivated mushrooms can be made more interesting by adding a few dried *cèpes* or dried *shiitake* (look for dark caps with lighter cracks all over), soaked in water for 30 minutes before use.

mustards It should be easy to find at least the basic types: strong, pale Dijon-style mustard; mild, which is less strong (e.g. Bornibus); and Meaux mustard with whole crushed grains. Mustard may also be flavored, for example with green peppercorns *(moutarde au poivre vert),* lime *(moutarde au citron vert).* Good delicatessens will have at least the basic kinds; the others can be improvised by adding flavorings.

oil Oils may be flavored. For chili oil, use 5 split chili peppers, preferably dried, with their seeds, or more to taste, per quart of oil. For garlic oil, use a similar number of whole, unpeeled cloves. If using fresh ingredients, heat the oil with the ingredients in it in a bath of boiling water for 30 minutes. Leave several weeks before using. See also hazelnut, olive and walnut oils.

olive oil The best quality is "extra-virgin" from the first, cold pressing: *huile d'olive*

extra-vierge première pression à froid. It is usually greenish and slightly cloudy, and tastes strongly of olives. Later pressings, extracted with steam, have less flavor, and the final pressings, extracted with solvents, are so dirty that they have to be completely deodorized. Always use a good, flavorful olive oil. Inferior kinds are a waste of money: peanut and other good vegetable oils are cheaper and better.

olives *(olives)* Much used in southern French dishes. There are innumerable types from many countries. Green olives are picked unripe and are more bitter than ripe black ones. Flavor is quite independent of size. Olives can be kept immersed in vegetable oil, to which they give a pleasant flavor so that it can be used afterwards.

onions Large, white Spanish and Bermuda onions have a mild, sweet flavor; use them unless otherwise specified. Purple or red onions, sometimes called Italian onions, are mild in flavor and are particularly attractive when sliced. Some recipes call for fresh onions with green stems; if these are unavailable use a Spanish onion and a couple of scallions.

orange zest, dried A common flavoring in Provençal cooking. Make *zeste d'orange sec* yourself by drying strips of rind (including pith, best from Seville oranges) in the sun or a very low oven. Store in a jar in a cool, dark place.

parsley Use Italian or flat-leafed parsley wherever possible as it has more flavor. With any parsley the stems have a stronger flavor and should never be thrown away as they are excellent in a *bouquet garni* (see above), or as a bed for baked fish.

peppercorns *(poivre)* Apart from ordinary black and white pepper, unripe, milder flavored green pepper *(poivre vert)* is sold canned in brine or dry. Pink pepper *(poivre rosé)* comes from a different plant. It has a sharp tang, but lacks the depth of flavor of true pepper. Two of the real reasons for its popularity are its attractive color and simple novelty. It should be used in moderation, because it is slightly poisonous.

pistou A Provençal sauce made from garlic, basil, tomato, cheese and olive oil; actually a French adaptation (name and all) of Genoese pesto, with tomatoes. Both are often added to soups. See the recipe on page 89.

poitrine roulée Pork belly rolled up and cured raw. Hard to find; substitute the more widely sold Italian *coppa di Parma,* or any raw ham. Both of these are leaner and less "streaky."

potatoes Most French potato recipes call for waxy potatoes which maintain their shape when cooked. Round-white or round-red "boiling" potatoes are suitable for use here. Some recipes in this book do require starchy "baking" potatoes; this is stated.

10

Pont l'Evêque See cheeses.

poudre à colombo French West Indian mixed spice similar to mild curry powder. Hard to find. Use mild curry powder as a substitute.

praline Crunchy sugared nut mixture. Roast ⅔ cups hazelnuts (filberts) in a dry pan over a medium heat, rolling around, until brown. Let cool, then rub off the skins. Put three tablespoons sugar in the pan, and heat gently until melted and lightly caramelized. Add the nuts, stir to coat and tip onto an oiled tray. When cool, smash it.

purslane (*pourpier*) See salad greens.

quatre-épices Common French mixed spice powder. If unavailable, make your own from equal amounts of ground black pepper and ginger, and half that amount of ground cloves and nutmeg. Buy or make only a little at a time, as it needs to be fresh.

rouille See the recipe on page 37.

salad greens (*salades*) Dandelion leaves (*feuilles de pisenlit*): French greengrocers sell forced dandelion leaves, grown in the dark to blanch them and reduce bitterness. Wild dandelion leaves are good until the end of April, when they become coarse and bitter. Pick the whole clump and discard the outer leaves. Escarole (*scarole*) is a semi-curly endive, available during the cool months. Substitute curly endive (chicory) or crisp lettuce. Red-leaf lettuce, with its purple-red crinkly leaves and red-tipped leaf lettuce can be substituted for the decorative French *feuille de chêne* (oak-leafed) lettuce. Purslane (*pourpier*) is sometimes sold by specialist food shops which sell fresh produce, or by gourmet greengrocers. The nearest substitute is watercress. Radicchio (*trévis*) is a red, bitter variety of chicory, now easily found in good supermarkets.

salt Some recipes call for coarse cooking salt (*sel gris*) or sea salt (*sel de mer*). Both, especially the second, are stronger tasting than ordinary salt and slightly bitter; use up to half the usual amount.

samphire (*pousse-pierre*) Wild seaside plant found on flat coastal land and at estuaries. It is now foraged commercially and exported from France and may occasionally be bought fresh in specialty fish markets. There is no real substitute for its tangy, salty taste.

shallots Small brown bulbs of the onion family with a rounder taste than onions. The best, but not very good, substitute is a mild Spanish onion blanched in boiling water for 3 minutes to tone down the flavor. French chefs prefer *echalotes grises* (literally gray shallots though actually they are violet), but these are very hard to find outside France.

stocks (*bouillons, consommés, fonds,* etc.) See the recipes – meat and poultry (pages 39 and 100), fish and shellfish (pages 33 and 62) or vegetables (page 76) – and also aspic (page 40). There is also a general discussion of stocks for soups in the introduction to that chapter. The color of meat stock is determined by whether or not you roast the ingredients before making it (give the bones 30 minutes in a 450°F oven; add the vegetables for the last 10 minutes). White stock is made from chicken and veal without roasting.

sugar cane syrup See cane sugar syrup.

tomatoes French tomatoes are incomparably better than most American ones. In the US, it is often only possible to get round, woolly tasteless ones or the large, solid but almost equally tasteless beefsteak tomatoes. In recipes where tomatoes are cooked to a pulp, canned ones are actually better. Otherwise, look out for fresh Italian plum tomatoes or the flavorful cherry tomatoes, both of which can be grown at home.

Tomme See cheeses.

truffles Subterranean funghi. French cooks almost always use the black kind. The best truffles are fresh; they are also available in jars from gourmet food shops. Either way they are extremely expensive. Cheaper are truffle peelings, essence or juice, sold in cans; you can also get truffle-flavored oil. Truffles are often counterfeited with little bits of black "horn-of-plenty" mushrooms (*trompettes des morts*), with or without real truffle flavoring.

vadouvan A North African blend of spices and garlic, with a slightly hot but not harsh taste. Hard to find. If unavailable use garam masala, from an east Indian market, and add some garlic.

vanilla sugar This can be bought but it is easily made by keeping an unsplit vanilla bean in a jar of sugar.

verjuice *Verjus* is a vinegary bottled juice made from unripe grapes widely used in the cooking of south-west France. It is very difficult to buy it. If you can find unripe grapes, make your own. Press the grapes and pour the juice into clean bottles. Top with a little oil to exclude air, and cork. It will keep for 2-4 months in a dry, cool place. You can make it keep for longer by sterilizing the filled bottles in boiling water for 2 hours. Substitute tart apple juice or lemon juice.

vinegars It is easy for American cooks to imagine that all imported wine vinegar is good. Actually the difference between good and bad wine vinegar is immense: always use good, naturally prepared vinegar. Basic French types are made from white wine (*vinaigre de vin blanc*) or red wine (*vinaigre de vin rouge*). Vinegar is also made from other wines including sherry (*vinaigre au xeres*) and from cider (*vinaigre de cidre*), sometimes flavored with honey. There are many kinds of vinegar with added flavorings, and you can make these yourself: see recipes, page 14. You can also substitute plain wine vinegars. Store vinegar in a cool, dry, dark place.

walnut oil Excellent nutty flavor. Available under the name *huile de noix* from specialty food stores, but rather expensive. Any vegetable oil can be used as a substitute, but the flavor will be missed.

walnut liqueur See liqueurs.

walnut wine (*vin de noix*) A delicious sweet, dark red wine, hard to find outside France. Substitute port or Madeira wine.

SAUCES

SHALLOT SAUCE (see page 17)   VINAIGRETTE (see page 15)

FLAVORED VINEGARS

A wide range of flavored vinegars, especially fruit ones like raspberry and blueberry vinegar, have become available from fine grocers in recent years. It is worth experimenting with other flavors at home: green peppercorns, dill, mint, shallots and lemon, for example, all give interesting effects. Wine essences may be made along the same lines.

There is as much scope with oils: thyme for beef, tarragon and sage for poultry, fennel or rosemary for grilled fish, garlic for seasoning salads and casseroles (see page 12 for the basic method).

HERB AND PEPPER VINEGAR
Vinaigre aux herbes et poivre vert

3 large sprigs of tarragon
2 teaspoons dry green peppercorns
1 quart white wine vinegar

MAKES I QUART
PREPARATION TIME: IO MINUTES

Rinse a 1 quart wine bottle. Plunge the tarragon into boiling water for 2 seconds. Dry it immediately. Trim the sprigs so that they will fit upright into the bottle and push them in stem first. Crush the peppercorns lightly and add. Top up with vinegar.

Seal with a clean cork and store upright in a cool, dark place. Leave to infuse for 1 month.

SHALLOT AND ONION VINEGAR
Vinaigre aux échalotes et oignons

3 shallots*
1 whole scallion
2 small fresh onions with green stems
1 quart red wine vinegar, preferably aged

MAKES I QUART
PREPARATION TIME: IO MINUTES

Chop the vegetables and put them in a rinsed 1 quart wine bottle. Top up with vinegar, seal and store (see left) for 1 month or longer.
Variations: add 2 cloves of garlic, peeled and crushed with the back of a knife, and/or 3 or 4 chili peppers and a fresh bay leaf.

VINAIGRETTE

The classic French vinaigrette is made with red or white wine vinegar, a vegetable oil and seasoning. Although very simple to make, there are two important points – the salt must be fully dissolved before the oil is added and both the oil and vinegar must be of good quality.

This basic dressing is only a starting point. The bite of vinegar, so good with sweet tomatoes or cucumber, can swamp the lusciousness of a mild cheese or *foie gras* and kill a good wine. Lemon, lime or orange juice give a slightly sweeter tang (see opposite) and a fruit or vintage vinegar a mellower taste. Likewise, while a fruity olive oil is delicious with many dishes, it can be mixed with, or replaced by grapeseed, peanut or sunflower oil for a more neutral effect alongside delicate flavors. Mustard, added before the oil, gives a smooth dressing that is especially good with potatoes, celeriac or cauliflower.

HONEY AND LEMON JUICE DRESSING
Sauce vinaigrette au miel

1 small clove of garlic
salt and freshly ground black pepper
a tiny drop of honey
1 tablespoon lemon juice
1 tablespoon cider vinegar
2 tablespoons olive oil
2 tablespoons corn or peanut oil

SERVES 6
PREPARATION TIME: 5 MINUTES

Paul Corcellet's Parisian grocery, which is a gourmet landmark, stocks some twenty-five vinegars, the same number of mustards (including star anise, olive and anchovy) and nearly as many honeys. He suggests this mixture for leaf or romaine lettuce, Belgian endive, chicory and dandelion.

Rub the salad bowl all over with the halved clove of garlic. Put in the salt and the honey. Dissolve in the lemon juice and vinegar. Add the pepper. Pour in the two kinds of oil and whisk to combine all the ingredients evenly.

This dressing is less likely than a classic vinaigrette to clash with the taste of a good wine drunk with the meal. If you prefer, you can reduce or omit the cider vinegar for more mellowness.

YOGURT AND CREAM DRESSING
Sauce au yaourt et crème

finely grated zest of ¼ lemon★
a tiny drop of orange blossom or other honey
salt
pinch each of cayenne and white peppers
1 tablespoon white vinegar
2 tablespoons thick plain yogurt
1 tablespoon heavy cream
2 sprigs of chervil
1 sprig of flat-leafed parsley

SERVES 4-6
PREPARATION TIME: 10 MINUTES +
TIME TO REFRIGERATE

Salads made with this dressing are best served chilled. Refrigerate the salad leaves and the main ingredients for the dressing separately before mixing at the last minute, otherwise the lettuce will go limp.

Grate the lemon zest into the salad bowl on top of the honey, salt to taste and peppers. Add the vinegar and mix thoroughly before stirring in the yogurt and cream. Beat vigorously to make a smooth, light sauce. Put in the lettuce, toss lightly, and snip the herbs into the bowl with scissors. Serve at once.

This dressing is excellent with tender hearts of butterhead lettuce.

WALNUT AND ALMOND DRESSING
Sauce aux noix

4-6 shelled walnuts
salt
1 tablespoon wine vinegar
1 tablespoon walnut oil
2 tablespoons peanut oil
freshly ground white pepper
1 tablespoon slivered almonds

SERVES 4
PREPARATION TIME: 5 MINUTES

Coarsely hand crush the walnuts.

Dissolve the salt in the vinegar and add the two oils. Stir well or shake in a jar to combine into an emulsion. Add pepper, and the almonds and walnuts. Leave to marinate for a few minutes, and stir or shake again before using.

A good dressing for spinach.

CLASSIC VINAIGRETTE
Vinaigrette de base

1 tablespoon wine vinegar
pinch of salt
2½-3 tablespoons oil
coarsely ground black pepper

SERVES 4
PREPARATION TIME: 1 MINUTE

For a classic vinaigrette, use 1 tablespoon vinegar, in which the salt should be dissolved, to 2½ to 3 tablespoons oil. Add coarsely ground black pepper to taste. If prepared in advance, the dressing can be kept in the refrigerator.

SUBTLE COMBINATIONS

– Olive oil, vintage red wine and herb vinegar (for all kinds of green salad).
– Walnut oil (1 part), corn oil (2 parts) and lemon vinegar (for Belgian endive, spinach, romaine lettuce and chicory).
– Hazelnut oil★ and sunflower oil with an aromatic vinegar (for red-leaf or other lettuce, Belgian endive and purslane★).
– Olive and peanut oils with herb vinegar (for mixed green leaves and watercress).
– Peanut oil and cider vinegar with honey (for lettuce).
– Grapeseed oil and white wine vinegar with green peppercorns (for green salads with delicate dishes). A neutral flavored oil such as peanut, corn or sunflower with raspberry or blackberry vinegar (for romaine lettuce, spinach, or red-leaf lettuce).
– Olive oil and anchovy paste, but no vinegar (for Belgian endive, celery and chicory).
– Cold-pressed olive oil and lime mustard (for a potato salad dressed while the potatoes are still hot – as made at the Tour d'Argent, one of Paris's oldest restaurants).

SAUCES FOR GRILLED AND ROAST MEAT

These sauces for grilled and roast meat require no tricky techniques. French *jus de rôti* acquire their delicious taste by the boiling down of the cooking juices, which concentrates the flavor and gives them body. Butter, cream or alcohol are usually added at the end for a little richness and punch. If you are adding wine to any of these sauces, remember that it is usually better to boil it first to evaporate the alcohol: this reduces the sharpness with white wine and mellows the flavor with red wine. On the other hand, liqueurs or spirits with a volatile flavor, are best added at the last minute to preserve their taste.

TIPS FOR CORRECTING MEAT SAUCES

If the flavor seems bland: add a sharp ingredient to liven it up – a dash of lemon juice or a few drops of good quality red wine vinegar to draw out the character of the juices. Check the seasoning: you may need more salt.

If there is a bitter or even sour taste: add a pinch of sugar or a dash of sweet wine (such as port), and possibly a little *crème fraîche.*★

If the flavor lacks fullness: whisk in a few pieces of butter to draw out the taste.

If the gravy lacks body and/or color: add a little meat (or fish) glaze, a twist of the pepper mill and perhaps a splash of Armagnac or Cognac. Mustard provides flavor as well as body; fresh herbs, color and flavor.

SHALLOT SAUCE
Sauce échalote

3 shallots
7 tablespoons butter
1 tablespoon wine vinegar
2 tablespoons red wine
2 tablespoons olive oil
2 tablespoons finely chopped flat-
leafed parsley
salt and freshly ground black pepper

SERVES 6
PREPARATION TIME: 5 MINUTES
COOKING TIME: 10 MINUTES

Chop the shallots and soften them in the butter over a gentle heat for 5 minutes. Add the vinegar and the wine and reduce for 5 minutes. Then stir in the olive oil and parsley and season to taste.
Variation: For a slightly different sauce that is good with grilled steaks and chops, fry bacon gently and use the rendered fat to replace some of the butter.

TARRAGON SAUCE
Sauce estragon

5 oz (1¼ sticks) butter
2 tablespoons Meaux mustard
1 tablespoon chopped tarragon

SERVES 4
PREPARATION TIME: 1 MINUTE
COOKING TIME: 2 MINUTES

Melt the butter in a small saucepan, but do not let it brown at all. Add the mustard and tarragon. Serve with grilled meats.

CHASSEUR SAUCE
Sauce chasseur

5 oz wild or cultivated mushrooms
2 shallots
2½ tablespoons butter
scant ½ cup dry white wine such as
Pouilly
⅔ cup clear beef stock (see page 39)
2 tablespoons fresh tomato purée (see
page 26), or 2 tomatoes
salt and freshly ground black pepper
1 sprig each of chervil, tarragon and
flat-leafed parsley

MAKES ABOUT 1 CUP
PREPARATION TIME: 15 MINUTES
COOKING TIME: 30 MINUTES

Remove the earthy base of the mushroom stems. Wipe the mushrooms, then chop them. Chop the shallots very finely.

Melt half the butter in a heavy-based saucepan over a low heat. Add the mushrooms and shallots, and soften without browning. Add the white wine, and cook uncovered until the liquid is reduced by half.

Heat the stock and add it. Also add the fresh tomato purée, or two tomatoes peeled, deseeded and crushed. Season to taste.

Discard the stems of the herbs, and mix the chopped herbs with the rest of the butter.

Spoon a little of the cooking liquid, but no solids, into a small bowl and briskly beat in the herb butter. Add this to the sauce, stir and pour into a heated sauceboat.

ROASTING JUICES

The best roasting juices are usually found in home cooking: the professional chef tends to create elaborate sauces, which ruin the straightforward flavor and quality of juices or gravy. Meat, poultry, game or fish which have been roasted in the oven in a good-sized pan all leave juices at the bottom which can then be deglazed and reduced (see below) for delicious *jus de rôti*.

Before cooking a roast brush it with a mixture of half oil and half butter, 1 tablespoon of this mixture to each pound of meat. The reason for this is that oil can withstand higher temperatures than butter, and it slows the breaking down of the butter.

Preheat the oven before putting in the meat. After 10 minutes of cooking, baste the roast with the juice which has already been released, and turn it as soon as the top has browned. Repeat this operation several times. When cooking has finished, remove the roast and cover it. Check that the juices in the bottom of the pan have browned sufficiently, but make sure that they never turn black, which would make the sauce bitter. Partially skim with a spoon; about a quarter of the fat should be left, as this helps the sauce to thicken.

Deglaze the juices: add double the amount of hot water or light stock to the amount of gravy you wish to obtain and scrape the solidified juices from the bottom of the pan with a spoon so that they dissolve in the hot water. Boil until reduced by half, allowing 2 tablespoons of gravy per person. Correct the flavor (see left).

You can also brown in the pan with the roasting meat a few sawed-up veal bones for a veal or beef roast, a few lamb bones for a leg or rack of lamb, or a few chicken carcasses for poultry.

THICKENING SAUCES WITH CRÈME FRAÎCHE

A simple way of thickening sauces and gravies is to bring the roasting juices, or liquid base, and *crème fraîche* to a boil and reduce to obtain a consistency that is neither too creamy nor too thick. Many cooks wrongly think *crème fraîche* should not be boiled or it will curdle. This is not so. When it first begins to boil, it does go through a worrying stage: it becomes runny, rises to the surface and seems to separate. But this is normal. The cream then reconstitutes itself, reduces and reaches the desired smooth, thickened consistency.

To make a successful sauce, the *crème fraîche* should be of the best quality and absolutely fresh (it is quite easy to make at home – see page 9), otherwise it will not reduce well and will remain runny. The quantity of juices should not be much more than that of *crème fraîche*. If there is too much liquid, the cream will be "drowned" and won't be able to reduce. Don't stop the reduction too soon, otherwise the sauce will remain a sort of creamy stock. Don't overreduce or the cream will turn to butter and disintegrate and you will have a fatty, lumpy mixture which is thoroughly unpleasant.

Both of these sauces are particularly good with grilled, poached or plainly baked fish, or with poultry if you stir in the cooking juices.

CRÈME FRAÎCHE SAUCE
Sauce crème fraîche

1 cup *crème fraîche**
salt and freshly ground white pepper
juice of 1 lemon
chives

MAKES JUST OVER 1 CUP
PREPARATION TIME: 5 MINUTES
COOKING TIME: 10 MINUTES

Place the *crème fraîche* over a gentle heat. Season to taste and reduce until smooth and creamy. Add the lemon juice and chopped chives. If you have deglazed meat, poultry or fish juices, stir them in slowly with the lemon juice, which will give you a thinner, creamy sauce rather like a gravy.

Tarragon, chervil, chives or marjoram make a good addition to this sauce. You can mix the herbs, but do not use them all together. Each herb has its own taste and should be respected. A purée of watercress gives a delicious green sauce (see right).

CÈPE SAUCE
Sauce cèpes

10 oz fresh or canned *cèpes**, or 3½ oz dried *cèpes**
7 tablespoons butter
½ clove of garlic
scant 1 cup water or stock
1 cup *crème fraîche**
freshly ground black pepper
chopped parsley

SERVES 6
PREPARATION TIME: 5 MINUTES MIN
SOAKING FOR DRIED *cèpes*
COOKING TIME: 25 MINUTES

Many country French households gather and preserve their own cèpes, *fleshy mushrooms with a slightly nutty flavor. Dried* cèpes, *or Italian* porcini, *easily bought in specialty stores and delicatessens, are quickly revived by a few minutes of soaking in warm water or wine. They give sauces a delicious lift.*

If you are using dried *cèpes*, soak them, following the instructions on the package. Chop the mushrooms, and wilt them in the butter. Mince the garlic and add to the pan, together with the water

or stock. Simmer for 20 minutes over low heat. Stir a little of the liquid into the *crème fraîche* to thin it, then pour the mixture back into the pan. Add a little pepper and the parsley.

Of course, you can use fresh cultivated button mushrooms instead of *cèpes*. Since they do not have the same strength of flavor you might like to add wine with the stock.

CRÈME FRAÎCHE SAUCE▶

BÉCHAMEL

A béchamel sauce is one of the most basic elements in the classic French repertoire, not only as a master recipe for a family of sauces, but also as the basis for croquettes, soups, soufflés and other dishes. It is named after its inventor, a seventeenth-century financier who became chief steward of Louis XIV. In the early nineteenth century the recipe was brought to perfection by the famous chef Antoine Carème, widely regarded as the father of *grande cuisine*. Then, béchamel was often a richer sauce made with cream and white stock; today it is made only with milk, flour, and butter, seasonings and other flavorings.

For a good flavor, the milk should be infused with bay leaves, an onion stuck with cloves, parsley stems and peppercorns; the roux of melted butter and flour which thickens the sauce is cooked well so that there is no lingering taste of raw flour; finally, the sauce is beaten well as the milk is slowly added to give a smooth sauce with a glossy finish.

Mornay and velouté sauces are very close variations of béchamel. A Soubise sauce – named after the general who invented it – starts differently, but uses essentially the same method.

BÉCHAMEL SAUCE
Sauce Béchamel

7 tablespoons butter
9 tablespoons sifted flour
4 cups scalded milk, still hot
small pinch each of salt, cayenne pepper and grated nutmeg

MAKES 4 CUPS
PREPARATION TIME: 5 MINUTES
COOKING TIME: 15 MINUTES

Infusing the scalded milk with bay leaves, an onion stuck with cloves, parsley stems and peppercorns enormously improves the flavor of a béchamel sauce.

If it has to be kept for a while, trail a piece of very cold butter all over the surface, or cover with plastic wrap, to prevent any skin from forming.

Melt the butter in a heavy-based pan over a low heat. Tip in the flour all at once and stir continuously with a wooden spoon until the mixture becomes pale and frothy. It will take about 4 to 5 minutes over a low heat to produce a properly smooth, uncolored *roux*, as this mixture is called.

Remove the pan from the heat and pour in all the hot milk. Beat vigorously with a whisk to obtain a smooth, lump-free texture.

Put the pan back on a low heat, add salt, pepper and nutmeg (omit the last if the sauce is for a spicy dish), and cook for about 10 minutes, stirring constantly.

MORNAY SAUCE
Sauce mornay

4 cups of béchamel
1¼ cups grated Comté* or Emmental cheese
4 egg yolks from large eggs
2 tablespoons *crème fleurette**
salt and freshly ground white pepper

PREPARATION TIME: 10 MINUTES
COOKING TIME: 20 MINUTES

This exquisitely rich sauce can be used to coat fish and shellfish as well as vegetables, gratin dishes, and to top poached eggs and crêpes. If you are using it with poultry or seafood, it is a good idea to replace the cream with a little of the cooking liquid from the dish it is to accompany.

Take the pan of béchamel off the heat and stir in the grated cheese. When it is blended in smoothly, add the yolks one by one, beating hard with a wooden spoon.

Return the pan to a very low heat and, still stirring, bring barely to simmering point. Remove at once: if cooked any more the yolks will coagulate. Stir in the *crème fleurette* and season to taste with salt and white pepper.

For a lighter sauce, omit 1 or 2 egg yolks.

VELOUTÉ SAUCE
Sauce velouté

2 tablespoons butter
3½ tablespoons sifted flour
2 cups poultry or veal stock (see page 39) or fish fumet (see page 33)
1-2 tablespoons cream, according to taste
salt and freshly ground white pepper

MAKES 2 CUPS
PREPARATION TIME: 5 MINUTES
COOKING TIME: 30 MINUTES

Velouté is made from a base of sauce blanche – that is, béchamel made with stock instead of milk. It is enriched with a little cream.

Put a heavy-based pan over a low heat. Melt the butter and sprinkle in the flour gradually. Stir well with a wooden spoon until smooth, then leave to cook very slowly for 7 to 9 minutes. This roux should not be allowed to color so watch it carefully.

Let it cool slightly. Heat the stock or fumet, and pour it in gradually, whisking. Put the pan back on a low heat and simmer for 20 minutes, stirring occasionally.

Let the sauce cool slightly before adding the cream. Season.
Variation: for sauce aurore, add ⅔ cup fresh tomato purée (see page 26) to béchamel or velouté.

ONION CREAM SAUCE
Sauce Soubise

1 lb onions
6 tablespoons butter
¼ teaspoon salt
5 tablespoons flour
1½ cups milk
1½ cups light cream
salt and pepper
pinch of grated nutmeg
2 tablespoons softened butter

MAKES ABOUT I CUP
COOKING TIME: APPROX. 45 MINUTES

Finely slice the onions and sweat them in butter with the salt for 20 to 30 minutes in a covered heavy-based pan until well softened but not brown.

With the pan still over a low heat, stir in the flour. Keep stirring for 3 minutes while you scald the milk in another pan. Take the pan of sauce off the heat, and gradually stir in the milk.

Return to the heat and simmer, stirring occasionally, for 15 minutes. Purée the sauce in a blender and then return it to the pan. Bring it back to simmering point, and stir in the cream. Heat but do not let the sauce reach simmering point again. Season, add the nutmeg and, just before serving, stir in the butter, making sure it melts.

FLAVORED BUTTERS

The idea of flavored butter melting into a simple hot sauce over plain grilled meat and steaks – or boiled and steamed vegetables – is often overlooked. For herb butters, like tarragon, dill or the classic *beurre maître d'hôtel* (with parsley, lemon juice, salt and pepper), the herbs need to be very finely chopped. Alcohol can also be used. See, for example, the Calvados butter on page 63.

BUTTER WITH GREEN AND PINK PEPPERCORNS
Beurre aux deux poivres

½ level teaspoon green peppercorns
1 teaspoon pink peppercorns
salt
a little grated lime zest★
7 tablespoons butter

MAKES ABOUT ½ CUP
PREPARATION TIME: 5 MINUTES

This aromatic, peppery butter, from Charles Reynal of La Cremaillère restaurant in Brive-la-Gaillarde (see also page 126), is especially good with grilled steak or shellfish.

Grind or crush the green and pink peppercorns. Add salt to taste and a little grated lime zest. Work into the butter, then rub through a sieve and refrigerate until serving. The pepperiness of the flavor will depend on the fineness to which you crush the peppercorns. In any case, pink and green peppercorns are rarely overpowering.

COLD EMULSION SAUCES

Mayonnaise, that "beautiful shining golden ointment," as Elizabeth David calls it, is the best known of the emulsions. It has a certain mystique, but it is not difficult to make, providing that the eggs and oil are at room temperature and that you concentrate on adding the oil very gingerly, drop by drop, until the mayonnaise "catches" to make a smooth yellow cream with no beads of oil on the surface. Once the mayonnaise has caught, the oil can be added in a steady trickle and the sauce needs much less careful handling. Some very fruity olive oils give a flavor which is too dominant; if this is so, or it is not to your taste, it can be mixed with another, more bland vegetable oil.

MAYONNAISE
Sauce mayonnaise

2 egg yolks from large eggs
pinch of fine salt
large pinch of freshly ground white
pepper
1 teaspoon mustard powder
few drops plus 1 teaspoon lemon juice
or red wine vinegar
1¼ cups peanut oil

SERVES 4 WITH MOST DISHES
PREPARATION TIME: 15 MINUTES + 1
HOURS WAIT BEFOREHAND

The standard proportions for mayonnaise are scant ⅔ cup of oil for each egg yolk, but there are no hard and fast rules. Simply stop adding the oil when you have reached the consistency you want, remembering that the mayonnaise will become thicker and more buttery as the oil is added. It can be thinned along the

way or at the end for a creamier texture, with lukewarm water, lemon juice or a little wine. The idea of using a wooden spoon rather than a whisk, so that the sauce is begun more gently, comes from Paul Bocuse. Leave the eggs, the oil and the mixing bowl together in the kitchen for a good hour before you begin.

Put the yolks in the bowl and add the salt, pepper, mustard and few drops of lemon juice or vinegar. Mix well with a wooden spoon, then trickle in the oil in a very thin stream, stirring quickly until the mayonnaise doubles in volume and becomes thick (see above). Stir in a sparing teaspoon of lemon juice, which will help to keep the sauce from curdling.

Coating consistency: stir 1 tablespoon hot water into the finished mayonnaise.

Green mayonnaise: strip the leaves from a bunch of fresh tarragon or chervil, reserving one sprig. Tear out and discard the midribs of a generous handful of spinach. Wash, drain and dry the herb leaves and spinach.

Whirl them briefly in a blender and squeeze hard in a fine cloth over a bowl to extract as much juice as possible. Heat the bowl in a *bain-marie* (put it over a pan of simmering water) for 10 minutes, which will ensure a very bright green color.

Filter the liquid and add to the mayonnaise to color it. Chop the reserved herbs, and add them.

GARLIC MAYONNAISE
Sauce aïoli à la provençale

3 cloves of garlic with shoots
salt
1 hard-cooked and 2 raw egg yolks
from large eggs
1¼ cups extra virgin cold-pressed olive
oil
freshly ground white pepper
a trickle of pastis★ or lemon juice

MAKES 1½ CUPS
PREPARATION TIME: 15 MINUTES

This delicious garlicky mayonnaise, a relation of Catalan ail-o-oli (garlic and oil), can be served as "un grand aïoli," surrounded by plates of poached white fish – in Provence sometimes salt cod and squid – and a mixture of cooked vegetables – potatoes and sweet peppers, for example, served at room temperature.

Remove the shoots from the garlic if you prefer. Crush the garlic with a little salt in a mortar. When it is reduced to a pulp, add the hard-cooked egg yolk and crush, then stir in the 2 raw egg yolks one at a time. Beat as for a mayonnaise, adding the olive oil gradually. Add pepper to taste and a dash of pastis or lemon juice. This can be kept in the refrigerator in an airtight jar for a few days.

A milder version of this can be made with blanched, puréed garlic mashed with the yolks.

HOT EMULSION SAUCES

Hot emulsion sauces should ideally be served as soon as they are made, or may be kept warm for one hour over hot – not simmering – water. Essentially, a hollandaise is a hot mayonnaise, with butter replacing the oil, while béarnaise is a tangy hollandaise flavored with vinegar and shallot. *Beurre blanc* is the trickiest of all the emulsions because it lacks the stabilizer of egg yolk or mustard. The butter used in hot emulsions must be fresh to avoid it going oily.

HOLLANDAISE SAUCE
Sauce hollandaise

1 tablespoon water
2 egg yolks from large eggs
7 tablespoons butter

MAKES ABOUT ½ CUP
PREPARATION TIME: 2 MINUTES
COOKING TIME: 10 MINUTES

A recipe for a classic hollandaise to go with fish, eggs and asparagus from Jean Moussié, who was chef and owner of Bistro 121, a much loved Parisian family restaurant (see pages 128 and 194 for other recipes).

Add the water to the egg yolks, place over a very gentle heat indeed, or over a hot but not even simmering *bain-marie* (pan of hot water or double boiler). Whisk continuously to obtain a smooth cream.

Meanwhile, gently melt the butter in a separate pan. It is the whey that makes the sauce curdle, so when the butter is melted skim the white bits off the top and pour the clear butter slowly out of the pan into a bowl, leaving the watery whey in the bottom. Whisk the butter into the egg yolks a little at a time as for a mayonnaise.

To retrieve a separated hollandaise: if it has just begun to separate, a spoonful of cold water will often save it. If this fails, remove the oily film of butter, add another egg yolk and begin whisking all over again. The sauce will become smooth; add more fresh butter (never use the butter just skimmed off) and it should emulsify again.
Variation: for a mousseline, beat in 2 heaping tablespoons of whipped cream.

BÉARNAISE SAUCE
Sauce béarnaise

2 shallots
scant ½ cup wine vinegar
1 tablespoon chopped tarragon
2 tablespoons water
salt and freshly ground black pepper
2 egg yolks from large eggs
7 tablespoons butter

MAKES A LITTLE OVER ⅔ CUP
PREPARATION TIME: 15 MINUTES
COOKING TIME: 15 MINUTES

Because a béarnaise has a stronger flavor than a hollandaise, it is served with steaks as well as fish, eggs and asparagus. The recipe is from Gilbert le Coze (see below).

Chop the shallots. Simmer them in the vinegar, without letting them brown, until the vinegar is completely evaporated. Add the tarragon shortly before this point.

Remove the pan from the heat. Add the water, salt and pepper to taste and the egg yolks. Whisk vigorously until the mixture is frothy. Place over a very gentle heat. Whisk in the softened butter a small piece at a time. The sauce should become thick, and is now ready to serve. If it separates, try the remedies for hollandaise.

WHITE BUTTER SAUCE
Beurre blanc

3-4 shallots
scant ½ cup vinegar
scant 1 cup white wine
1¾ sticks fresh slightly salted butter
freshly ground black pepper

MAKES ABOUT 2 CUPS
PREPARATION TIME: 5 MINUTES
COOKING TIME: 20 MINUTES

Traditionally served with pike, this classic sauce from the Loire valley is now more often eaten with salmon, but it is equally good with other poached fish (see page 76). There are different versions – for example, some regions use salted and others unsalted butter (mildly salted tends to work better); some chefs add aromatics like peppercorns (see page 11) and Alain Senderens, one of France's leading chefs, even uses light beer to replace half the white wine vinegar.
Always keep the heat constant. If it drops, the sauce separates and becomes oily. This recipe comes from Gilbert le Coze, a Breton fish chef now working with his sister Magne in New York.

In a heavy-bottomed saucepan, simmer the chopped shallots in the vinegar and wine. When the liquid has evaporated whisk in a few small pieces of butter one at a time, adding another one only when the sauce has become creamy. (You can use cold butter for this initial stage, but the butter added later must be at room temperature.) Whisk vigorously, keeping the sauce over the heat.

Once the pieces of butter have melted, remove the saucepan from the heat and stir in the rest of the butter. The contents of the saucepan will be hot enough to emulsify it. Add pepper to taste.

The shallots may be left in the sauce, which enhances the flavor, but it is more usual to strain it.

TARTARE SAUCE
Sauce tartare

4 hard-cooked egg yolks from large eggs
1½ tablespoons pale Dijon-style mustard
¼ teaspoon salt
1 cup olive oil
1 tablespoon lemon juice or wine vinegar
3 tablespoons each chopped dill, pickle, capers and mixed flat-leafed parsley and chives
2-3 sieved hard-cooked egg whites (optional)

SERVES 4 WITH MOST DISHES
PREPARATION TIME: 15 MINUTES

A tartare sauce is something of a rogue among the emulsion sauces. It is made rather like a mayonnaise, but it uses the yolks of hard-cooked eggs. Some recipes suggest simply adding the herbs and other flavorings to a mayonnaise, but the hard-cooked yolks do add a subtly different flavor and texture. It is good served with fish and cold foods.
Make sure that the capers have been soaked well or the brine will kill the other flavors.

Mash the egg yolks with the mustard and salt until smooth.

Add the oil drop by drop, stirring constantly, as if making mayonnaise. When all the oil is amalgamated, gradually stir in the lemon juice, then the chopped cucumbers, capers, herbs and, if you wish, the egg whites.

◀WHITE BUTTER SAUCE

FRESH TOMATO SAUCES

A tomato sauce made with good sun-ripened tomatoes can never be replaced by one made with canned tomatoes or purées. Nevertheless, a spoonful of purchased tomato paste can be a useful addition if your tomatoes lack sweetness and flavor. Some cooks recommend adding a teaspoon of sugar, or, in the south-west of France and in Provence, a little orange zest. Of the two sauces here, the one with uncooked tomatoes gives a very fresh, clean taste and is particularly good with fish and vegetables or noodles; the fully cooked sauce is excellent with cold meats and poultry or as a soup base, and will keep for several months. Elsewhere in the book there are recipes for a tomato and wine sauce (page 164) and a spicy hot tomato sauce (page 90).

FRESH TOMATO PURÉE
Coulis de tomates crues

4½ lb tomatoes
3 white onions
1 clove of garlic
2 tablespoons olive oil
5-6 sprigs of flat-leafed parsley
3 leaves of mint
pared zest of 1 lemon*
3 tablespoons olive oil
salt and freshly ground black pepper

MAKES ABOUT 2 QUARTS
PREPARATION TIME: 30 MINUTES +
TIME TO COOL
COOKING TIME: 10 MINUTES

This recipe makes enough to be used for several recipes or stored for later use.

Put the tomatoes in a bowl, pour boiling water over them, and leave for 30 seconds; drain. Or put them under a broiler to char the skins. Peel them and remove the seeds.

Chop one of the onions and the garlic clove very finely. Soften them in the oil, without browning, in an enamel or heatproof glass pan over a very gentle heat, stirring from time to time. If you don't like the garlic flavor to be too strong, crush the clove without peeling it, add it to the onion and remove it later. Otherwise, peel, chop and add it in the usual way.

You can also remove the green shoot to make it less powerful.

Finely chop the parsley, mint, the other two onions and the lemon zest and put them in a bowl. Rub the peeled tomatoes through a sieve or pass them through a vegetable mill held directly above the bowl. Stir in the fried onion and garlic when they have cooled a little. Whisk in the oil. Add salt and pepper to taste.

To store leftover sauce, put it in a clean jar and cover it with at least ½ inch of olive oil. When you use the sauce, either mix the oil in or remove it and use it for other applications. It will have a delicious flavor.

THICK TOMATO SAUCE
Coulis de tomates

2 onions
1 small carrot
1 small stalk of celery
3 tablespoons olive oil
2¼ lb tomatoes
a few sprigs of flat-leafed parsley
1 clove of garlic
1 bay leaf
salt and freshly ground black pepper

MAKES ABOUT 1½ QUARTS
PREPARATION TIME: 10-20 MINUTES
COOKING TIME: 1 HOUR 10 MINUTES

Roughly chop the onions, carrot and celery. Soften in 1 tablespoon of olive oil. Deseed and coarsely chop the tomatoes, peeled or unpeeled depending on whether you want a strong taste or not, and add to the pan. Cook over a very high heat for 15 minutes, stirring occasionally.

Add the parsley, peeled garlic, bay leaf and remaining olive oil. After simmering over a low heat for 45 minutes, remove the garlic and bay leaf. Purée the sauce, then sieve out tomato skins if necessary and season well. Divide the sauce among sterilized canning jars, seal, and process in a bath of boiling water for 15 minutes. The sauce will keep for several months in unopened jars.

FRESH TOMATO PURÉE ▶

SOUPS

White Garlic Soup *30*
Onion Soup *30*
Michel Guérard's Herb and Vegetable Bouillon *31*
Cream of Asparagus *31*
Sorrel Soup with Curried Cream *32*
Green Lentil Soup with Port *32*
Croûtons *32*
Fish Fumet *33*
Sole Soup *34*
Mussel Soup with Saffron *34*
Provençal Fish Soup with Rouille *37*
Fish Soup from Sète *37*
Beef Bouillon *39*
Chicken Bouillon with Watercress and Mussels *39*
Clarified Consommé *39*
Fennel, Herb and Yogurt Soup *40*
Dodin-Bouffant's Crab Soup *40*
Meat Aspic *40*

SORREL SOUP WITH CURRIED
CREAM (see page 32)

FISH FUMET (see page 33)

VEGETABLE SOUPS

Now that blenders and food processors have replaced the old-fashioned wooden spoon and sieve or foodmill, there is an unhappy temptation to reduce all soups to a predictably even consistency at the flick of a switch. Yet one of the great qualities of soup with character should be a carefully judged texture. Here are six soups with very different textures: three of them light – a clear *bouillon* from Michel Guérard, a slightly thickened broth and traditional French onion soup – and three of them thick – a smooth *crème*, a green herby velouté and a thick lentil purée. The last two are both chefs' versions of old country recipes.

WHITE GARLIC SOUP
Tourin blanchi à l'ail

2 large onions
1 head of garlic
2 tablespoons goose fat★ (or butter)
pinch of flour
salt and freshly ground black pepper
4 cups chicken stock (see page 39)
few leaves of sorrel
4 thick slices stale bread
1 egg yolk from a large egg
2 teaspoons vinegar

SERVES 4 AS A FIRST COURSE
PREPARATION TIME: 20 MINUTES
COOKING TIME: 20 MINUTES

Tourin – *known also as* tourri *and* tourain *in different localities – is a surprisingly mellow garlic soup from the southwest of France. It is traditional to "faire Chabrot," that is, to add a little wine to the last spoonful of soup and drink it from the bowl.*

Chop the onions and garlic and brown them in the goose fat. As soon as the mixture is golden brown, add the flour, salt and pepper to taste.
Pour in the chicken stock. Bring to a boil and simmer for 10 minutes. Cut up the sorrel and add this. Dice the stale bread and put these in the soup tureen. Pour on the soup. In a separate bowl, combine the egg yolk and vinegar. Add a few tablespoons of soup, then stir the mixture into the tureen and serve piping hot.

ONION SOUP
Soupe à l'oignon

4 large, strong onions
4 tablespoons butter
1 teaspoon flour
4 cups beef or chicken stock (see page 39)
scant ½ cup dry Banyuls or port wine
salt and freshly ground black pepper
a little grated nutmeg
12 slices of French bread
1¾ cups grated Comté★ or Emmental cheese

SERVES 4
PREPARATION TIME: 10 MINUTES
COOKING TIME: ABOUT 45 MINUTES

A steaming earthenware marmite *of onion soup is a classic French bistro snack, especially at the end of an evening out or as a cure for a hangover! In fact, it has become something of a French culinary cliché, endlessly depicted sitting on a bistro table next to a bottle of red wine. But it is worth making properly, at home, too.*

Chop the onions finely. Heat the butter in a cast iron or other heavy-based pot. Put in the onions and gently soften them over a low heat until just beginning to color.
Sprinkle in the flour and stir constantly for 2 or 3 minutes, until the flour is slightly browned. Pour on the stock, cover and simmer gently for at least 30 minutes, Preheat the oven to 400°F.

Add the Banyuls or port wine, season to taste, grate in a little nutmeg and cook for another 5 minutes. Meanwhile, dry the slices of bread in the oven, then turn it up to maximum.
Divide the soup into 4 ovenproof bowls. Sprinkle in a little grated cheese, drop 3 slices of bread into each bowl, cover them with the rest of the cheese and put the bowls in the oven for 5 minutes to brown the top. If you want a very crisp top, heat the broiler, and give the soup 2 or 3 minutes of browning on top, watching to make sure it does not burn.

30

MICHEL GUÉRARD'S HERB AND VEGETABLE BOUILLON
Bouillon de petits légumes d'Eugénie

½ cup chicken stock (see page 39)
1½ inch piece of leek white
1 stalk of celery
2 small carrots (about 2 oz)
2 oz mushrooms
½ lemon
1 large ripe tomato
2 sprigs of flat-leafed parsley
2 sprigs of fresh chervil
1 sprig of fresh tarragon
ground white pepper
4 teaspoons *crème fraîche*★ (optional)
speck of grated nutmeg (optional)

SERVES 4 AS A FIRST COURSE
PREPARATION TIME: 20 MINUTES
COOKING TIME: 15 MINUTES

Michel Guérard was inspired to develop his world-famous cuisine minceur after he moved from Le Pot-au-Feu, in the suburbs of Paris, to Eugénie-les-Bains, the small spa town in the southwest of France where his wife came from. This soup, an aesthetic delight low in calories, typifies Guérard's minceur approach, and combines all the fragrances of the herb gardens there.

The chicken stock should be prepared in advance as for chicken consommé (see page 39), and strained and skimmed.

Cut the trimmed and cleaned leeks, celery and carrots into very fine julienne strips 1½ inch long and 1/10 inch wide or, if you have neither the time nor the patience, put them through a food processor or grate them. If you need to wash the mushrooms, give them time to dry. Use a stainless steel knife to slice them finely. Squeeze lemon juice over them immediately to prevent any discoloration.

Bring the chicken consommé to a boil and put in the vegetables, beginning with the leek and adding the mushrooms last. Simmer three-quarters covered for 15 minutes, or until the vegetables are just cooked but still retain their shape and color.

Meanwhile, peel, deseed and crush the tomato. Cut the herbs with scissors; do not chop them. Add the tomato to the simmering soup and turn off the heat. Sprinkle in a little pepper, but no salt because the stock is already salted. Serve at once sprinkled with herbs.

Michel Guérard likes to present the soup in four individual bowls. You can put in a dollop of *crème fraîche* and a hint of nutmeg if you wish. And you can add your own little variations, but be careful not to destroy the delicate aroma of this delicious soup by including anything with an overpowering flavor.

CREAM OF ASPARAGUS
Crème d'asperges

2¼ lb asparagus (you can use the bottom parts of the asparagus cut into pieces the size of a pea and a few green tips)
6 cups water with
1 chicken bouillon cube
1 egg yolk from a large egg
⅔ cup *crème fraîche*★
freshly ground white pepper
pinch of grated nutmeg
10 sprigs of chervil
croûtons★ (see page 32), to serve

SERVES 4 AS A FIRST COURSE
PREPARATION TIME: 20 MINUTES
COOKING TIME: 30 MINUTES

If there is any suspicion of bitterness, peel the asparagus for this soup or its flavor will be ruined. Of course, if you do have real chicken stock on hand, it is preferable to artificial stock. This soup is very good served cold, especially since it is thickened without flour; you will probably need to add extra seasoning.

Cut up the asparagus spears and cook them in the chicken stock for 30 minutes. Add the tips 10 minutes before the end. There is no need to add more salt as the stock is usually salty enough. Reserve the tips, then purée the rest in a blender or food processor. Rub the purée through a sieve. In a preheated soup tureen, combine the egg yolk and *crème fraîche*. Add a little pepper and nutmeg, and whisk in the purée. Add the still slightly crunchy asparagus tips, and sprinkle with chopped chervil.

Serve with little croûtons hot from the oven, but not toasted too much because their taste would overpower the delicate flavor of the asparagus. If you prefer fried croûtons, make sure all the excess oil is wiped off first. This soup should be light and delicate.
Variation: another subtle *crème* can be made on a base of chicken stock with 4 small zucchini, half a bulb of fennel, the white of a leek, plenty of fresh dill and cream beaten with an egg as a thickener.

SORREL SOUP WITH CURRIED CREAM
Velouté d'herbes gratiné au curry

3 cups oxtail stock (see pages 39 or 146)
5 egg yolks
1½ cups *crème fraîche**
freshly ground white pepper
5 oz sorrel leaves
2½ oz purslane* or watercress
7 tablespoons butter (at room temperature and broken up into small pieces)
pinch of curry powder

SERVES 4 AS A FIRST COURSE
PREPARATION TIME: 20 MINUTES
COOKING TIME: 18 MINUTES

PHOTOGRAPH ON PAGE 28

You would never guess that this creamy, smooth, refined soup is an adaptation of a fine old French country recipe for herb soup. Jacques Cagna, a chef working in Paris, whose restaurant is in a seventeenth-century house and who is an avid reader of old cook books, reinvented this light, subtle soup from old family recipes. The base of this soup is stock from oxtail cooked as for a pot-au-feu (meat and vegetable stew, see page 123) with vegetables and a bouquet garni. The stock is reduced and the fat skimmed off. You can use a ready-made stock base, but it won't taste the same. Note that the oxtail and vegetables can be eaten as a separate dish, either hot, or cold as part of a salad.

Heat the stock. Combine the egg yolks with 1¼ cups *crème fraîche* and a little white pepper. Stir into the stock as for custard and cook, without allowing the mixture to boil and stirring continuously with an up-and-down motion, folding in the egg mixture. French chefs call this technique *vanner*. The soup is ready when it coats the spoon.

Cut up the sorrel and purslane or watercress with scissors and wilt over a low heat in 2 tablespoons butter. Stir this into the soup and cook for a couple of minutes. The mixture should now be a lovely jade-green color. Beat in the rest of the butter.

Preheat the broiler. Whip the remaining *crème fraîche* until thick. Divide the soup among four bowls, filling them to the brim. Place a tablespoon of stiffly whipped cream on top of each one, sprinkle with a pinch of curry powder and place under the broiler for a few seconds. The heat will make the whipped cream spread, rise and turn golden. The soup is now ready: serve it at once.

GREEN LENTIL SOUP WITH PORT
Soupe aux lentilles vertes avec porte

1 onion
1 tablespoon butter
4 cups beef bouillon (see page 39)
¼ cup green lentils
dash of port wine
few sprigs of chervil

SERVES 4 AS A FIRST COURSE
PREPARATION TIME: 10 MINUTES
COOKING TIME: 25 MINUTES

Jean Paul Lacombe, who succeeded his father at the renowned Léon du Lyons, is known for highly imaginative new dishes and a light touch with classic Lyonnais cooking. This soup uses the renowned green lentils of Le Puy, sometimes called the caviar of the poor.

Finely chop the onion and sauté gently in the butter in a heavy-based saucepan. Pour on the beef bouillon, bring to a boil and then lower the heat until it is simmering. Add the lentils and cook till they are soft. Purée the soup in a blender, food processor or *mouli-légumes*, then add a dash of port wine and a sprinkling of chopped chervil.

CROÛTONS

These small triangles of fried or toasted bread are used mostly as a garnish for soup, to which they add an interestingly contrasting crunchiness. They are also a very good addition to salads.

Texture is all important: soggy croûtons are simply nasty. To stay crisp, they must be properly made from the right kind of bread. If possible, use French bread, or at least a superior white bread with real body and texture. Mass-produced flabby white bread will not make good croûtons. The bread can be slightly stale; this does not matter.

Cut it into ¼ inch slices, discard the crusts and cut little triangles no more than ¾ inch long. Sauté these slowly in a generous amount of clarified butter, turning, until golden.

Lighter croûtons can be made by dipping the bread in beaten egg white and cooking in a slow oven till golden. The egg makes the croûtons waterproof, so that they stay crisp even in soup.

FISH SOUPS

France boasts wonderful fish soups and stews. The fumets, bisques and veloutés served in Parisian restaurants tend to be light, sophisticated first courses, based on good stock and delicate fish.

Those which are eaten around the coast are, by contrast, often a meal in themselves, having evolved as cheap everyday food around the catches of the local fishing. From the northern coasts – *le pays du beurre* – come creamy Flemish *waterzooi* (see page 88), *caudière*, *marmite Dieppoise* and Breton *cotriade*. South of the Loire the spicing becomes stronger, the colors, aromas and flavors, more forceful: in the Charente and Morbihan region there is *chaudrée*, made with the local white wine and from the Basque country comes peppery *ttoro*. The Mediterranean coast – *le pays d'huile* – is the home of the best known of all the French fish soups – bouillabaisse – as well as *aïgo-sau*, *bourride* and many other more local soups. It is worth bearing in mind the spirit of these recipes and concentrate on the soups in which you can use a mixture of locally available, good fresh fish rather than trying to recreate authentic soups for which you need expensive, imported rarities. None of the fish called for here should be difficult to buy fresh from a good fish merchant or supermarket.

FISH FUMET
Fumet de poisson

2¼ lb fish heads and tails
1 large leek, including some of the green top
1 carrot
2 shallots
¼ lb button mushrooms
1 small clove of garlic
1 onion stuck with a clove
1 teaspoon olive oil
1 teaspoon butter
6 cups dry white wine
1 bouquet garni*
10 white peppercorns
sea salt

SERVES 4 AS A SOUP BASE, OR CAN BE USED TO COOK 1¼-1¾ LB FISH
PREPARATION TIME: 25 MINUTES
COOKING TIME: 35 MINUTES

PHOTOGRAPH ON PAGE 29

A fumet is a court bouillon (see page 76) to which fish trimmings and bones, heads and tails or even whole fish are added to boost the depth of flavor. It may then be used as a base for soups and sauces or on its own as a simple, quick soup with wine, pasta or tapioca added to it.

The cooking liquid may be water, white wine, hard cider or water with lemon juice or vinegar. Either the fish and vegetables are placed directly in the liquid or they are sautéed in oil or butter first to bring out their flavors. If you are using more than one type of fish, separate those with firm and those with delicate flesh; the delicate fish should be added only just before the end of the cooking time. A few shellfish may also be added at this point.

Peel and finely slice all the vegetables, except the garlic and onion. Mince the garlic and leave the onion whole.

Heat the oil and butter in a saucepan and put in all the fish heads and tails with all the vegetables except the onion and the bouquet garni. Leave to sweat over a medium heat for 5 minutes.

Moisten with the wine. Add the bouquet garni and the onion with its clove. Add water to cover the ingredients by about 1½ inches. Cover, turn down the heat and cook for 15 minutes.

Crush the peppercorns, tie up in a piece of cheesecloth and add to the liquid together with salt to taste. Cook for another 15 minutes.

Strain the stock through a fine sieve, without squeezing the ingredients, to obtain a clear stock. Alternatively, you can remove the peppercorns and press the ingredients through the sieve with the back of a wooden spoon, or put them through a food mill. Then strain the stock through a fine sieve, pressing it a little to produce a thick stock.

For other ideas on flavoring a fumet, see the suggestions given for the court bouillon on page 76.

33

SOLE SOUP
Soupe de soles

2 carrots
1 mild onion (or the white of a leek for a more subtle flavor)
¼ lb mushrooms
juice of 1 lemon
2 tablespoons slightly salted butter
6 good-sized fillets of sole, with the bones and trimmings
salt
1 teaspoon green peppercorns, crushed
6 cups clear fish fumet (page 33), made with dry white wine or hard cider
4 sprigs of chervil or flat-leafed parsley
pinch of grated nutmeg

SERVES 6 AS A FIRST COURSE
PREPARATION TIME: 15 MINUTES
COOKING TIME: 18-20 MINUTES

The sole fillets are very lightly poached just before the soup is served to preserve their delicate texture, but the soup may be prepared up to that point ahead of time.

Finely dice the carrots, and cut the onion into thin rings. Finely slice the mushrooms and pour lemon juice over them.

In a heavy pot, heat the butter until golden and put in the onion and carrots. Cook over a gentle heat for 5 minutes.

Put the sole bones and trimmings in a piece of cheesecloth and secure well. Add the mushrooms to the pan and cook for 5 minutes, until the juice begins to come out. Add salt to taste and the peppercorns, stir well and add the fumet. Put in the bag of fish trimmings. Once the mixture begins to simmer, cook 6 to 8 minutes more. Meanwhile chop the herbs.

Add the nutmeg and half the chopped chervil. Put in the sole fillets. As soon as the liquid begins to simmer again (but it is important not to let it boil), count 1 minute and no longer, then remove from the heat.

Discard the fish trimmings, add the rest of the chervil and serve immediately, accompanied by a dry hard cider or a light, fruity white wine.

MUSSEL SOUP WITH SAFFRON
Soupe de moules safranée

¾ lb bones from white fish such as sole and flounder (but not any of the oily fish, which would ruin the delicate flavor)
1 tablespoon olive oil
5 cups water
1 bouquet garni★
1 large carrot
2 onions
1 stalk of celery
3 lb mussels
2 teaspoons *crème fraîche*★
1 saffron thread
salt and freshly ground white pepper

SERVES 4-6 AS A FIRST COURSE
PREPARATION TIME: 15 MINUTES
COOKING TIME: ABOUT 1 HOUR

A great classic, this soup can be the best or the most ordinary of dishes. But here, Bernard Loiseau, the young and talented chef of La Côte d'Or restaurant in Saulieu, offers an entirely new recipe which has a subtle blend of seaside aromas. Saulieu is just south of Chablis, in Burgundy, on the route Napoléon, and has a long tradition as a place for eating well because of the number of coaching inns there when it was an important staging post.

Brown the fish bones for 5 minutes in half the oil. Then add the water to the pan, put in the bouquet garni, cover and simmer for 25 minutes.

Meanwhile, dice the vegetables and sauté for a few minutes on all sides in a wide saucepan with the rest of the oil until golden. Strain the fish stock through a fine sieve over the vegetables. Bring to a boil and simmer over a gentle heat for 15 to 20 minutes. Scrub the mussels, discarding any opened shells, then heat the mussels in a non-stick pan, shaking it so that the mussels open quickly and all at the same time. Discard the shells (and any mussels that remain closed), but reserve the juice, which should be strained and added to the stock. Put a few mussels in each soup plate. Stir the *crème fraîche* and the saffron into the soup, and taste and adjust the seasoning if necessary. Pour it over the mussels and serve.

SOLE SOUP▶

MEDITERRANEAN FISH SOUPS

Gertrude Stein made a good point when she wrote of bouillabaisse, "The fish should be more than fresh, it should be caught and cooked the same day." This is, of course, an ideal that is almost impossible to meet for bouillabaisse if you are not very close to Marseilles since you need, among other ingredients, the local rockfish such as *rascasse* (scorpion fish). So it is useful to know about other Mediterranean fish soups, which are less demanding but still full of the flavors of the Mediterranean.

Aïgo-sau is a simple white soup traditionally eaten with *rouille* (see page 11), and also good with aïoli (see page 22). The soup from Sète, a fishing port in the Languedoc known for its fine chefs and for its distinctive traditional fish recipes, is richer and more robust, flavored with olive oil, wine, garlic and saffron.

FISH SOUP FROM SÈTE

PROVENÇAL FISH SOUP WITH ROUILLE
Aïgo-sau

1¾-2¼ lb cheap fish (whiting,
flounder, etc.)
2 onions
1 clove of garlic
1 bouquet garni*
1 tomato
3 sprigs of flat-leafed parsley
1 sprig of herb fennel
1 tablespoon olive oil
1 stalk of celery
strip of dried orange zest*
salt and freshly ground black pepper
2 potatoes (optional)
4 cups water
slices of toast or stale bread
rubbed with garlic and olive oil
rouille

SERVES 4 AS A MAIN COURSE
PREPARATION TIME: 25 MINUTES
COOKING TIME: 15-25 MINUTES

Aïgo-sau is Provençal for "salted water." This is a simple recipe for a soup made from everyday fish, similar to the cotriade *from the Charentes region but with the addition of garlic and herbs.*

Gut the fish but reserve any roe. Scale as necessary and wash them, then cut into large chunks.

Chop the onions, and mince the garlic; put them in a saucepan with the bouquet garni, the crushed tomato and the herbs. Pour on the oil and add the chopped celery and the orange zest. Season to taste. At this time you can also add potatoes, cut into large rounds (the true recipe includes both potatoes and bread). Pour in the water and bring to a boil over a medium heat. Simmer for 10 minutes from when the liquid begins to boil, or 20 minutes if using potatoes. Put toast or stale bread rubbed with garlic and olive oil in the soup tureen. Pour the soup on top of it, straining it through a sieve. Serve the choicest pieces of fish and the vegetables separately with the potatoes and the *rouille*.

For the rouille: Parboil 2 oz sweet red pepper and a small chili pepper with its seeds left in. Add 4 cloves minced garlic and 1 teaspoon thyme, basil or herb of your choice. Pound in a mortar. Add one of the soup potatoes. Mix to a smooth paste.

FISH SOUP FROM SÈTE
Soupe comme à Sète

1¼ lb monkfish
1¼-1¾ porgy or red snapper
½ lb eel, cut from the head end
1 sweet green pepper
1 sweet yellow pepper
4 tomatoes
1¾ cups dry white wine
4 cloves of garlic
pinch of brown sugar
1 small onion, preferably with its stalk
if fresh and green
1 tablespoon olive oil
salt and freshly ground white pepper
4 cups thick fish fumet (see page 33)
pinch of saffron threads
sprig of flat-leafed parsley
toasted croûtons (see page 32), to
serve

SERVES 6 AS A MAIN COURSE
PREPARATION TIME: 45 MINUTES
COOKING TIME: ABOUT 1 HOUR

Ask the fish merchant to fillet the monkfish and the porgy, but keep the bones and trimmings. Cut the monkfish into 4 pieces; cut the eel into 3 pieces.

Blanch the sweet peppers whole in boiling water for 6 minutes; blanch the tomatoes for 30 seconds. Peel these vegetables.

Put the wine with the trimmings from the fish and the pieces of eel in a saucepan, and leave to reduce over a gentle heat.

Meanwhile, deseed and crush the tomatoes. Split the garlic cloves at the base without peeling them. Add them to the wine in the saucepan together with one crushed tomato and the brown sugar. Cook, uncovered, over a medium heat.

Finely slice the onion. Gently heat the oil in a large pot. Add the onion and slowly soften. Put in the rest of the tomatoes and three-quarters cover the pot. Deseed the peppers. Cut them into strips, then add to the pot. Season to taste with salt and pepper. Push the vegetables to the side of the pot and in the center place the pieces of monkfish. Allow the water from the fish to evaporate. Turn over with a spatula and pour on the fish fumet. When this begins to simmer, cover and turn the heat down as low as possible.

Remove the garlic and eel from the wine. Shred the eel on a plate and remove the bones and skin. Hold the bones and skin in a fine sieve over the pot of soup, and press with the back of a wooden spoon to squeeze as much juice as possible into the pot. Discard the skin and bones. Crush the cooked garlic into the pot, add the saffron and boil a little longer.

Place the porgy fillets in the soup. They only need to simmer lightly for 1 or 2 minutes. Taste and adjust the seasoning. Add the shredded eel. Turn off the heat. Carefully pour into a soup tureen, sprinkle with parsley and serve immediately with croûtons.

BOUILLONS

Home-made bouillons take a little time and trouble, but once made are endlessly adaptable, and if all the fat has been skimmed off they can be frozen until needed. Hot, they can be eaten simply with a little sherry or Madeira wine stirred in, or with any number of garnishes: julienne vegetables and homemade noodles, called *spetzle* or *petits moineaux* (small sparrows), are good for example. Miniature stuffed ravioli with shellfish, *cèpe*, cheeses and other fillings are a current favorite with French chefs, an idea which can be adopted without too much work by using small fresh stuffed pasta from good specialty stores. Cold consommé is also delicious (see opposite for details on clarifying consommé).

BEEF BOUILLON
Bouillon de boeuf

1 oxtail
1 calf's foot
3 lb beef top round or shank
14 cups cold water
1 onion
2 or 3 cloves
2 leeks
parsley stems
3 carrots
1 stalk of celery
piece of turnip
1 bouquet garni*
1 clove of garlic
sea salt
black peppercorns

SERVES 8-10
PREPARATION TIME: 30 MINUTES
COOKING TIME: 4-5 HOURS

Beef and chicken bouillons are made in a very similar way, and many of the same herbs and vegetables are used. But beef bouillon has a stronger taste than chicken, is darker in color and takes longer to prepare. It requires careful skimming to make it perfectly clear. Both make excellent bases for soups and sauces, bearing in mind the different strengths of flavor.

Break up the oxtail, and split the calf's foot in two lengthwise. Put all the meat in a large pot and pour over the cold water. Bring slowly to a boil.

After about 10 minutes, start to skim the froth which has formed on the surface and continue skimming until the stock is clear.

Meanwhile, stud the onion with the cloves. Tie the leeks together, and tie up the parsley stems. The stock should be clear by now. Add the vegetables, parsley stems, bouquet garni, garlic, salt to taste and a few peppercorns. Cover the pan, leaving a small gap, and bring back to a boil. From this point, allow 3 or 4 hours of very gentle cooking. Then remove from the heat and allow to cool.

Remove the meat and vegetables. Pour the stock into a metal container and refrigerate. The fat will rise to the surface and harden. Remove as much as possible, then strain the stock through a jelly bag or paper coffee filter. It is now ready for all sorts of uses. Keep refrigerated.

CHICKEN BOUILLON WITH WATERCRESS AND MUSSELS
Bouillon de volaille au cresson et aux moules

½ bunch of watercress
4 cups chicken stock
2 sprigs of flat-leafed parsley
pinch of saffron threads
cayenne
¼ cup heavy cream
1 quart mussels
juice of ½ lemon
1 clove of garlic
1 tomato

SERVES 6-8 AS A FIRST COURSE
PREPARATION TIME: 40 MINUTES
COOKING TIME: 10 MINUTES

BEEF BOUILLON WITH NOODLES
AND JULIENNE VEGETABLES

Remove the stems from the watercress and reserve the three best sprigs.

Heat the stock. As soon as it is about to boil, put in the watercress, except for the sprigs that have been set aside. As soon as the stock begins to boil again, turn off the heat. Remove the watercress with a slotted spoon and leave to drain.

Finely chop the parsley. Add the saffron threads and a little cayenne to the heavy cream and leave to infuse.

Scrub the mussels, discarding any open ones, and put them in a high-sided wide pan with the lemon juice, the chopped garlic and the crushed tomato. Heat until the mussels begin to open.

The minute they open, put them in a strainer over a clean bowl. Discard any mussels that remain stubbornly closed. Slowly pour the juices from the pan into a tall heatproof glass (sand and other impurities will sink to the bottom). Remove the mussel shells, working over the strainer over the bowl to catch the juices in the bowl. Set the mussels aside. Strain the juices and the liquid in the glass into the soup.

Reheat the soup. Purée the watercress with a few of the mussels in a blender or food processor, and pour into the soup. Add the rest of the mussels. Do not let the soup boil.

Garnish with the watercress sprigs and the flavored cream.

CLARIFYING STOCK FOR CONSOMMÉ
To clarify 1 quart, put 1 cup of lukewarm stock in a bowl, add 2 egg whites and beat with a wire whisk. Always beating, boil the rest of the stock, add to the mixture slowly and heat gently. When it begins to simmer, stop beating. Move the pan so that one side of the liquid simmers and turn a quarter turn every 5 minutes three times. Slowly ladle (do not pour) the stock into a cheese-cloth-lined colander over a bowl.

CHILLED SOUPS

Many soups are as good, if not better, eaten cold as warm, providing the seasoning is emphasized. The cream of asparagus (page 31) or zucchini soup would be excellent chilled. Cold consommés (page 39), of course, are a classic. Beef consommé could be flavored with a fresh herb like tarragon and a slice of lemon. For chilled chicken consommé, try adding cooked diced sweet peppers and chopped mild onion, then pour in a trickle of olive oil and wine vinegar. Or try the rich meat aspic below.

FENNEL, HERB AND YOGURT SOUP
Soupe au fenouil, aux herbes et yaourt

2 cups water
sprig of thyme
1 fennel bulb
2 cloves of garlic
2 sprigs of flat-leafed parsley
salt and freshly ground white pepper
1 biscotte*
1 egg yolk
⅔ cup plain yogurt
paprika

SERVES 4 AS A FIRST COURSE
PREPARATION TIME: 20 MINUTES + AT
LEAST 2 HOURS REFRIGERATION
COOKING TIME: 15 MINUTES

Bring the water to a boil with the thyme. Trim off the tough outside skin of the fennel and peel the garlic. Purée in a blender or food processor. Pour the purée into the boiling water. After the mixture has begun to boil again, simmer for 10 minutes.

Pour it back into the blender and add the parsley leaves stripped from the stems. Purée it again. Season to taste with salt and pepper and leave to cool slightly.

Add the biscotte, egg yolk and yogurt to the purée, blend briefly once more, then allow to cool before pouring into a tureen. Chill before serving, sprinkled with paprika.

DODIN-BOUFFANT'S CRAB SOUP
Soupe d'Irène

4 slices of cooked ham
4 hard-cooked eggs
3 small cucumbers
bunch of herb fennel
meat from 1 freshly cooked crab
5 teaspoons Meaux mustard
2 quarts water
juice of 3 lemons
salt and freshly ground black pepper

SERVES 8-10 AS A FIRST COURSE
PREPARATION TIME: 25 MINUTES + 24
HOURS REFRIGERATION

Dodin-Bouffant is a popular Parisian fish restaurant known for its superb oyster and shellfish bar, and for its relaxed brasserie atmosphere. This soup comes from their excellent varied menu.

Put the ham, eggs and the peeled and deseeded cucumbers through a meat grinder, or use the coarse grater disk of a food processor. Chop up the fennel with scissors, and flake the crabmeat.

Dissolve the mustard in the water. Whisk in the lemon juice and season to taste. Mix in all the other ingredients, and refrigerate for 24 hours. This soup is better when it has been prepared the day before.

Just before serving, add ice cubes and adjust the seasoning.

If fresh crab is not available use one small can of crabmeat in its place.

GELÉE (ASPIC)
A recipe by Maurice Casanova of Le Fouquet, Paris. Use 1 calf's foot split in half and tied together with string, 2 lb cracked veal bones, 1 veal knuckle and ¼ lb couenne*. Add a few carrots, 1 leek, 1 onion, 1 bouquet garni*, lots of pepper and a little salt. Cover with water, bring to a boil, skim, half cover and simmer for at least 5 hours, skimming until clear and reducing to about 1 quart. Strain, leave to settle, skim off the fat and reheat with ¼ cup lean ground beef, the green of a leek, 2 teaspoons chervil and 1 egg white. Stir until it boils, then take off the heat. Leave for 15 minutes, strain, and add ¼ cup port wine.

DODIN-BOUFFANT'S CRAB SOUP ▶

CHEESE AND EGGS

BAKED EGGS ON A BED OF
PURÉED GREENS (see page 54)

FRESH GOAT'S CHEESE WITH
HERBS (see page 45)

GOAT'S CHEESE CRACKERS
Sablés de biquette

2½ cups flour
1½ sticks lightly salted butter, slightly softened
2 extra large eggs
about ½ lb fresh goat's cheese★
⅓ cup sugar
pinch of salt

MAKES 20-30, DEPENDING ON SIZE
PREPARATION TIME: 25 MINUTES + 2
HOURS RESTING THE DOUGH
COOKING TIME: 10-12 MINUTES

It is difficult to go wrong with these crackers as long as the dough is left for at least 2 hours before cooking.

Their delicious flavor comes from the pungent taste of goat's cheese. Alternatively, a ewe's milk cheese (like Provençal Brousse) or a low-fat fresh cow's milk cheese may be used. In the Anjou region, this recipe would be made with a very ripe cheese, but it is advisable to try first with a fresh, mild one. Later, when you are hooked, you can try a dryish but still creamy cendré★ goat's cheese coated with ash (scrape off the outside), which gives you crackers with a very pungent flavor.

Put the flour in a bowl and make a well in the center. Cut the butter into small pieces and put in the well together with the beaten eggs and the cheese, crumbled or crushed with a fork. Add the sugar and salt. Rub together all the ingredients with your fingertips, or use a pastry blender, gradually drawing in the flour from the sides to form a ball of dough. Put the dough on a pastry board and flatten it with the heel of your hand. Roll it into a ball again, cover with a cloth and leave to rest in a cool place for 2 hours.

Preheat the oven to 375°F. Lightly grease a baking sheet.

Roll out the dough to a thickness of ¼ inch, then cut out rounds and place them on the baking sheet. Bake for 10 to 12 minutes, no longer, until the crackers are a golden brown color.

The crackers can be eaten warm, but will also keep for a week in an airtight can or jar. They are good served with a dry white wine.

SPINACH, WALNUT AND GOAT'S CHEESE ON STICKS
Petites bouchées aux épinards

24 young spinach leaves
6 oz fresh goat's cheese★
freshly ground black pepper
olive oil
24 walnut halves

MAKES 24
PREPARATION TIME: 20 MINUTES
COOKING TIME: 10 MINUTES

Dip the spinach leaves, one at a time, in boiling salted water for a second, and lay them on paper towels immediately. Cool slightly.

In the center of each leaf place a small piece of goat's cheese. Sprinkle each with pepper and 2 drops of olive oil.

Wrap the cheese in the spinach leaf and secure it with a toothpick spearing the walnut half.

These make excellent simple canapés.

SOFT CHEESE MIXES

In France there are many *fromage aux herbes* or *fromage à la paysanne*, flavored soft cheeses sold in the cheese shops and made at home. The herbs, seasonings and other aromatics vary from region to region.

From the Lyonnais area, for example, comes claqueret or canut de cervelle, made with olive oil, wine vinegar and wine as well as a mixture of fresh herbs. *Bibbeleskäs*, from Alsace, is a mixture of *fromage blanc* and *crème fraîche* seasoned with coarsely ground black peppercorns, fresh parsley and chives, finely chopped garlic and onion.

These are three other ideas, originally published as picnic recipes, to be eaten with bread or crudités, or used in stuffings and the like (see page 82). *Fromage blanc*, a creamy-textured white cheese, is available with very varying fat contents expressed as a percentage per 100 grams of cheese. A figure below 10% is a low-fat cheese, something between 40% and 60% has the same fat content as a cheese like a Brie or Camembert (see page 8 for substitutes). Once mixed, the cheeses will keep for two to three days in a cool place.

It is also possible to make a light, unsalted cream cheese with *fromage blanc* and *crème fraîche* (see page 48).

CREAM CHEESE WITH OLIVES
Olivade de fromage blanc

1 lb 2 oz (about 2¼ cups) fresh, good quality *fromage blanc**
1 heaping cup ripe black olives
1 tablespoon capers
1 tablespoon olive oil
freshly ground black pepper
1 large mild onion

SERVES 6
PREPARATION TIME: 20 MINUTES +
TIME TO CHILL

Tapenade, a Provençal olive paste, gives this cheese a fairly powerful flavor.
If you are in a hurry, you can make this with 3½ oz bought or previously prepared tapenade *(see page 164) instead of the olives, capers and oil.*

Pit the olives and purée them with the capers and olive oil in a blender or food processor. Combine this with the cheese and season to taste with pepper. Do not add salt, as the olives are already salty. Put in a salad bowl and garnish with onion rings and a few extra olives. Serve chilled with a red wine – nothing too fine.
Variations: any of the additions to the *tapenade* on page 164 can be used here, as could a flavored oil.

FRESH GOAT'S CHEESE WITH HERBS
Chèvre frais aux herbes

1 lb 2 oz (about 2¼ cups) fresh goat's cheese
2 small scallions
about ½ cup dry white wine
3 tablespoons olive oil
salt and freshly ground black pepper
chopped herbs of your choice: parsley, chervil, tarragon, chives, basil, coriander (cilantro) leaves

SERVES 6-8 AS AN APPETIZER
PREPARATION TIME: 10 MINUTES + A
FEW HOURS REFRIGERATION

PHOTOGRAPH ON PAGE 43

French goat's cheeses made with unpasteurized milk mature sometimes almost day by day, from mild, soft fresh cheeses to hard ones with a pungent flavor. Experiment with the ripeness you prefer.

If the cheese is a little dry, add some milk or light cream, working it in gradually with a fork. You may also need to cut off the cheese skin or rind and discard it.
Finely chop the scallions and combine them with the cheese, wine, olive oil and seasoning to taste. Add the chopped herbs and put the mixture in an airtight container. Refrigerate for a few hours before serving with crackers or French bread. If possible make this cheese one or two days before eating it as the flavors will blend and mature.

Goat's cheese needs a dry wine with good flavor.

CREAM CHEESE WITH ANCHOVIES
Fromage blanc aux anchois

1 lb 2 oz (about 2½ cups) fresh, good quality *fromage blanc*★
8 anchovy fillets
2 tablespoons capers
1 teaspoon ground cumin
1 teaspoon mustard powder
small bunch each of chives and flat-leafed parsley
paprika

SERVES 6
PREPARATION TIME: 10 MINUTES + AT LEAST 2 HOURS REFRIGERATION

Anchovy fillets are usually found in oil in this country. In France they are also available whole, packed in brine. These have an excellent flavor. If you find them, rinse in water and remove the backbone. Anchovies in oil do not need to be drained so thoroughly.

Thoroughly beat the *fromage blanc*. Chop the anchovies and add these. Add the capers, cumin, mustard, most of the chopped chives and all the chopped parsley. Refrigerate for a few hours.

Just before serving sprinkle with paprika and chopped chives. Serve with a light, cheerful red wine.

CHEESE AND WHITE WINE SPREAD
Fromages au vin: pâte fondue

1 ripe Pont-l'Evéque cheese or 14 oz Camembert, Brie, Coulommiers or Chaource★ cheese
scant 1 cup dry white wine
7 tablespoons butter
1 clove of garlic (optional)
coarsely ground black pepper

MAKES ABOUT 1 LB 2 OZ (2¼ CUPS)
PREPARATION TIME: 25 MINUTES + OVERNIGHT MARINATING

Cancaillote, a pungent, runny, wine-flavored cheese traditional to the Franche-Comté region in the French Alps, is produced commercially there and sold in small pots. Cheese lovers prefer to make it themselves.

Since the Franche-Comté and neighboring Savoy border Switzerland it is hardly surprising that some of the local cheeses are of the Swiss type. The best known is Comté, a large round wheel of cheese resembling Gruyère or Emmental, but as good in its own way as either. The most illustrious cheese of the entire region is probably Vacherin du Mont d'Or, a big, round, flat cheese enclosed in a wooden hoop. When ripe it has an inimitable rich softness.

Another specialty of Franche-Comté, which this region shares with Switzerland, is raclettes, for which the cut surface of half a large cheese is grilled in front of an open fire, and delicious little curls of half-melted cheese scraped off.

Remove the rind and put the cheese in a bowl, packing it in well. Pour on the white wine, which should cover the cheese. Cover with a cloth and leave to marinate overnight, or for at least 6 hours, in a cool place.

The next day, pour off any wine that has not been absorbed, and reserve. Transfer the cheese to a large, deep bowl that is heatproof. Set the bowl over a saucepan of hot water (the water should not touch the bottom of the bowl) and add the butter, which should be at room temperature.

Use a wooden spoon to work the cheese and butter into a smooth cream. The purpose of the hot water is to soften the cheese, not to cook it, so do not overheat. Add a little of the reserved wine. If you like garlic, mince the clove and add it to the mixture. Slowly beat in more wine until the mixture is smooth and elastic, but not runny. Add pepper to taste.

Pour into ramekins or plastic bowls and cover with an airtight lid. Heat through just before serving, or serve at room temperature, with crusty bread and a salad. This preparation can be kept for 3 or 4 days in the refrigerator.

FONDUE

Fondue is originally a Swiss dish, but the French border areas – Alsace, Franche-Comté and Savoy – have their own versions. Some combine full fat and lower-fat cheeses, others add eggs and butter. Traditionally fondues are made in a *câquelon* or *câclon*, a clay pot glazed only on the inside, but any flameproof dish which distributes the cooking heat evenly will do if you don't have a fondue set.

If the cheese and wine do not seem to be blending after the cheese has melted, you could follow a tip from Edouard de Pomiane, the great French food writer. On the advice of a Genevan cook, he recommended adding half a teaspoon of potato flour dissolved in a little of the wine to ensure a smooth cream.

CHEESE FONDUE
Fondue Comtoise

1 clove of garlic
2 lb Comté★ or Gruyère cheese
2¼ cups very dry white wine
salt and freshly ground white pepper
¼ cup kirsch liqueur (optional)
cubes of bread
1 extra large egg

SERVES 6
PREPARATION TIME: 15 MINUTES
COOKING TIME: 15 MINUTES

Peel the garlic and rub the inside of an earthenware fondue dish with it; discard the garlic. Cut the cheese into fine slivers or grate it. Put it in the fondue dish and pour in the wine.

Set the dish on a heat diffuser over a very gentle heat. Cook, stirring constantly with a wooden spoon, until the cheese has completely melted. Care is needed beyond this point so that the cheese does not become stringy. Add very little salt, as the cheese is already salted, and pepper to taste, and stir in the kirsch liqueur at the last minute. Mix well.

Place the fondue dish in the center of the table over a burner and keep the wooden spatula within reach to stir the fondue from time to time. Spear pieces of bread with a fork and dip these in the fondue until the bread is coated with cheese.

When the dish is almost empty, make a *gratin*: add the egg and the remaining bread to the dish and cook over the flame until golden. The perfect final mouthful!

EGGPLANTS STUFFED WITH HERBED CHEESE
Aubergines farcies

4 eggplants
peanut oil for frying (optional)
½ cup *fromage blanc*★
1 clove of garlic, minced
small bunch of flat-leafed parsley
sprig of fresh mint
pinch of caraway seeds
salt and pepper
1 large egg
1 tablespoon olive oil

SERVES 4
PREPARATION TIME: 35 MINUTES
COOKING TIME: 35-40 MINUTES

Eggplants are stuffed in all kinds of ways in France. This recipe dates from before the French Revolution.

Cut the eggplants in half lengthwise without peeling them. Either poach them in salted water for 10 minutes or cook them in a little peanut oil, uncovered, over a medium heat.

While the eggplants are cooking, prepare the stuffing. Lightly beat the cheese and gradually add the minced garlic, chopped herbs (reserve the stems), caraway seeds and seasoning to taste. Mix without beating again.

Drain the eggplant halves on paper towels and as soon as they have cooled a little, scoop out the flesh with a teaspoon without damaging the skin. Purée the flesh, add it to the cheese mixture and mix until smooth. Bind with the egg.

Preheat the oven to 375°F. Lightly oil an ovenproof dish. Make a bed of parsley and mint stems.

Fill the eggplant skins with the cheese mixture and arrange them close together, head to tail, in the dish. Moisten with the olive oil and bake for 25 to 30 minutes.

FRESH CREAM CHEESE SALAD
Fromage blanc en salade

10 oz (about 1¼ cups) *fromage blanc**
scant ½ cup *crème fraîche**
4 ripe tomatoes
mixed salad greens: various types of
lettuce, chervil and flat-leafed parsley
1 clove garlic
salt and crushed black peppercorns
¼ cup olive oil
1 tablespoon red wine vinegar
1 tablespoon lemon juice
1 tablespoon mixed herbs cut up with
scissors
1 tablespoon capers
a few leaves of basil

SERVES 4
PREPARATION TIME: 30 MINUTES +
OVERNIGHT DRAINING IN ADVANCE

Start preparing this salad 24 hours in advance. Whisk the cheese and the *crème fraîche* together and hang this up to drain in a jelly bag overnight. Then put the cheese between two wooden boards to finish draining it. Leave it like this until it is time to make the salad. Peel, deseed and crush the tomatoes. Wash and dry the salad greens and keep them cool.

Prepare the dressing: crush the garlic, preferably with salt, using a mortar and pestle. Gradually add the oil and dilute with the vinegar and lemon juice. Lastly add the chopped herbs and pepper to taste. Season the tomatoes and arrange them on each plate together with the salad greens. Slice the cheese and arrange 2 or 3 slices on the salad greens on each plate.

Sprinkle with the capers and basil leaves, and pour on the dressing. Accompany with lightly toasted brown bread and a fairly robust wine to stand up to the vinaigrette: Minervois, Corbières, Provence red or rosé or Côtes de Roussillon, for example.

If you do not wish to make your own cheese, you can always use a bought mild semi-soft cheese.

OMELETTES

There are said to be over a hundred types of omelette in France. Some are flat and some are rolled; others, like *pipérade*, are thick cakes with vegetables stirred in like a Spanish omelette or souffléd by whisking the whites separately from the beaten yolks; in yet others the eggs are beaten with cheese and cream.

A PERFECT ROLLED OMELETTE

The pan is as important as the eggs. It needs to be heavy, with a flat base (no ballooning in the center) to spread the heat evenly and to ensure even cooking. Use a cast-iron omelette pan and cook only omelettes in it. Most important of all, it must be the right size. If it is too small, the base of the omelette will toughen to a leathery skin before the top is cooked; if it is too large, the omelette will be very thin and cook too quickly. For a rolled omelette, two eggs need a 7 inch pan; three to four eggs need a 8 inch pan; six eggs need a 10 inch pan.

Some cooks maintain that the eggs should be beaten quite lightly, with a knife, and that a little water and melted butter should be added for lightness and flavor. They do give a more yielding texture, but do not overdo this. Others swear they should be beaten vigorously with a fork to whisk in air. All agree that they should never be salted while they are being beaten: it makes the omelette hard. Always beat the eggs at the last minute; it hardly takes any time and eggs beaten in advance make a heavy, sad omelette.

Make sure that the pan is absolutely clean and smooth; then there is no danger of the omelette sticking. Heat the pan with a pat of butter until it is sizzling; pour surplus butter into the egg. Once the eggs are poured in, work quickly. Shake and tip the pan rather than stir the eggs for a good texture. Begin to roll the omelette while there is still enough liquid for it to be moist and creamy in the center. A little melted butter, perhaps mixed with lemon juice and fresh herbs, gives a nice shine on the top.

The cooking mixture may also be lard, or chicken or duck fat, and it is always a good idea to include a very little light oil – like peanut oil – to help the butter keep from browning and to encourage the omelette to slip easily from the pan.

FRESH CREAM CHEESE SALAD ▶

CLASSIC ROLLED OMELETTE
Omelette baveuse

6 extra large eggs
salt and freshly ground white pepper
2 tablespoons butter
a trickle of oil

SERVES 4
PREPARATION TIME FOR BASIC
OMELETTE: 3 MINUTES
COOKING TIME: 5 MINUTES

A good rolled omelette is said to be baveuse – literally dribbling. Alexander Dumas wrote apologetically, "Excuse the use of this last word, but each art has its own language." The notes on page 49 summarize French opinions on the art of perfect omelette-making.

Break the eggs into a bowl. Add a few grinds of pepper and a tablespoon of water or milk, etc. Stir until well mixed, but no more.

Heat the butter with a trickle of oil in a perfectly clean omelette pan over a high heat. When the butter is hot, tip in the eggs. They should begin to set at once. Keep the heat high so that the omelette cooks quickly, pulling the cooked edges of the omelette into the center of the pan with a fork every few seconds so that the egg which is still liquid runs through the prongs and flows under the cooked parts. But do not stir the eggs. While there is still enough liquid for the omelette to be moist and creamy in the center slide it onto a warm dish in such a way that it folds itself into three.

Variations: flavorings to mix into the eggs include flaked tuna, anchovies, crisply fried bacon, grated cheese, a *fines herbes* mixture or any other fresh herbs you like.

INDIVIDUAL OMELETTES
Les petites omelettes

For each omelette:
3 tablespoons butter
6 extra large eggs
salt and freshly ground black pepper

Spinach:
10 oz fresh bulk spinach

Sweet pepper:
1 sweet green pepper
1 sweet red pepper
1 cup shelled fresh peas (optional)
1 onion

Tomato and mozzarella:
2 tomatoes
¼ lb mozzarella cheese
a few leaves of fresh basil

SERVES 6 AS A MAIN COURSE
PREPARATION TIME: 5-15 MINUTES
COOKING TIME: 5-15 MINUTES

These flat, rather cakelike omelettes with a creamy texture and a variety of flavorings are left to cool before being neatly sliced so that they can be eaten more easily. They can also be served as an entrée accompanied by a salad or make a sandwich filling in a lovely, fresh loaf of French bread. Three large omelettes, or up to twelve small omelettes, can be made from the recipes here. These recipes come from Cecconi's, a restaurant which used to be on the Champs-Elysées.

Wilt the trimmed spinach in a little of the butter. Stir in the beaten eggs and seasoning to taste. Make one or two omelettes, depending on the size of the pan, using the remaining butter. Cook until the omelette is still slightly moist. Cut into slices when cold.

Make the sweet pepper omelette.

Broil the sweet peppers on all sides to char and loosen the skin. Peel and deseed them, then cut the flesh into julienne strips. Blanch the peas, if using.

Chop the onion and soften in the butter in a large skillet. Add the peppers and the peas. Cook for 1 minute, then stir in the beaten eggs with seasoning to taste. Make the omelette moist. Leave to cool and slice.

Meanwhile make the omelette with the tomato and mozzarella. Peel, deseed and finely dice the tomatoes. Dice the mozzarella. Mix into the beaten eggs, season to taste and add the coarsely chopped basil.

Cook the omelette in the butter in a large skillet until slightly moist. Leave to cool and slice.

INDIVIDUAL OMELETTES▶

TRI-COLORED LAYERED OMELETTE
Cubes d'omelette froide

6 extra large eggs
2 tablespoons *crème fraîche*★
¼ cup Gruyère cheese
salt and freshly ground black pepper
grated nutmeg
2 tablespoons chopped herbs (parsley,
tarragon, chives, basil)
3 tablespoons tomato paste
a little beaten egg

SERVES 2-3 OR MAKES ABOUT 36
PREPARATION TIME: 10 MINUTES +
TIME TO COOL
COOKING TIME: 30 MINUTES

This is a cake of thin omelettes, with three differently flavored layers. It is good cut into wedges or cubes, either as a light dish or a snack to eat with drinks.

Break 2 eggs into a bowl and add 1 tablespoon *crème fraîche*, the grated Gruyère, and salt, pepper and nutmeg to taste. In another bowl, beat 2 eggs with the remaining *crème fraîche* and the chopped herbs. Beat the remaining eggs with the tomato paste, salt and pepper.

Preheat the oven to 350°F.

Make a thin omelette from each of the egg mixtures.

Lay the omelettes on top of each other on a baking sheet with a little beaten egg between them to stick the omelettes together. Bake for 15 minutes, then leave to cool. Cut into cubes and serve on toothpicks.

POACHED, BOILED AND BAKED EGGS

EGGS POACHED IN RED WINE
Oeufs en meurette

12 extra large eggs
12 shallots
3 tablespoons butter
1 bottle (750 ml) of good red
Burgundy wine
2 thick slices smoked bacon
12 pearl onions
1 teaspoon sugar
salt and freshly ground black pepper
1 bottle (750 ml) of red table wine
garlic croûtons (see page 32)

SERVES 6
PREPARATION TIME: 25 MINUTES
COOKING TIME: ABOUT 1¼ HOURS

*This is a wonderful Burgundian recipe.
Like many apparently simple dishes it
depends on good quality produce – in this
case the wine and eggs.*

Chop the shallots and brown them
in half the butter. Pour in the
Burgundy and simmer,
uncovered, over a gentle heat for
45 minutes.

Meanwhile, cut the bacon into
matchsticks and brown.

Peel the pearl onions and
simmer them in a small amount of
water. When tender, sprinkle
them with the sugar. Pass the wine
and shallots through a sieve, or
blend, to make a sauce. Add the

bacon and the drained onions.
Season to taste with salt and
pepper. Stir in the rest of the
butter to bind the sauce.

Make the croûtons (see page
32), frying them in garlic oil.

Bring the ordinary red wine to a
boil with a little salt and pepper.
When it begins to simmer, break
the eggs into it (cook them in
batches according to the size of the
pan). As soon as they rise to the
surface, they are cooked. Remove
with a slotted spoon, drain well
and arrange on a flat dish.

Pour on the sauce and serve
with garlic croûtons.

SOFT-COOKED EGGS IN ARTICHOKE SHELLS
Oeufs mollets en coques d'artichauts

4 globe artichokes
lemon juice
2 sprigs of flat-leafed parsley
1 tablespoon heavy cream
salt and freshly ground black pepper
cayenne pepper
1 cup grated Gruyère cheese
4 large eggs
butter

SERVES 4
PREPARATION TIME: 45 MINUTES
COOKING TIME: 25 MINUTES

*An inspired idea for a rich first course or
for a light meal served with bread and a
good salad.*

*Oeufs mollets, that is, eggs boiled for
a hard white but a creamy soft yolk, are
often used for their contrast of textures in
hot French savory dishes. For example,
eggs Florentine (eggs on a bed of spinach
with a mornay sauce), may be made with
oeufs mollets or poached eggs.*

*For a more traditional way of stuffing
artichokes, see page 152.*

Remove the hard outer leaves and
the hairy chokes from the
artichokes. Cut off the top halves
of the remaining leaves. Cook the
artichokes in boiling water with
plenty of lemon juice or, if you
prefer, in a *blanc* – water with
flour, salt and vinegar – until the
leaves will pull away easily. Turn
the artichokes upsidedown to
drain and keep them hot.

While the artichokes are
cooking, finely chop the parsley
and season the cream with salt,
pepper and cayenne. Add half the
parsley and a third of the cheese to

the cream.

Preheat the oven to 375°F.

To soft-cook the eggs, put them
in a pan of boiling water and count
about 5 minutes from the time the
water comes back to boil. The
yolk should be thick but still
runny. Cool quickly in cold water,
then roll them on a flat surface to
crack the shell. Peel without
breaking the egg.

Pour half the cream mixture
into the center of the artichoke
hearts, place an egg in each, and
cover first with the rest of the
parsley, then the rest of the cheese
and finally with slivers of butter.
Preheat the broiler. Place the
artichokes in a greased flameproof
dish and broil for 3 minutes to
brown the tops. Serve at once. Use
the artichoke leaves to dip into the
egg.

SOFT-COOKED EGGS IN
ARTICHOKE SHELLS▶

BAKED EGGS ON A BED OF PURÉED GREENS
Les oeufs au vert

6 young onions with green stems (or 1
bunch scallions)
3 tablespoons butter
large bunch of flat-leafed parsley
2¼ lb fresh bulk or frozen spinach
¼ lb sorrel
½ Swiss chard or beet top leaves
a few leaves of chervil, tarragon or
basil
salt and freshly ground black pepper
tiny pinch of grated nutmeg
1 cup *crème fraîche*★
6 or 12 extra large eggs

SERVES 6
PREPARATION TIME: 15 MINUTES
COOKING TIME: 5 + 30 MINUTES

PHOTOGRAPH ON PAGE 42

*The green purée is made with summer
vegetables, ideally spinach and sorrel,
but you can also use watercress, Swiss
chard leaves, lettuce or other greens. It
needs the flavor of the chervil, tarragon
or basil. Count one or two eggs per
serving, depending on whether the dish is
being served as an appetizer or main
course.*

Chop the onions and their green
tops, and soften gently in the
butter. Blanch the parsley and
drain well. Add the spinach,
sorrel, Swiss chard leaves and
parsley to the onions and cook for
15 minutes, stirring continuously.
Preheat the oven to 350°F.

Add the tarragon or basil and
seasoning to taste, and purée in a
blender. Add the nutmeg and half
the *crème fraîche*. Pour the mixture
into an ovenproof dish. Make a
little hollow for each egg. Break
the eggs one by one into a cup and
place them in the hollows.
Sprinkle with salt and pour on the
rest of the *crème fraîche*. Bake for 5
minutes until the whites have set
but the yolks are still runny. Serve
very hot.
   If you are serving this as a main
course, it would be good with
bread, butter and a few slices of
jambon cru.★

HERB CUSTARDS
Flans aux herbes

8 extra large eggs
1 cup milk
3 tablespoons *crème fraîche*★
salt
6 tablespoons chopped mixed basil,
flat-leafed parsley, chervil and chives

SERVES 6
PREPARATION TIME: 10 MINUTES + 20
MINUTES COOLING
COOKING TIME: 20 MINUTES

Preheat the oven to 400°F. Beat
together the eggs, milk and *crème
fraîche* with a little salt. Add the
herbs and mix well. Pour into six
buttered ramekins and cook in a
pan of hot water in the oven for 20
minutes. Leave to cool before
serving.
Variation: for Parmesan cheese
ramekins, proceed in the same
way but substitute 1 cup freshly
grated Parmesan cheese for the
herbs, and flavor with a little
grated nutmeg.

QUICHES

The family of French savory tarts, or quiches, is almost invariably represented in cook books by the classic but much distorted quiche Lorraine. A quiche should properly be made with cream; once it is made with milk it becomes a flan. Jean Moussié of Bistro 121 suggests bringing the milk for a flan filling to a boil and pouring it onto the yolks, just as you would for a sweet custard, for the best consistency. If you are making a quiche or flan ahead of time and are worried about soggy pastry try self-rising flour for a soft, but very dry, nonabsorbent pastry.

Here are three rather different recipes for easily made savory tarts. One is an everyday quiche; another is a marvelous creation from a young chef. The third, without a crust, is a savory version of an egg and cream fruit clafoutis. It makes a particularly good first course because it is so light.

TOMATO AND ONION QUICHE
Flans aux tomates et aux oignons

6 tablespoons butter
2¼ lb onions
1½ lb tomatoes
1 tablespoon peanut oil
salt and freshly ground black pepper
cayenne
1 egg yolk from an extra large egg
8 whole extra large eggs
5 tablespoons flour
½ cup *crème fraîche*★
1 cup milk
sprig of fresh savory

For the pastry:
2¾ cups flour
½ lb (2 sticks) butter
scant ½ cup water

SERVES 8-10
PREPARATION TIME: 35 MINUTES +
TIME FOR PASTRY TO REST
COOKING TIME: ABOUT 40 MINUTES

This can be made by pouring the filling directly into a buttered pie dish, but that requires a fairly large quantity of flour to make the quiche "hold", and as a result it is less delicate. It is better to use a pie crust or pastry case, rolling out the dough as thinly as possible and baking it unfilled in advance.

Prepare the pastry (see page 202) and let it rest for at least 30 minutes, before rolling it out thinly.

Preheat the oven to 375°F. Melt about 2 tablespoons butter and use it to grease two 10 inch flan pans, preferably with detachable bases. Line the tart or quiche pans with the pastry, which should come well above the rim, pressing it down well over the bottom and around the sides. Fold over the edges, pinching the dough between your fingers.

Prick the pastry cases with a fork and cover with lightly buttered baking parchment, or with foil and dried beans. Bake for 20 minutes.

Meanwhile, finely chop the onions. Peel, deseed and drain the tomatoes. Heat the remaining butter and the oil without browning and soften the onions, stirring occasionally. This should take about 15 minutes. Add the tomatoes, salt to taste and cayenne (a tiny pinch is enough). Cook for another 10 minutes without covering to allow the moisture to evaporate. Remove from the heat.

By now the pastry cases should be cooked. Remove them from the oven. Beat the egg yolk with a little water and brush all over the pastry cases. Put them back in the oven for 2 minutes to dry out the egg yolk glaze.

Beat the eggs, discarding two of the whites for greater smoothness if desired, with salt to taste and a pinch of pepper. Sift in the flour, beating all the while, and when the eggs and flour are smoothly blended, gradually add the *crème fraîche* and the milk.

Add the onions and tomatoes to the egg and cream mixture with the finely chopped savory. Mix well and pour into the pastry cases. Handling with care so as not to spill the mixture, put the quiches in the oven. If your oven is big enough, cook them both together. Otherwise, add the filling to the second pastry case only when the first quiche is cooked. Bake for about 40 minutes.

About 10 minutes before removing the quiches from the oven, brush the edges of the pastry with the remaining egg yolk glaze. Serve hot or cold.

CREAM OF WALNUT AND *CÈPE* QUICHE
Tarte aux cèpes et à la crème de noix

2½ lb fresh *cèpes** or mushrooms
1 shallot
1½ tablespoons butter
1 large egg
2 oz *jambon cru**
½ inch thick slice of French baguette,
soaked in milk and squeezed
½ cup grated walnuts
½ cup light cream
salt and freshly ground black pepper
1 clove of garlic

For the pastry:
1¼ cups flour
7 tablespoons butter
2½-3 tablespoons water

SERVES 6-8
PREPARATION TIME: I HOUR + 45
MINUTES WAIT
COOKING TIME: 20 MINUTES

Michel Bras, one of the French chefs whose dishes are most inspired by regional cooking, has chosen to live and work in the small village of Laguiole on the plateau of Aubrac in the southern Massif Central. Bras uses almost entirely local ingredients, here walnuts bought in the nearby market of Rodez and cèpes from the local hills. Large open cultivated mushrooms will replace the fresh cèpes. For other recipes by Michel Bras, see pages 77, 78 and 192. They all have the same sense of sophistication rooted in simplicity.

Make the pastry with the flour, butter and water, the day before if possible following the method given for French pie pastry on page 202. Avoid kneading it too much.

Trim the *cèpes*, blanch them in boiling salted water for 5 minutes and drain. Chop the shallot and soften in a little of the butter. In a blender or food processor combine the egg, ham, bread, grated walnuts and the shallot. Add the walnuts last to prevent the oil separating. Process until smooth and refrigerate for 45 minutes to set, then stir in the cream. Adjust the seasoning.

Preheat the oven to 425°F. Roll out the dough as thinly as possible, ¹⁄₂₀ inch, following the instructions given on page 202, then use to line a 12 inch fluted quiche mold. Spread the filling over the pastry. Thinly slice the *cèpes* and arrange over the filling. Melt the remaining butter with the split clove of garlic and brush over the surface. Bake for 20 minutes.

LEEK AND HAM CLAFOUTIS
Clafoutis aux poireaux et jambon

2¼ lb leeks
1 lb 2 oz (about 2¼ cups) low-fat
fromage blanc★
4 extra large eggs
¼ cup freshly grated Parmesan cheese
1 clove of garlic
salt and freshly ground black pepper
6 slices of cooked ham
melted butter or flavored oil (see
page 10)

SERVES 6
PREPARATION TIME: 20 MINUTES
COOKING TIME: ABOUT 20 MINUTES

This recipe, by Nathalie le Foll, a Parisian working mother, was published in an article on quick family meals made in less than forty minutes. The idea of savory clafoutis has also been taken up by chefs in recent years.

Cook the leeks in boiling water for 12 minutes. While they are cooking, blend the *fromage blanc* and the eggs, then add half the freshly grated Parmesan and the minced garlic. Season to taste. Chop the ham coarsely.
Preheat the oven to 400°F.

Drain the leeks thoroughly, chop with a knife and combine with half the egg and *fromage blanc* mixture. Butter an ovenproof dish and put in the chopped ham. Pour on the leek mixture and stir with a fork. Cover with the rest of the egg mixture. Sprinkle on the remaining Parmesan cheese and moisten with a little aromatic oil or melted butter. Bake for 20 minutes. Serve hot with a salad and a fruity dry white wine.

SAVORY CRÊPES

Crêpes, large, thin pancakes, can be bought everywhere in France now that the crêperie, just like the pizzeria, has become a universal feature of town life. But they remain a specialty of Brittany where they are still made with buckwheat flour and washed down by the local hard cider. One good Breton tip is to add a little soda water or lager beer as part of the liquid for the batter; this lightens the crêpes.

BRETON CRÊPES
Crêpes bretonnes ou galettes de sarrasin

2 cups whole wheat or 2½ cups buckwheat flour
1 extra large egg
1 teaspoon sea salt
2 cups water
2 tablespoons lard + more to cook

MAKES 12; SERVES 4
PREPARATION TIME: 15 MINUTES + AT LEAST 2 HOURS TO REST
COOKING TIME: ABOUT 20 MINUTES

Whole wheat or buckwheat crêpes are traditionally eaten instead of bread by the Bretons. They are served cold with a hard slicing sausage or andouille (*a sausage made of chitterlings*), *or with* rillettes (*potted meat*) *or sardines in oil.*

Put the flour in a large bowl. Make a well in the center. Break in the egg, add the salt and mix while you gradually pour in the water. Stir with a wooden spoon to make a loose batter, then beat hard with a whisk or in a mixer or food processor. Leave to rest for at least 2 hours, or overnight.
Melt the 2 tablespoons of lard and beat it in: this makes the batter spread more readily.
Grease a griddle or a thick, flat skillet with a bit of lard or a twist of paper towel soaked in melted lard. Heat it, then drop on a small dollop of batter and spread this out with a circular sweep of a broad spatula. When the edges solidify and begin to color, lift them with the spatula. Turn over the crêpe (use your fingers) and cook through.
Crêpe with ham and eggs: for each crêpe you will need a small pat of slightly salted butter, 1 large egg, salt and freshly ground black pepper and 1 slice *jambon cru,*★ chopped.
When cooking the second side of the crêpe, drop on a little butter and break the egg on top. When the egg is just set, season, spread the ham all over the crêpe and fold into four. Serve at once with well chilled hard cider.

HOT SAVORY SOUFFLÉS

Every cook is tempted to try hot soufflé. But it can be an ordeal – in case it collapses like a burst tire! Precision is required. Here are some chefs' guidelines and a very precise master recipe for a classic cheese soufflé from the Troisgros brothers.

CHEESE SOUFFLÉS
Soufflés au fromage

6 tablespoons butter
2½ tablespoons flour
2½ tablespoons potato starch
1 cup milk
salt
4 eggs
½ lb Gruyère cheese

SERVES 4
PREPARATION TIME: 15 MINUTES
COOKING TIME: 30 + 12 MINUTES

This recipe comes from the late Troisgros brothers, who, through their restaurant in Roanne, had a great influence on other chefs (see page 112).

Make a béchamel: melt 5 tablespoons of the butter in a small saucepan, then add the flour and starch and beat with a whisk. Cook, without letting the mixture brown, for 3 minutes. Gradually mix in the milk, beating constantly. Add a little salt. When the mixture begins to boil, turn the heat down very, very low and continue cooking for 20 minutes, beating from time to time to prevent the sauce from sticking.
 Preheat the oven to 400°F. Grease 4 ramekins. Separate the eggs. Beat the egg whites until stiff – the mixture should hang from the beater in a single blob. As soon as the whites are ready, add the yolks and grated Gruyère cheese to the hot sauce and stir vigorously. Add a quarter of the whites and mix again. This thins the sauce, making it easier to incorporate the rest. Then use a spatula to fold in the remaining egg whites.
 Fill four individual soufflé dishes four-fifths of the way up. Place them on a baking sheet over heat on top of the stove for 2 minutes. Then put them into the oven and turn off the heat. The oven will remain hot enough for the soufflés to cook, which takes about 10 minutes for individual dishes. Serve immediately.

Vegetable soufflés

All sorts of vegetables can be added to a basic soufflé mixture: carrots, cauliflowers, asparagus, mushrooms etc. Cut the vegetables into julienne strips and gently soften them. They must be carefully drained, or, if you are using a purée, heated to remove all moisture, to enable them to rise with the soufflé. Add a little grated cheese, which brings out the flavor of the vegetables, and a few chopped herbs, such as parsley or chives.

Meat, fish or shellfish soufflés

These soufflés are generally more durable than those made with vegetables: they are unlikely to collapse before reaching the table! The meat or fish must be flaked quite finely for the soufflé to rise.

Chefs' tips

Small soufflés are more likely to be a success so try your hand first with them.

Most chefs recommend using half flour and half potato starch or rice flour for thickening the béchamel to be sure of success. If the béchamel mixture is still warm it will cook more quickly and rise more easily.

Never put soufflés in the oven until everyone who will be eating has arrived, allowing 8 to 12 minutes for individual soufflés and 15 to 20 minutes for larger ones.

To give a soufflé an initial boost and help it on its way, put it on a baking sheet on a hot stovetop for 2 minutes before placing it in the oven, or put it on a heated baking sheet in the oven.

Try to make sure there are no other dishes with awkward timing.

COLD SAVORY SOUFFLÉS

The fundamentals of a cold soufflé are always the same: a purée to which whipped cream, stiffly beaten egg whites, a light béchamel (see page 20) or gelatin are added. For a savory soufflé the purée can be made from chicken, fish, shellfish, vegetables or herbs. A charlotte, soufflé dish or a hollowed vegetable is used and the sides are raised by wrapping a sheet of wax paper, folded in half and buttered, around the dish and tying it in place. The soufflé is chilled by placing it in the refrigerator, *never* in the freezer, even in an emergency when you need to speed things up. Only once it is set can the soufflé be put in the freezer for 30 minutes to make it firmer. It should be served on very cold, refrigerated plates.

CHILLED TOMATO AND AVOCADO SOUFFLÉ IN TOMATO SHELLS
Soufflé aux tomates et avocats

7 large, well-flavored tomatoes
salt and freshly ground white pepper
3 avocados
tiny pinch of mustard powder
lemon juice
1½ tablespoons unflavored gelatin
(1½ envelopes)
2 tablespoons chicken stock *(page 39)*
¼ cup *crème fraîche**
sprig of chervil, or pinch of *fines
herbes**

SERVES 6
PREPARATION TIME: 30 MINUTES + 4
HOURS TO SET

Gerard Besson's cooking at his restaurant of the same name, in Paris, combines impeccable classic technique with originality. Here he has replaced a traditional soufflé mold with tomato shells.

Cut the tomatoes in half, hollow them out, salt them and turn upsidedown to drain. Purée seven of the tomato halves in a blender or food processor, and season to taste. Dice another tomato half. Reserve half the purée.

Purée the flesh of 2½ avocados with the mustard and seasoning to taste. Finely dice the other avocado half and squeeze lemon juice over it. Dissolve the gelatin in the heated chicken stock. Leave to cool a little, then stir half the mixture into each purée. Whip the cream with a tiny pinch of salt and stir half into each mixture.

Wrap each of the remaining tomato halves in a strip of wax paper 2 inches high, and fasten it. Pour the two purées, a spoonful at a time, into each tomato cup. Refrigerate for 4 hours.

Mix the reserved tomato purée with the chopped chervil or *fines herbes*, and divide between the serving plates. Remove the paper from the tomatoes and place the soufflés in the center of the plates. Sprinkle with diced avocado and tomato. Serve with a chilled rosé wine.

SHELLFISH

PRAWNS AND SHRIMP WITH
COUNTRY BREAD (see page 63)

SHELLFISH FRIED IN THEIR
SHELLS (see page 67)

HOW TO BUY SHELLFISH

Crustaceans
The name "shellfish" is misleading for crustaceans. They are creatures with legs: lobsters, crabs etc. All spoil very quickly. For this reason, small crustaceans, such as shrimp, are often cooked or frozen on the fishing boat itself. The shell should be firm and shiny and the smell pleasant. Large crustaceans, such as lobsters, should, if possible, be bought alive. It is not hard to give them a merciful death (see page 66). The best crustaceans come from cold seas. Shrimp and giant prawns imported from the tropics are often frozen, or worse still thawed and refrozen. If they are on a bed of ice in the fish merchants, take care. Feel the shells, which should be firm, make sure that the creatures are not crushed and that they do not have a dubious smell.

Bivalve shellfish
These are mollusks with two shells, such as mussels, cockles, clams and oysters. They should be tightly closed and have a good fresh smell, like the sea. Any with a broken shell, or an open one that does not close immediately on being touched should be discarded ruthlessly.

It can be hard to find scallops still in their shells, but it is preferable since it is a good guarantee of their freshness. Scallops are easily opened by heating for only a minute or two, flat shell upwards, in a skillet, steamer or baking pan in the oven.

Oysters should be tightly shut and when prised open should respond to the slightest touch. They should be full of liquid and have a fresh smell.

Gastropod shellfish
These are mollusks with one shell, for example, whelks and periwinkles. They are closely related to snails. When buying, make sure they are alert; this is a sign of perfect freshness. At the slightest sign of danger, the creature should withdraw into its shell. It should be aware of its surroundings and cautious. When lightly touched, it should recoil.

Squid etc.
Squid, cuttlefish and octopus are also mollusks (they have little shells inside). Squid and cuttlefish should be pearly white. They turn grey when they lose their freshness. All these creatures should be odorless.

Note: Ideally shellfish should be prepared just before it is required rather than by the fish merchant. Preparation of frozen shellfish is more delicate than for fresh. They should be thawed gently (microwave ovens are unbeatable for this) and cooked with great care, as freezing slightly "cooks" the delicate meat and it is easy to overcook.

Cleaning shellfish
Shellfish feed by filtering nourishment out of sea water. This makes them particularly liable to pick up waterborne pollution, which can give you a nasty attack of food poisoning. The chief offenders are mussels. Even if you buy locally caught mussels in a place where you know that the water is clean, they may be polluted by natural organisms.

To clean mussels, or any marine mollusks that are bought alive, put them in a clean bucket of cold water. Sprinkle in a little salt, cover with a cloth, and leave in a cool place overnight for them to rinse themselves. Next day discard any that are not firmly shut. If open, they are dead; if the shell halves can be slid sideways they will be full of grit.

COURT BOUILLON

2 cups dry white wine
1 onion
1 carrot
green leaves of 3 leeks
1 *bouquet garni*★
1 clove of garlic
1 clove
1 teaspoon sea salt
1 teaspoon crushed black peppercorns
3 cups cold water

MAKES 2½ PINTS
PREPARATION TIME: 5 MINUTES
COOKING TIME: 35 MINUTES

This is a lightly flavored liquid for poaching shellfish. The recipe below is suitable for delicate flavored shellfish like shrimps. For extra flavorings, see page 76.

Put all the ingredients in a saucepan and bring to a boil. Turn down the heat to minimum and simmer for 30 minutes. Skim the surface occasionally. Turn off the heat and leave to cool.

Reheat when you are ready to cook the shellfish.

The white wine can be replaced by lemon juice or cider vinegar.

Stocks based on court bouillon:
Fish and shellfish stocks based on court bouillon can be made from almost any sea creature, and flavored with any vegetables or herbs that you feel are suitable for the dish. They range from very light *nages* (discussed on page 76) to concentrated fumets which are used to flavor a fish velouté sauce (see pages 33 and 21).

PRAWNS AND SHRIMP

Good quality fresh shrimp are well worth seeking out. It is unlikely you will see whole live shrimp for sale, but fresh shrimp – raw or cooked, sold headless with or without shell – are shipped all over the United States. Avoid frozen shrimp (or so-called "fresh" shrimp that has been frozen and thawed) because the flavor will be bland and the texture mushy. The size of shrimp can range from the tiny ones weighing less than 1/10 ounce to huge ones at over a pound each! Medium shrimp average 30 to the pound, and jumbo shrimp are 6 to 15 per pound.

If you do find good quality, fresh, uncooked prawns and shrimp they are at their best in plentiful quantities freshly simmered in seawater (use salted water as a substitute) or court bouillon and served in a large mound, just as they are. Simple but superb. On the table with them you need only have good crusty bread and butter – in France it would probably be unsalted – chilled white wine and, perhaps, a bowl of mayonnaise. Here are two other simple French ways of cooking and serving them, both of which highlight rather than drown out the flavor. Suggestions for adapting the recipes to cooked shrimp are given at the end of each one.

SHRIMP WITH COUNTRY BREAD
Bouquets, crevettes et tartines

2½ pints court bouillon (see opposite), or water with sea salt, pepper and a *bouquet garni**
5 oz shelled shrimp (mixed medium and small, if desired)
slightly salted butter
a little chopped flat-leafed parsley
a few crushed peppercorns
a few drops of Calvados
4 slices of mixed grain bread

SERVES 4
PREPARATION TIME: 10 MINUTES
COOKING TIME: 5 MINUTES

PHOTOGRAPH ON PAGE 60

This is a useful basic method for cooking shrimp to be eaten cold, or used cooked in other dishes. If you are peeling the shrimp, put the shells back in the cooking water and simmer for a further 20 to 30 minutes to give a delicious shellfish stock for use in fish soups.

Bring the court bouillon to a boil and put in the shrimp. When the liquid begins to boil again, remove from the heat and leave for a few minutes.

Meanwhile, combine the butter with the parsley, pepper and Calvados and spread it on the bread. Drain the shrimp and arrange them on top of the bread while still warm.

If you are using cooked shrimp do not try to heat them through. You could remove any shrimp roe – this is delicious – and mix it into the Calvados butter.

FRESH SHRIMP SAUTÉED IN BUTTER
Crevettes chaudes au beurre

½ lb raw shrimp
7 tablespoons butter
salt and freshly ground black pepper
bread and butter, to serve

SERVES 4 AS AN APPETIZER
PREPARATION TIME: 5 MINUTES
COOKING TIME: 3 MINUTES

Fry the shrimp in the butter for 3 minutes, shaking the pan constantly. Season to taste and serve hot with bread and butter. For cooked shrimp, fry simply enough to heat through the shrimp.
Variations: for lovers of food with spice, the shrimp can be sautéed in olive oil with slivers of garlic and chopped fresh chili pepper (with the seeds removed!). Freshly snipped chives are another possibility – the green looks wonderful with shrimp – or sautéed sweet white or red onions.

63

LANGOUSTINES

Freshwater crayfish, or *écrevisses*, and the saltwater Dublin Bay prawns, or *langoustines* (also called Norway lobster) are great favorites with the French, served *à la nage* (meaning literally, swimming), in an aromatic court bouillon, in creamy *bisques* or to garnish other dishes with a sauce Nantua. Crayfish recipes have also crossed the Atlantic to the Creole and Cajun cooking of Louisiana, where there are plentiful supplies from the Mississippi delta.

Generally, fresh crayfish are a rare find and one usually has to resort to the frozen variety. Here are two ideas for *langoustines*, one with the flavors of southwest France, the other in the nouvelle cuisine tradition with an oriental influence.

LANGOUSTINES STEAMED WITH GINGER
Langoustines au gingembre

3 tablespoons peanut oil
3¼ lb *langoustines*, cleaned
½ cup of fresh tomato purée (page 26), diluted with 1½ cups of water
2 cloves of garlic
5 stalks of chive
1½-2 inch piece of fresh gingerroot, peeled and cut into thin matchsticks
salt and freshly ground black pepper
pinch of cayenne
1 cup dry white wine

SERVES 6
COOKING TIME: 20 MINUTES

When you season the langoustines, *bear in mind that dishes with ginger need very little salt.*

Find your largest, heavy-based skillet or other shallow pan. Pour in the oil, heat to sizzling and put in as many *langoustines* as will fit. Fry over a fierce heat for 4 to 5 minutes, turning them over with a slotted spatula and checking that they are seized on both sides. Remove them to a heavy-based, lidded casserole, in which they will fit.

Moisten with the diluted tomato purée, then add the minced garlic, snipped chives and ginger. Toss gently. Season and finally add the cayenne and wine. Put on the lid, place the pan over high heat and bring to a boil, shaking frequently so that all the seafood soaks up the flavor of the sauce. They will be ready in 5 minutes.

LANGOUSTINES IN WALNUT AND WHITE WINE SAUCE
Langoustines en blanquette

1 large onion
3 cloves of garlic
⅓ cup olive oil
scant 1 cup dry white wine
grated zest of 1 lemon*
1 bay leaf
3 dozen large raw *langoustines* or jumbo shrimp
1 tablespoon ground walnuts
1 tablespoon capers
1-2 sprigs of flat-leafed parsley
salt and freshly ground black pepper
lemon wedges
toast

SERVES 4 AS AN APPETIZER
PREPARATION TIME: 15 MINUTES
COOKING TIME: ABOUT 15 MINUTES

The ground walnuts should be crushed in a pestle and mortar or finely chopped; the heat of mechanical grinding encourages the oils to separate out.

Chop the onion and garlic. Heat half the oil in a saucepan and put in the chopped onion. When it has softened, add the garlic. Turn down the heat and continue cooking gently for 1 or 2 minutes. Moisten with the white wine, add the lemon zest and bay leaf and allow to reduce by half. Meanwhile, peel and devein the *langoustines*.

Add the ground walnuts, capers, finely chopped parsley, salt and plenty of pepper to the sauce. Heat the rest of the oil in a skillet and when it is very hot, put in the *langoustines* for 20 seconds, turning once with a slotted spatula. Use the spatula to lift the *langoustines* from the pan, and lay them on paper towels to drain. Then add them to the sauce. Shake the pan gently.

Remove the bay leaf and serve in heated individual dishes with a wedge of lemon, toast and a chilled light white wine.

LANGOUSTINES STEAMED WITH GINGER▶

SHRIMP AND SPINY LOBSTER SALAD
Salade de crevettes et de langouste

3 oz very fine green beans
few drops of vinegar
10 young spinach leaves
1 live spiny lobster weighing
1¾-2¼ lbs
3 quarts court bouillon★ (see page 62)
6 raw jumbo shrimp in shell
10 sprigs of samphire★ (optional)
1 slice of smoked salmon
8 cherry tomatoes
toast
slightly salted butter
lime wedges

For the dressing:
1 hard-cooked egg yolk from a
large egg
2 tablespoons walnut oil
1 tablespoon peanut oil
1 tablespoon sherry vinegar★
tiny pinch of mustard with green
peppercorns
salt and freshly ground black pepper
tiny pinch of cayenne

SERVES 4
PREPARATION TIME: 40 MINUTES
COOKING TIME: 20 MINUTES

Alan Davidson comments in
Mediterranean Seafood *that many
people consider langouste to have a more
delicate flavor than lobster. Known as
rock or spiny lobster in the United States
and as crawfish in the United Kingdom,
it lacks the large claws of a lobster and
has a darkish red shell before it is
cooked. Enormously popular in France,
it is imported from as far away as North
Africa and South America. Different
varieties of spiny lobsters are found in the
Atlantic and Pacific Oceans and in the
Gulf of Mexico.*

*Samphire, or pousse-pierre, a wild
seaside plant with thin glassy green stalks
and an aromatic salty taste had all but
disappeared from French tables until it
was brought back into vogue by chefs, to
be eaten uncooked or lightly boiled.*

Trim the green beans, then cut them in half lengthwise and blanch them in very salty boiling water for 4 minutes. Drain and place on absorbent paper to dry, then transfer them to a plate and sprinkle with a little vinegar. Trim the spinach by pulling the stalks towards the tips. Rinse under cold running water, drain and dry.

Plunge the spiny lobster into the boiling court bouillon and it will die instantly. Cook for 12 minutes, no longer. Leave to cool in the liquid, then drain and remove the meat from the shell. (The shell can be reserved to flavor a shellfish sauce or fish soup.)

Reheat the court bouillon and put in the shrimp. Simmer for 4 minutes, then drain and peel as soon as they have cooled a little. Cut the spiny lobster meat into slices ½ inch thick, and cut the shrimp in half lengthwise.

Arrange them in a dish on a bed of spinach, green beans and samphire (if used). Cut the salmon into slivers and arrange among the other ingredients, together with the cherry tomatoes.

To make the dressing, chop the egg yolk and beat it with the oils, then add the other dressing ingredients and pour over the salad. Serve on chilled plates, with hot toast and slightly salted butter, wedges of lime and a chilled dry white wine.

SPICY CARIBBEAN CRAB PURÉE
Purée de crabe aux piments

1½-2¼ lb crab meat
½ lb (about 10 slices) bread, crusts
removed
3½ tablespoons white rum
2 small chili peppers
½ lb onions
3 cloves of garlic
1 teaspoon *poudre à colombo,*★ or mild
curry powder
salt and freshly ground black pepper
2 egg whites from extra large eggs

SERVES 6
PREPARATION TIME: 25 MINUTES

*In the French Caribbean, this recipe is
made with land crabs, which are
fattened, often with coconut, a few days
before the sacrifice in the same way that
the French fatten snails and poultry.
Either crab or spider crab can be used,
but for large amounts this can be
expensive, and the recipe is almost as
good made with canned crab meat,
lightened with stiffly beaten egg whites.
If you are using fresh crab meat, you can
use the lower-priced flake meat instead of
lump meat.*

Soak the bread in water, then squeeze it dry and soak it in the rum in a bowl. Deseed the chili peppers and purée in a blender with the onions and garlic. Add the drained crab, *poudre à colombo* and a little salt and pepper, and blend for a few more seconds. Add the bread soaked in rum and blend for 2 or 3 seconds more. Transfer the mixture to the bowl the bread was soaked in.

Beat the egg whites with a pinch of salt until stiff. Carefully fold the egg whites into the crab mixture to obtain a light, fluffy preparation. Keep in the refrigerator until required – but do not freeze.

This makes a good first course served with lime wedges and ripe tomatoes, in which case allow only 2 oz crab meat per person instead of 4 to 6 oz, as allowed here.

MUSSELS AND CLAMS

Mussels are eaten in large quantities in France, from north to south: at Lille there is even an annual festival which results in huge heaps of shells in the cathedral square. Since recipes for *moules marinières* abound, here are two less well known dishes from the north of France. *Moules à la biere* is particularly popular, filling the bistros from Dunkirk to Amsterdam with its pungent smell.

Clams, too, are farmed in France, and are greatly enjoyed. They may be used instead of mussels – or in addition to them – in the following recipes.

SHELLFISH FRIED IN THEIR SHELLS
Poelée de coquillages

For each serving:
1 pint mussels and clams
1 tablespoon olive oil or butter
1 tablespoon dry white wine
freshly ground black pepper
bread with oil and garlic, or with herb butter (see page 21), to serve

PREPARATION TIME: 15 MINUTES
COOKING TIME: 5 MINUTES

This is a marvelously simple way of cooking clams or mussels from master fish chef Paul Minchelli of Le Duc (see page 90). Paul and his brother Jean started their first restaurant on the Ile de Ré off the west coast, close to the shellfish farms of Marennes and the Vendée. Fresh clams tend to be better quality in the colder months (from September through May), although some can be found in the market place the rest of the year.

Scrub and rinse the shellfish. Sauté them in the oil or butter over a fairly high heat, and sprinkle with the wine and pepper to taste. Remove them from the pan as they open. Eat them with your hands, with bread rubbed with olive oil and garlic, or toasted and spread with herb butter.

CRÊPES FILLED WITH MUSSELS IN CREAM
Pannequet aux coquillages

1 quart small mussels
1 *bouquet garni**
1 sprig of rosemary
2 small pinches of cayenne pepper
scant 1 cup dry white wine or hard cider
1 fresh onion with its green stalk
2 tablespoons butter
2 large eggs
2/3 cup heavy cream
1/3 cup grated Gruyère cheese
salt
pinch of cayenne
oil for frying
1 sprig of flat-leafed parsley

For scant 1 pint batter:
1 2/3 cup flour
1 1/2 cups water and cooking juices from shellfish
1 tablespoon peanut oil
2 large eggs

SERVES 4
PREPARATION TIME: 15 MINUTES
COOKING TIME: ABOUT 20 MINUTES

These little crêpes, filled with shellfish and a sauce and then browned in the oven; can be prepared in advance. This recipe comes from the Boulogne area.

Be ruthless about discarding any mussels which are open when you scrub them or which do not open on heating.

Scrub the mussels and heat with the *bouquet garni*, the rosemary, 1 pinch of cayenne and the white wine until they open. Drain, reserving the cooking liquid. Remove the mussels from their shells, working over a bowl to catch the juice. Strain the juice and cooking liquid. Make the crêpe batter, which may not need salt because the mussel juices will be salty.

Finely chop the onion and its green stalk separately. Soften the onion in the hot butter. Remove from the heat, then add the chopped green top.

In a bowl, lightly beat together the eggs and two-thirds of the cream. Add the onion, mussels and half the grated cheese. Taste, and adjust the seasoning.

Make the crêpes, which always taste better when cooked just before they are needed. Meanwhile, preheat the oven to 375°F. Lay out each crêpe in turn, spread the filling on and roll it up. Fit all the crêpes tightly into a *gratin* dish. Pour on the remaining cream mixed with the rest of the cheese, and sprinkle with a tiny pinch of cayenne. Bake the crêpes for 8 to 10 minutes, until golden brown. Sprinkle with chopped parsley. Serve piping hot with a green salad and chilled dry hard cider.

MUSSELS STEAMED IN BEER
Moules à la vapeur de bière

6 quarts mussels, scrubbed
2 tablespoons butter
2 shallots
3 sprigs of flat-leafed parsley
3½ tablespoons flour
1 level teaspoon curry powder
scant 1 cup lager or other light beer
⅓ cup water
2 egg yolks from large eggs
salt and freshly ground black pepper
1 cup *crème fraîche*★

SERVES 4-6
PREPARATION TIME: 25 MINUTES
COOKING TIME: ABOUT 25 MINUTES

This steamed version of mussels in beer is adapted from a recipe by Jacques Manière (see page 137).

Gently heat the butter in the bottom of a steamer. Finely chop the shallots and soften them in the butter. Strip off the parsley leaves and reserve both stems and leaves separately. When the shallots begin to color, sprinkle them with the flour and stir well. Wait for 3 or 4 minutes until the flour is well cooked, then add the curry powder and parsley stems and stir again. Add the beer and water. Put in the steaming basket full of mussels, cover and cook for 3 to 4 minutes, shaking the basket two or three times. (It may be necessary to cook them in two or three batches.) Keep the cooked mussels hot.

When all the mussels are open and keeping hot, make the sauce. Cut up the parsley leaves. Put the egg yolks in a bowl and whisk with a pinch of pepper, a little salt and the *crème fraîche*. Strain the cooking juices into the bowl, rinse out the pan and pour in this sauce. Bring to a boil, whisking vigorously all the time. Turn off the heat, add the parsley and whisk again until the sauce cools a little. Pour it over the mussels, or serve the sauce separately if you prefer.

SCALLOPS

Coquilles Saint-Jacques take their French name from the medieval pilgrims who wore scallop shells as a talisman in their hats on their journey to Santiago da Compostella, the great shrine of Saint James in northern Spain. Since scallops are now rather costly, almost on a par with oysters, two of the recipes here, with wine sauces, are frankly extravagant.

TOUTOUNE'S SCALLOP AND APPLE SALAD
Salade Toutoune de pétoncles et de pommes

4½ lb sea scallops in shell
3 Granny Smith apples
½ lemon
4 stalks of celery, with leaves
crusty white bread, to serve

For the mayonnaise:
2 egg yolks from large eggs
1 teaspoon English mustard powder
1 cup grapeseed oil
1 tablespoon dry white wine
salt and pepper
1 tablespoon curry powder

SERVES 4
PREPARATION TIME: 25 MINUTES +
TIME TO MAKE MAYONNAISE
COOKING TIME: 1 MINUTE

Toutoune is the nickname of Colette Dejean, who runs Chez Toutoune, a Paris restaurant serving excellent, unpretentious food with a regional accent. The pétoncle *is a smaller relation of* coquilles Saint-Jacques, *but any kind of scallops can be used.*

Scrub the scallops and open them by steaming for 1 minute (see page 62). Leave them to cool.

Meanwhile, peel the apples and cut them into large cubes. Squeeze lemon juice over them immediately to prevent them turning brown. Cut up the celery. (Toutoune uses only the leaves, but you can use the stalks as well, provided that they are tender.) Put the apples and celery in a bowl. Refrigerate the salad while you prepare the mayonnaise, using white wine instead of the usual vinegar. Season lightly with salt and pepper, add the curry powder and stir in.

Shell the scallops and add them to the salad. Pour on the mayonnaise, mix carefully and leave in the refrigerator until required. Serve with crusty bread and a chilled medium-dry Chablis or other good white wine.

MUSSELS STEAMED IN BEER▶

OYSTERS AND SCALLOPS WITH BOUZY WINE SAUCE
Huîtres et coquilles Saint-Jacques au Bouzy

12 large live oysters
12 shelled sea scallops
12 spinach or Swiss chard leaves
2 tablespoons butter
30 grapes, preferably muscat
3 shallots
½ bottle (about 3 cups) young red
Bouzy or other light red wine
salt and freshly ground black pepper
scant 1 cup *crème fraîche*★
7 tablespoons butter, at room
temperature
chopped chervil (optional)

SERVES 4
PREPARATION TIME: 50 MINUTES
COOKING TIME: 35 MINUTES

Gerard Besson, a young chef who is also a wine fanatic (the cellar of his restaurant holds some 45,000 bottles of fine wines), makes this with Bouzy, a grand cru wine. It is a quiet, fairly dry red wine. However, it would not spoil the dish if you were to make it with a less exalted wine, although you should drink the same wine with the meal. Besson has adapted the recipe for home cooks. Another recipe by him is on page 59.

Cook the spinach leaves in the hot butter just 4 to 6 seconds on each side until wilted. Drain and lay out on a board spread with paper towels.

Peel and deseed the grapes. Open the oysters and put them, still in their shells, in a saucepan. Bring the oysters to a boil, then keep the oysters hot, covered. (At this point Besson takes them out of their shells, removes the beard and gently scrapes off any grains of sand.)

Finely chop the shallots and put them in a stainless steel pan with the liquor from the oysters, the wine, and salt and pepper to taste. Bring to a simmer and reduce by half.

Clean and debeard the scallops, rinse under running water to eliminate all the sand and cut the scallops in half horizontally.

Take the reduced sauce off the heat and let it cool slightly, then add the scallops. Cover and leave to poach for 2 minutes.

Having removed the oysters from their shells, place each one in the center of a spinach leaf. Fold over to make a little parcel. Remove the scallops from the sauce with a slotted spoon and place them on a warm serving plate with the oyster parcels. Add the grapes.

Continue simmering the sauce over a high heat and whisk in the *crème fraîche*. Reduce the sauce to 1¾ cups. Taste and adjust the seasoning – usually the oyster juices make it salty enough. Divide the butter into small pieces and whisk it in. The sauce should froth and have the consistency of a mayonnaise. Pour it over the dish and put it under a very hot broiler for a minute to heat it up rather than brown it. Sprinkle with chopped chervil if you like, and serve on very hot plates.

SCALLOPS WITH SABAYON SAUCE
Sabayon aux coquilles Saint-Jacques

12 large sea scallops in shell
about 1 pint court bouillon★ for
shellfish (see page 62)
1 cup dry white wine
3-4 threads of saffron
4 egg yolks from extra large eggs
juice of ¼ lemon
freshly ground white pepper
¼ cup *crème fraîche*★
a few lettuce leaves, to garnish

SERVES 6
PREPARATION TIME: 15 MINUTES
COOKING TIME: 20 MINUTES

Open the scallops (see page 62). Separate the white meat from the coral (if any). Cut the whites of the scallops in half, and reserve any coral.

Put the scallop meat in a saucepan wide enough to take them in a single layer. Heat the court bouillon in a separate pan, adding wine just until the liquid covers the shellfish, and, when barely simmering, pour gently over the scallops. Add the saffron. Cover and simmer gently for 2 minutes. Remove from the heat, immediately drain the scallops and reserve the cooking liquid. Return it to the pan and reduce to scant 1 cup. Transfer it to a jug, and put 1 tablespoon separately in a cup to cool. Keep the scallops warm. Preheat the broiler.

Put the egg yolks, the scallop corals, the cooled spoonful of cooking liquid, the lemon juice and a little pepper in a bowl that you can set over simmering water without the base touching the water (or use a double boiler). Whisk until creamy (preferably with an electric beater). Set the bowl over the hot water, add the rest of the cooking liquid and whisk until the mixture foams up. Take it off the heat. In another bowl, whip the *crème fraîche* until frothy but not stiff. Fold this into the egg mixture.

Arrange the scallops on a warmed serving dish, pour the sauce over them and color the top under the broiler. Decorate with lettuce leaves.

SCALLOPS WITH SABAYON▶

SQUID

Squid and cuttlefish appear under a number of names in France – as *calmars*, *seiches*, and *encornets*, as *supions* in the Languedoc and as *chipirones* on the southern Atlantic coast. Small squid are very often gently sautéed in olive oil and braised in wine until they are tender; the larger, less tender ones are stuffed or stewed. Cooking times vary between 10 minutes for frying small, tender squid and several hours for stewing larger ones. Do not be put off by the idea of cleaning squid. It is neither difficult nor unpleasant – the method is given in the marinated squid recipe below.

MARINATED SQUID
Calamars marinés

1 lb 2 oz small squid
2 tablespoons olive oil
a little chopped garlic
salt and freshly ground black pepper
hot pepper sauce
juice of ½ lemon
1 level teaspoon chopped fresh basil

SERVES 4 AS AN APPETIZER
PREPARATION TIME: 15 MINUTES +
COOLING
COOKING TIME: 5 MINUTES

If you cannot find the very tender small squid you may need to increase the cooking time – judge by testing them in the pan for tenderness. The same recipe can be used for shrimp, which can be peeled before serving.

Clean and trim the squid, and cut into slices ¾ inch thick. Cut off the tentacles so that they are attached together by a ring of flesh at the base. Sauté in the olive oil over a high heat for 5 minutes with the garlic. Season to taste, and add a few drops of hot pepper sauce and the lemon juice. Leave to cool in the cooking juices. Stir in the basil.

Cleaning squid: cut off and reserve tentacles. Pull off head; remove everything inside body. Peel away outer membrane. Rinse.

SQUID IN GREEN SAUCE
Calamars en sauce verte

1¼ lb squid or cuttlefish
scant 1 cup dry white wine
1 tablespoon oil
small bunch of fresh chervil
small bunch of flat-leafed parsley
1 cup court bouillon (see page 62)
sea salt
freshly ground white pepper
tiny pinch of cayenne pepper
1 clove of garlic, minced
scant 1 cup water
2 tablespoons slightly salted butter
3 large Swiss chard leaves, without stems, or ¼ lb fresh bulk spinach

SERVES 4
PREPARATION TIME: 30 MINUTES
COOKING TIME: ABOUT 40 MINUTES

Poaching squid in court bouillon makes a pleasant change from the usual fried squid recipes.

Clean the squid, make a 1-inch slit in the bodies and reserve these and the tentacles, which cut off at the level of the eyes. Rinse well.

In a saucepan, combine the white wine and oil; add chervil and parsley stems along with the court bouillon, a little salt, the cayenne and minced garlic. Add the water and bring to a boil.

Separately, boil some water. When the court bouillon mixture begins to boil, put in the tentacles and add enough of the boiling water to cover them. Bring back to a boil and simmer gently for 10 minutes. Chop the parsley and chervil leaves. Steam them for 3 minutes and drain well.

Now add the squid bodies to the pan and cover with more boiling water if necessary. Cover and simmer for 10 minutes.

Heat half the butter in a skillet. When it begins to color, add the Swiss chard and the herbs. Wilt over a gentle heat, shaking the pan from time to time, for about 6 to 8 minutes, then add a generous ladleful of stock from the squid pan. Cook for another 5 minutes.

Purée the Swiss chard and herbs and put them back in the pan for a few minutes to reduce even more, still over a gentle heat and without covering. Whisk in the remaining butter. Adjust the seasoning, and spread the sauce over the bottom of a heated dish. Drain the squid and arrange on the sauce.

SQUID IN GREEN SAUCE ▶

FISH

CAPITAINE SEYCHELLOISE (see page 90)

ROAST MONKFISH (see page 81)

BUYING, CLEANING AND COOKING FISH

Freshness is always essential in fish. Very fresh ones may be sold whole and uncleaned. The most reliable way of establishing their freshness is to press with your fingers: if they are fresh, the supple flesh will spring back into shape. Another sure sign is appearance: the fish should be shiny, the gills red, the eyes bright. There should be no smell and the fish should be slightly sticky to the touch. Fresh warm-water fish keeps for 1 week if refrigerated, but cold-water fish will keep for only 3 days. It is particularly important to buy absolutely fresh fish for lightly cooked or raw dishes.

None of the fish used in this chapter should be impossible to find fresh, although alternatives are suggested for the more unusual tropical fish. If you want a particular fish it is always worth discussing it in advance with your fish merchant since they are often happy to take special orders if given notice.

Never wash fish: wipe with a damp cloth. Gut them, of course. Otherwise cleaning varies. Some fish, such as whiting, only require a light scraping, while others, like sea bass, should not be scraped at all. Do not scale fish that is to be broiled or grilled. The scales protect the flesh from the heat, which can make the flesh tough if too intense. When cooked, the scales and skin can easily be removed – preferably in the kitchen. For filleting, skinning and boning, refer to a good book on fish cooking.

There is some disagreement among chefs as to the best methods for cooking various types of fish: baking sealed or in sea salt, poaching in a court bouillon (page 62), steaming . . . the list could go on. So, for example, while some cook bass in a court bouillon, others disagree, saying that the fish loses its flavor and it is better to throw away the fish and use the court bouillon! Certainly, however, any very lightly cooked, raw or marinated raw dishes must not even be contemplated unless the fish has been caught that day.

How can you test if fish are cooked? Here are two tips: Breton chef Gilbert le Coze suggests inserting a trussing needle behind the head of the cooking fish and raising the needle to your lips. When it is slightly warm, the fish is cooked to perfection. Paul Minchelli of Le Duc advises checking near the head by pulling the small bones. If they come away easily, the fish is cooked.

POACHING FISH AND SERVING IT *À LA NAGE*

For poaching fish, use the court bouillon given on page 62, increasing the quantities so that there is enough to cover the fish. This will depend on the size of the fish kettle or pan you are using as well as the fish itself. The flavoring ingredients for a court bouillon can vary considerably as appropriate to the fish and finished dish. Extra flavorings could include fresh herb fennel, rosemary, basil, thyme or, for exotic fish, coriander (cilantro) leaves and cumin. Paul Minchelli of Le Duc uses a wine court bouillon flavored with garlic, chili pepper and cinnamon for fish with mild or even bland flavors, such as pollack, halibut, whiting, flounder, hake and cod. No single flavor should predominate.

During the poaching itself, the liquid should only tremble; if it

boils, the fibers of the fish will toughen.

After the fish has been removed, the stock may be boiled to concentrate its flavor. Now called a *nage* – more delicate than a fumet made with fish heads and tails – this may be poured back over the fish as a sauce, in which case the fish is said to be *à la nage* – or swimming. Once reserved mainly for *écrevisses*, small lobsters and other crustaceans, this has become popular among chefs as a way of serving all kinds of fish – sole, whiting, flounder, cod and hake, for example.

Final flavorings can be added after the *nage* has been concentrated. Minchelli, for example, adds fresh mint, grated ginger, chopped lemon grass, softened onion, parsley and a little fresh orange juice.

TROUT

Both of the following recipes come from Michel Bras (see also pages 56 and 192), who uses the produce of the Aveyron countryside, in the southern Massif Central, to create a wonderful personal repertoire which is entirely local in its influences. The nearby rivers are full of trout and Bras takes full advantage of the fact. Lagouiole, used in the first recipe, is a fairly hard cheese flavored with wild herbs, which is made in, and named after, the small village where Bras lives and cooks. A Cheddar-type herbed cheese will replace it.

Fresh trout is abundantly available so there is no need to buy frozen. Much of it is farmed; this gives fattier, less tasty flesh. There is little difference between white and pink fleshed trout, although white trout can have a muddier flavor.

TROUT FILLETS AU GRATIN
Gratin de filets de truite

1 large trout, weighing 14 oz, or 2
smaller ones
¼ lb shallots
1½ tablespoons butter
salt and freshly ground black pepper
coriander seeds
4 large cabbage leaves
1 level tablespoon goose fat★ (or 2
tablespoons butter)
¼ lb Laguiole cheese★

SERVES 2
PREPARATION TIME: 20 MINUTES
COOKING TIME: 50 MINUTES

This recipe can also be used for fillets of whiting, sole and flounder.

Fillet the trout and discard the skin. Coarsely chop the shallots and add them to the melted butter in a pan. Cover with salted water. Add pepper to taste and a few coriander seeds. Cook for 20 minutes.

Blanch the cabbage leaves, then cook them with the goose fat (or butter), a few coriander seeds, seasoning and water to cover for 15-20 minutes. Preheat the oven to 475°F.

Transfer the shallots and their liquid to an ovenproof dish. Then add the cabbage and its liquid. Put the trout fillets on top, cut in two horizontally if they are very thick. Salt lightly. Cover with slivers of cheese. Bake for 4 minutes.

77

FISH

TROUT FILLETS AND LEEKS WITH *AÏGO BOULIDO*
Filets de truite et poireaux à l'aïgo boulido

1 large trout, weighing 14 oz, or 2
smaller ones
4 young leeks
salt
4 cloves of young, fresh garlic or 2
cloves of old garlic
1 bay leaf
2 cloves
coriander seeds
black peppercorns
2 sprigs of flat-leafed parsley
1½ tablespoons butter
1 tablespoon walnut oil

SERVES 2
PREPARATION TIME: 20 MINUTES
COOKING TIME: 25 MINUTES

Aïgo boulido is the name of a Provençal specialty, a thin garlic and herb soup considered in the midi to be a great health tonic. Its name – meaning simply boiled water – reveals its origins as a very cheap, simple peasant soup. No doubt its reputation as a reviver comes from the garlic, which is eaten to kill germs and keep away colds. Note the difference in the quantities given for young garlic, available in the summer, and the stronger older garlic.

Fillet the trout. Cook the leeks in boiling salted water for 5 minutes. Drain, reserving 1¼ cups of this water; in it cook the minced garlic, the bay leaf, cloves, coriander, peppercorns, parsley and butter for 15 minutes.

Meanwhile, steam the trout fillets for 3-5 minutes, depending on their thickness.

Arrange the leeks and trout in a deep serving platter. Season with pepper. Pour on the garlic and herb soup through a strainer, and add a trickle of walnut oil. This finishing touch adds wonderfully to the final flavor.

LYONNAIS SALMON AND WHITING ROULADE
Cocon roulé

8-10 raw crayfish
1 large egg
3 egg yolks (from large eggs)
10 oz salmon fillet
salt and freshly ground white pepper
⅔ cup *crème fraîche*★
14 oz whiting fillet
3 oz mushrooms (wild if possible)
melted butter
oil or butter for frying

For the fish stock:
½ lb fish heads and tails
1 carrot
1 onion
1 *bouquet garni*★
scant 1 cup dry white wine

For the sauce:
scant ½ cup cognac (optional)
3 egg yolks from large eggs
1 cup *crème fraîche*★
pinch of *quatre-épices*★
bunch of chervil

SERVES 4
PREPARATION TIME: 50 MINUTES
COOKING TIME: ABOUT 1½ HOURS

This recipe from Lyon, for centuries the center of French silk weaving, is for a fish mousse which rises in the oven until it looks like a silkworm's cocoon.

Make the fish stock by simmering the ingredients for 30 minutes.

Discard any eggs (roe) from the crayfish and cook the crayfish in the boiling stock for 6 to 8 minutes. Remove with a slotted spoon. As soon as they have cooled, peel them and throw the shells into the stock, which should still be simmering. Lightly beat the whole egg and egg yolks together. Purée a third of the egg mixture with the salmon, salt and pepper to taste and a third of the *crème fraîche*.

Now blend the whiting to a purée with the rest of the egg mixture and *crème fraîche*. Season.

Finely slice the mushrooms and squeeze lemon juice over them. Sauté for 6 minutes gently.

Spread a piece of cheesecloth on a board. Using a spatula, first spread out the salmon purée on it, and then cover with the whiting purée. Arrange the crayfish and mushrooms on top, and add the mushroom juice to the stock. Fold over the purée on all sides to enclose the filling, then roll it up like a jelly roll with the help of the cheesecloth. Tie ends and center.

Place the "cocoon" on the rack of a fish kettle or in a pot and poach for 20 minutes in simmering water. Preheat the oven to 385°F.

Drain the cocoon and place it in a baking dish. Carefully remove the cheesecloth, and brush the cocoon with melted butter. Then bake until it rises and turns a light golden brown, about 20 minutes.

While the cocoon is baking, strain the stock into a clean saucepan, also rubbing the crayfish shells and vegetables through the sieve into the pan. To finish the sauce, add the Cognac (or omit it if you wish) and whisk the stock vigorously, gradually adding the *crème fraîche* and beaten egg yolks. Turn the heat down to a minimum and continue whisking to obtain a light frothy sauce. Add the *quatre-épices* and sprinkle with chopped chervil.

Serve the cocoon with the sauce poured around it.

TROUT FILLETS AND LEEKS WITH *AÏGO BOULIDO*▶

78

SEA TROUT AND POTATOES WITH PARSLEY AND *BEURRE BLANC*
Truite de mer au beurre de persil

1 sea trout, weighing about 2¼ lb or
2 smaller ones
1 lb 2 oz small potatoes
4 small white onions
1 clove of garlic
small bunch of flat-leafed parsley
1 stick slightly salted butter
scant 1 cup water
salt and freshly ground white pepper
10 green peppercorns

SERVES 4
PREPARATION TIME: 25 MINUTES
COOKING TIME: ABOUT 45 MINUTES

A simply cooked but refined dish from Jean-Pierre Billoux, whose restaurant is in Dijon, at the heart of gastronomic Burgundy. He lays great emphasis on shopping in the markets. "It trains and inspires your eye. I find it helps me to keep in contact with the rhythm of the seasons; that the juxtaposition of colors and smells is a wonderful source of inspiration. Also I like to try and find produce – freshwater fish, for example – that may have become underused because it is not available in every shop or supermarket."

You can cook the trout whole or divide it into 4 (or 8) fillets. Parboil the potatoes, onions and garlic. Remove the largest parsley stems and blanch the sprigs in boiling water. Heat 1½ tablespoons butter in a skillet and sauté the potatoes in it. Put the garlic and onion in a heavy-bottomed pan with 1½ tablespoons butter and place over a gentle heat. Cover and let them sweat for about 10 to 12 minutes.

Meanwhile, lightly brush the bottom of a non-stick skillet with very little butter. Set it over a medium heat and cook the fish: 3 minutes each side for fillets and 6 to 7 minutes for a whole fish.

At the same time, bring the water to a boil in a small saucepan. When the water boils, beat in the rest of the butter with a whisk or a fork to make a frothy sauce. Season to taste, and add the green peppercorns.

Arrange the trout on a serving dish with the potatoes, garlic, onions and blanched parsley. Coat with the sauce.

FISH

MONKFISH WITH DILL BAKED IN FOIL
Papillotes de lotte à l'aneth

4 lb monkfish
1¼ cups *crème fraîche*★
1 lemon
fresh dill weed, or dill seed

SERVES 6
PREPARATION TIME: 10 MINUTES
COOKING TIME: 25 MINUTES

This recipe was given in an article on good but speedy recipes to save time and trouble. Cooking fish in aluminum foil not only keeps the pan clean but also seals in the juices and aromas, giving the prized texture and taste of fish cooked en papillote – so you can be practical and perfectionist at the same time!

Monkfish, known in France as baudroie *and* lotte de mer *(but only by the second name once it is in the fish merchants), has a perfect texture for this cooking method.*

Ask the fish merchant to skin the monkfish, if necessary, and to remove the membrane, which otherwise shrinks around the fish and removes from its appearance.
Preheat the oven to 475°F. Cut the monkfish into 6 slices. Place each slice of fish on a piece of foil. Season to taste and add a share of the *crème fraîche*, a thin slice of lemon and a little dill. Seal the foil and bake for 25 minutes.
Serve with buttered pasta or potatoes, followed by a green salad. This is a good dish to serve after a rich or heavy first course.
Many other fish are good cooked by this simple method: hake, whiting, cod, flounder and lemon sole, for example. Cooking time depends on the thickness of the fish rather than the size of the slice.

ROAST MONKFISH
Gigot de mer de Palavas-les-Flots

1¾ cups olive oil
3 onions
¾ lb eggplants
½ lb zucchini
7 cloves of garlic
1 strip of dried orange zest★
1 sweet green pepper
1 sweet red pepper
1 sweet yellow pepper
1 lb 2 oz tomatoes
1 teaspoon fennel seed
sprig of thyme
3-4 needles of rosemary
salt and freshly ground black pepper
1 monkfish tail piece, weighing 3 lb
sprig of basil
1 teaspoon *pastis*★ (optional)

SERVES 8
PREPARATION TIME: 20 MINUTES
COOKING TIME: ABOUT 1 HOUR

PHOTOGRAPH ON PAGE 75

A gigot de mer, *or roast monkfish tail, is so called because after trimming it looks a little like a leg of lamb. Spiked with garlic and baked on ratatouille, it is one of the great Provençal fish dishes.*

Choose a heavy, oval flameproof pot with plenty of room for the fish. Put in half the oil, and set over a medium heat. Slice the onions, separate the rings and drop them into the hot oil.
Without peeling, cut the eggplants into slices ¼ inch thick and the zucchini into slices of ½ inch. Stir the onions and spread the eggplants and zucchini on top. Finely chop 3 cloves of garlic. Crush the dried orange rind. Sprinkle these over the vegetables.
Deseed the sweet peppers, cut into strips or rings and spread them on top. Peel the tomatoes by plunging them into boiling water for 30 seconds, quarter them, discard the seeds and spread them over the peppers. Pound the fennel seeds, thyme and rosemary in a mortar and pestle and sprinkle on top with the seasoning. Preheat the oven to 375°F.
Slice the remaining garlic no more than about one-tenth of an inch thick. Use a sharp pointed knife to make a row of little cuts all along the spine of the fish and insert the slices.
Push the top layers of vegetables aside to make a slight hollow, and put in the fish. Pour on the remaining oil. Cover the casserole and cook in the oven for 45 minutes, turning the fish over after half this time.
Five minutes before the end, bury the leaves of basil among the vegetables. Serve in the pot. Some enthusiasts like to sprinkle it with *pastis* at the last moment. This dish is equally good hot and cold.

81

PORGY

Porgies are a large family, most of which like warm southern waters. In France, *daurade* (called gilt-head bream in England), a golden yellow fish from the Mediterranean, is the most highly prized for eating. It is difficult to find *daurade* farther north, but red porgy or scup, striped mullet or bass, can all be used in these dishes. In any case, these are both marvelous recipes to adapt for stuffing any large whole fish.

STUFFED PORGY BRAISED ON A BED OF VEGETABLES
Dorade farcie braisée sur légumes

1 porgy, or other whole fish, weighing about 2¾ lb
3 shallots
3 tablespoons butter
¼ lb button mushrooms
juice of ½ lemon
1 lb green leaf vegetables in season (spinach, Swiss chard etc.)
5 oz whiting fillet
a few sprigs of flat-leafed parsley, chervil, herb fennel, thyme etc.
salt and freshly ground black pepper
2 teaspoons *vadouvan*★ (or curry powder with 1 crushed clove of garlic)
1 cup *crème fraîche*★
1 carrot
2 whites of leek
1¼ cups beer
10 green peppercorns
2 tablespoons cream

SERVES 4
PREPARATION TIME: I HOUR
COOKING TIME: 45 MINUTES

This is a dish from northern France, where it is made with freshwater fish, such as bream (porgy) and carp. Beer replaces wine in several northern dishes from Flanders and Alsace, coq à la bière from Alsace or moules à la bière, for example. The beer should be a light lager or British-type ale.

Scale the fish without damaging it. Cut off the fins with scissors. Using a sharp, pointed knife, remove the backbone by inserting the knife through the gills and sliding it down each side of the backbone to the tail. Do the same from the tail end. Take care not to slit the belly. Snip through the backbone at either end and pull it out, leaving the head and tail in place. The fish should open like a pocket. Gut, wash and dry it. It is now ready for stuffing.

Prepare the stuffing. (If you like, it can be made the day before and refrigerated, which will make it firmer; pack it tightly into a container and cover it with greased or oiled paper.) Chop 2 shallots as finely as possible and put them in a heavy flameproof pot with half of the butter. Remove the stems from the mushrooms and chop these; set the caps aside. Squeeze a little lemon juice over the chopped mushrooms and add to the shallots. Wilt over a very gentle heat. The mixture should soften, but not brown. Wash and dry the greens and cut up with scissors. Add them to the pot and remove from the heat at once. Leave to cool with the lid on.

Scrape all the flesh of the fish from the backbone and put it in a bowl. Chop the whiting and add it. Add the shallot and mushroom mixture, chopped herbs and salt and pepper to taste and the *vadouvan* or substitute. Mix well with a wooden spoon and gradually incorporate the *crème fraîche*. Mix until smooth. Slice the carrot into almost transparent rounds and the leeks into thin slices. Cut each mushroom cap into four. Slice the remaining shallot. Place in a fish kettle.

Preheat the oven to 400°F. Stuff the fish with the mixture, packing it in firmly. Sew up the opening or secure with wooden toothpicks. Put the fish on the bed of vegetables, then pour on the beer. Sprinkle with the peppercorns and slivers of the remaining butter.

Set the fish kettle on top of the stove, over a medium heat, uncovered. As soon as it is near boiling, cover and transfer it to the oven. Braise the fish for 20 minutes, basting from time to time. Tilt the lid to make the aromatic condensed water run back into the kettle. Turn off the oven and leave the kettle inside for 10 minutes with the door shut.

Before serving, take out a few spoonfuls of cooking juice, stir them into the cream and pour back into the casserole.

82

PORGY STUFFED WITH SPINACH, CREAM CHEESE AND ANCHOVIES
Dorade au fromage blanc

1 porgy, weighing 2¼ lb
1 onion
½ cup dry white wine
1 cup fish fumet (see page 62)
chopped flat-leafed parsley and chervil
lemon wedges

For the stuffing:
1 shallot
1 clove of garlic
1 tablespoon olive oil
¾ lb mixed greens (spinach, Swiss chard, a very little sorrel, chopped flat-leafed parsley and chervil)
4 canned anchovy fillets, soaked in milk to remove salt
5 thin slices stale bread, without crust
scant 1 cup dry white wine
grated zest of 1 lemon★
2 egg yolks from large eggs
⅔ cup *fromage blanc*★
salt and freshly ground black pepper

SERVES 4
PREPARATION TIME: 45 MINUTES
COOKING TIME: 35 MINUTES

Fromage blanc, *or any other cream cheese with 40 or 60% fat content, is a good binding agent. Green stuffings, usually based on sorrel, are often used for freshwater fish, meat and cabbage stuffings.*

Scale, clean and gut the fish, leaving the head on. Extend the slit to the tail. Loosen all the ribs, taking care not to damage the flesh. Pull out the backbone as close to the head as possible and snip it through at both ends. (Use this bone to make the stock.) Put the fish in the refrigerator until needed.

To prepare the stuffing, finely chop the shallot and soften it with the minced garlic in hot olive oil in a heavy pan for 2 minutes. Coarsely chop the greens and add to the pan. Wilt for 2 minutes, no longer, then add the parsley and chervil without cooking them. Remove from the heat and leave until required. Preheat the oven to 425°F.

Crush the anchovies in a bowl. Moisten the bread with a little white wine and combine with the anchovies and lemon zest, adding as much wine as you need to make a runny paste. Add the egg yolks, then the *fromage blanc*, and mix well. Add a little salt and pepper to taste; remember that the anchovies are quite salty. Drain the mixture in the pan, reserving the liquid, and add to the bowl. Mix together thoroughly.

Lightly pepper the inside of the fish, fill with the stuffing and carefully sew up the belly. Lightly oil the bottom of a large, deep, ovenproof dish. Finely slice the onion and spread it over the dish. Place the stuffed fish on this bed of onion, and pour on the white wine, the fish fumet and the juices from the cooking of the stuffing. Bake for 20 minutes, basting 3 or 4 times, and then turn the oven down to 350°F and cover the dish with oiled baking parchment. Bake for a further 10 minutes.

Transfer the fish to a hot dish and sprinkle with freshly chopped parsley and chervil. Strain the sauce and serve separately in a sauceboat. Serve the fish with lemon wedges, and accompany with a dry white wine, preferably the same as that used in the sauce.

MARINATED HERRING

The French are very fond of marinated herring. Those in spiced vinegar, known as Baltic herring or sometimes Bismarck herring (but not in France since 1870!), are usually bought in jars from the grocer or supermarket. Herring marinated in wine, sometimes replaced by hard cider, is an excellent dish to make at home. It is delicious eaten either as part of a mixed *hors d'oeuvre* or as a main course with crisp green salad leaves and a hot or cold potato salad.

In Alsace, where appetites are large, the herring would be accompanied by the local pickled turnips, sauerkraut salad, beets and dollops of sour cream or horseradish, to be eaten with a dry white wine, lager or ale. On the lighter side, a salad of sliced marinated herring, finely chopped white or red onion and a little grated tart apple, dressed with sour cream, red wine vinegar and a dribble of olive oil, is excellent for reviving sated or jaded appetites.

HERRING OR MACKEREL MARINATED IN WINE
Harengs ou maquereaux marinés au vin

2¼ lb small fresh herring or mackerel
1 handful sea salt
1 bottle (750 ml) of dry white wine,
such as Muscadet
2 onions
1 carrot
1¼ cups wine vinegar
10 black peppercorns
4 sprigs of thyme
2 bay leaves, preferably fresh
4 cloves
1 small chili pepper
2 sprigs of tarragon

SERVES 4
PREPARATION TIME: 25 MINUTES +
OVERNIGHT SALTING
COOKING TIME: 30 MINUTES

This simple recipe is a wonderful illustration of the adaptability of wine in cooking. The marinade can be made from either red or white wine, and used for mackerel and anchovies as well.

Fresh herring are widely available – make sure you choose fresh-looking fish with shiny eyes.

Gut the fish and cut off the heads. Cover them with salt without washing them. Refrigerate them overnight in a non-metallic container placed on a slightly sloping surface to drain away the juices from the fish.

Prepare the marinade by heating together the wine, the finely sliced onions and carrot, the vinegar, peppercorns, a sprig of thyme, a bay leaf, cloves and whole chili pepper. Simmer for 30 minutes. Cool.

Wash and dry the fish and lay them head to tail in a dish (not steel or aluminum). Put herbs between each layer, finishing with herbs. When the marinade has cooled a little, pour it over the fish. Leave to cool completely, then cover and refrigerate.
Variation: for a more pungent flavor, prepare the fish and the marinade as above, but let the marinade cool completely. Preheat the oven to 300°F. Put the fish in a deep ovenproof dish and pour on the marinade. Cover with aluminum foil and bake for 20 minutes. Leave in the oven to cool, then refrigerate with the marinade. In either case, drink with white wine.

SARDINES

It is hard to beat really fresh charcoal-grilled or fried sardines served with lemon and bread, although their smell lingers long after you have eaten them. Michel Guérard suggests baking them in salt, which locks in the cooking smells – it takes about 30 minutes.

Here are two of the many sardine recipes from the Mediterranean. One is a traditional Provençal recipe from Cagnes-sur-Mer, near Nice; the other comes from Algeria, a French colony until twenty-five years ago.

STUFFED SARDINES FROM CAGNES
Sardines à la mode de Cagnes

18 fresh sardines
sprig of flat-leafed parsley
2 leaves of basil
3 Swiss chard or spinach leaves
1 clove of garlic
scant 1 cup olive oil
salt and freshly ground black pepper
1¼ cups dry white wine or Provençal rosé
2 onions
1 tablespoon capers
1 tablespoon fresh bread crumbs
1 egg yolk from a large egg
chopped flat-leafed parsley
lemon wedges

SERVES 4
PREPARATION TIME: 30 MINUTES
COOKING TIME: 20-25 MINUTES

Most sardines served in restaurants are frozen, but fresh ones are sometimes available and the difference in texture and flavor is considerable. Look for fish with bright, shiny eyes.

Gut the sardines by cutting off the head and pulling; the innards will follow. Scale them and wipe the insides but do not wash them. Chop the herbs and chard.

Coarsely chop the garlic. Cook the herbs and garlic in very little oil with salt to taste until the moisture from the herbs has evaporated. Sprinkle with pepper and leave to cool a little.

Fillet two of the sardines and crush them with the herb mixture. Stuff the rest of the sardines with the mixture, pressing it in well. Arrange in a shallow pan. Pour the wine into the pan and poach the sardines for 2 minutes on each side. Turn them over carefully to prevent the stuffing from falling out. Remove the sardines from the pan and lay on paper towels to drain. Reserve the wine.

Preheat the broiler. Heat half the remaining oil in a flameproof dish and brown the chopped onions. Lay the sardines head to tail on the bed of onions. Scatter on half the capers and pour on a little of the reserved wine. Mix the rest of the capers with the bread crumbs, sprinkle the mixture over the dish, and moisten with the rest of the olive oil.

Put the sardines under the

broiler to cook for 3 minutes. Meanwhile, strain the remaining wine into a small saucepan. Add the egg yolk and whisk constantly over a low heat until the sauce becomes creamy. Pour the sauce over the sardines and put back under the broiler for 30 seconds to brown the sauce lightly.

Serve piping hot garnished with chopped parsley, with lemon wedges and a chilled dry white or rosé wine.

ALGERIAN SPICED SARDINES
Les sardines du Chenoua

24 fresh sardines
3 cloves of garlic
small bunch of flat-leafed parsley
tiny dot of *harissa*★
flour
oil for deep frying
lemon or lime wedges

SERVES 6 AS A STARTER; 4 AS AN
APPETIZER
PREPARATION TIME: 30 MINUTES
COOKING TIME: 10-12 MINUTES

These sardines, pinned together in pairs with a garlic and parsley stuffing, are good served with other North African dishes (see pages 128 and 167), and perhaps with an orange and olive salad. The sardines may also be flattened and the stuffing placed between the two fish.
This version was given to Marie Claire by Anouk Laitier; for other recipes by her see the index.

Remove the heads and tails from the sardines, gut them and wash them under the tap. Lay them on paper towels.

Finely chop the garlic and parsley and add the *harissa*. Stuff the sardines with the mixture and secure in pairs on wooden toothpicks. Flour them all over, but not too heavily. Plunge them into a pan of hot oil and cook on each side for 5 to 6 minutes. Drain on paper towels, and serve hot or cold.

FRESH TUNA *DAUBE*
Daube de thon

2 cloves of garlic
8 crushed black peppercorns
2 onions, chopped
5 anchovy fillets
1 round tuna steak, 1¼ inches thick, cut crosswise from the center of the fish
2 tablespoons olive oil
strip of dried or fresh lemon zest★
5 tomatoes
1 *bouquet garni*★ (sprig of flat-leafed parsley, sprig of thyme, celery leaves, sprig of herb fennel, ½ bay leaf)
pinch of cayenne pepper
½ teaspoon sugar
freshly ground black pepper
1 bottle (750 ml) of dry white wine
1 sweet green pepper
1 tablespoon capers

SERVES 4
PREPARATION TIME: 40 MINUTES + 1
HOUR TO MARINATE
COOKING TIME: 1 HOUR 10 MINUTES

In Provence, daubes *are by no means only made of meat. Tuna, caught off the Mediterranean coast between Marseilles and Corsica from summer to mid-winter, is a fish particularly suited to marinating and braising because it is so meaty in taste and texture. Indeed, Dumas wrote that it was described as "neither meat nor fish" and compared it to veal.*

Crush the garlic in a mortar with the peppercorns and half the onion. Rinse the anchovies under running water to remove excess salt, and pick out any visible bones. Make four incisions in the tuna steak with a knife and lard with four of the anchovies; that is, thread them through the steak with a larding needle.

Put the garlic and onion paste in a deep dish the size of the tuna steak, and place the fish on top. Pour on the oil, add the lemon zest and cover with a cloth. Leave to marinate for 1 hour.

Preheat the oven to 400°F. Finely slice the remaining onions. Peel, deseed and crush the tomatoes.

Choose a casserole barely bigger than the tuna steak. Drain the tuna in a strainer held over the casserole and scrape with the back of a knife to remove as much of the garlic paste as possible. Reserve the paste.

Pour the oil from the marinade into the casserole, place over a gentle heat and, as soon as the oil is hot, put in the sliced onion to soften and lightly brown (3-4 minutes). Remove the onion.

Now sauté the tuna, turning up the heat a little, for 3 minutes on each side. Return the onions, and after 2 minutes add the crushed tomatoes. Cook for 5 minutes. Add the *bouquet garni*, cayenne, sugar, lemon zest, and the garlic paste scraped off the tuna. Add pepper, but no salt because of the anchovies. Pour on the white wine so that the fish is completely immersed. Cover, and put in the oven, turning it down to 350°F for 25 minutes.

Meanwhile, char the skin of the sweet pepper over a gas flame or under the broiler, and peel it. Deseed it over a plate to catch any juice, and cut into strips. Add the sweet pepper and its juice, the last anchovy and the capers to the casserole and replace the lid. Turn the oven down to 325°F and cook for another 15 minutes, then switch off the oven. Leave the casserole in the oven for 10 minutes or so to cool a little.

FRESH TUNA *DAUBE* ▶

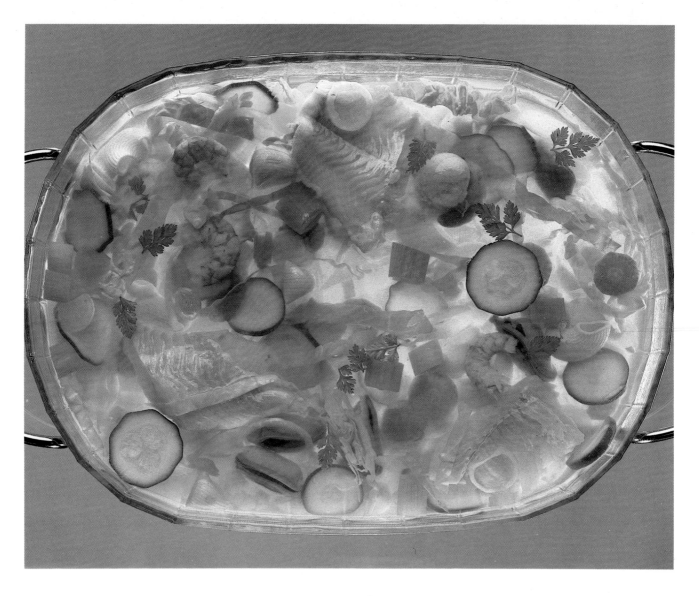

FISH *WATERZOOI*
Waterzooi de poisson

2¼ lb firm-fleshed fish fillets (whiting, monkfish, weakfish, etc.)
6 cups water
3 leeks
3 carrots
1 stalk of celery
2 turnips
1 onion
2 cloves of garlic
1 bay leaf
salt and pepper
1 quart mussels
¼ peeled shrimp (fresh or frozen)
6 large shelled sea scallops
1 stick butter or ½ cup *crème fraîche*★
6 sprigs of flat-leafed parsley or chervil

SERVES 6 AS A MAIN COURSE
PREPARATION TIME: 30 MINUTES
COOKING TIME: 35 MINUTES

A waterzooi is a Flemish dish, like a very solid soup, which is made with fish or chicken. The sauce is flavored with plenty of vegetables and has a rich buttery or creamy finish. This is only one of several Flemish fish stews. There is also a carbonnade made with smoked haddock and the famous eels cooked au vert, with a thick herby green sauce. Traditionally waterzooi was made with white fish only, but shellfish make a good addition. Serve simply, perhaps with green salad, bread and butter.

Put the water, the chopped vegetables, garlic bay leaf, and salt and pepper to taste in a saucepan and cook for about 20 minutes. Add the fish fillets and cook for a further 5 minutes.

Meanwhile, in a nonstick skillet, heat the scrubbed mussels to open them, then discard the shells. If any mussels are open when you clean them, or will not open when you heat them, then they should be discarded.

Add the shrimp (thawed if using frozen), the scallops and lastly the mussels to the soup. When it begins to boil again, taste and adjust the seasoning. Remove from the heat and add the butter or *crème fraîche* and the chopped parsley or chervil. Serve piping hot.

Variation: for a more filling dish, you could add ½ lb sliced potatoes or pasta.

FISH

MAXIM'S BREADED SOLE BAKED IN VERMOUTH
Soles Albert

6 Dover sole or gray sole (flounder),
each weighing ¾ lb
1 stick butter
4 shallots
1⅔ cups fresh white breadcrumbs
salt and freshly ground black pepper
1¾ cups dry vermouth
½ lemon
1 tablespoon each of chopped tarragon
and parsley (optional)

SERVES 6
PREPARATION TIME: 25 MINUTES
COOKING TIME: 15 MINUTES

Maxim's restaurant in Paris is famed as much for its clientele and its Art Nouveau decor as for its cooking. Now it is owned by Pierre Cardin. This dish was named after a legendary maître d'hôtel *there.*

Ask your fish merchant to draw and dress the fish, to remove the skins and to make an incision along the backbones.

Choose an ovenproof dish that will hold all the fish lying side by side. Melt 3 tablespoons butter in the dish, and keep 2 tablespoons at room temperature. Chop the shallots and spread them over the bottom of the dish. Preheat the oven to 425°F. Melt 3 tablespoons butter in a saucepan and dip the "white skin" side of each sole in it. Coat this side with breadcrumbs. Arrange the fish on the bed of shallots, breaded side

up. Season, and carefully pour in the vermouth down the side of the dish so that the fish are moistened but the bread is kept dry. Put the dish in the oven and bake for 10 minutes, then transfer the fish to a hot serving dish.

Pour the juices from the dish into a small saucepan and reduce rapidly until only 3 tablespoons of liquid are left. Remove from the heat, strain, and beat in the remaining soft butter to make a light frothy sauce. Add 1 to 2 drops of lemon juice and adjust the seasoning. Pour a little of this sauce over the sole and serve immediately, with the rest of the sauce in a sauceboat.
Variation: add the tarragon and parsley to the shallot bed. The flavor of the herbs nicely balances that of the vermouth.

SKATE WITH SWEET PEPPERS, POTATOES AND PISTOU
Raie au piment et pommes de terre

about 2 lb skate wings
2 large onions
4 sweet peppers
3 cloves of garlic
3 potatoes
2 tomatoes
sprig of basil
2 sprigs of flat-leafed parsley
3 tablespoons olive oil
1 dried chili pepper
salt and freshly ground black pepper
4 thin slices of crusty white bread

For the pistou:
2 cloves of garlic
3 sprigs of basil
½ teaspoon coarsely ground black pepper
salt
3½ tablespoons virgin olive oil
few drops of lemon juice

SERVES 4
PREPARATION TIME: 40 MINUTES
COOKING TIME: 20 MINUTES

This recipe comes from chef José Lampreia of La Maison Blanche restaurant in Paris. He says of the way he creates dishes, "I try to discard everything that is unnecessary to discover the correct taste; combine flavors which complement each other and at the same time provide a contrast; and lastly, introduce a third ingredient as much by way of punctuation as of a conclusion."

Clean the skate, rinse and dry with paper towels.

Finely slice the onions. Peel, de-seed and slice the sweet peppers. Crush the garlic. Cut the potatoes into strips which are not too thin. Peel and deseed the tomatoes and cut them into large segments. Strip the leaves from the basil, reserving the tip for decoration. Strip the parsley leaves too.

Heat the olive oil in a pot and brown the onions, sweet peppers, potatoes, tomatoes, garlic and

crumbled chili pepper; a little later add the basil and parsley. Cut the skate into four pieces and place these in the sauce. Cover with water. Season, cover the pan and cook for 20 minutes over a medium heat.

Meanwhile, prepare the pistou by crushing the garlic and basil together. Add the pepper and a little salt, and beat in the olive oil. Add the lemon juice. Toast the bread till lightly golden.

When the skate is cooked, transfer it to a serving dish, cover and keep hot.

Reduce the sauce over a high heat. Pour it over the fish and serve with the bread covered in pistou sauce.

SEYCHELLOIS RECIPES

When Paul Minchelli and his brother, Jean, opened a fish restaurant called Le Duc in Paris twenty years ago, the style of their cooking – with much of the fish and shellfish blatantly raw, very lightly grilled or baked so that it was still pink near the bone – caused a furor in the *monde gourmand*. Today, they still have animated fans and critics, but it is widely acknowledged that they have revolutionized French fish cooking.

Now there are two other branches of the restaurant, one in Geneva and the other, called le Château des Feuilles, on the island of Praslin in the Seychelles. Here two Seychellois cooks, trained by Minchelli in Paris, apply Minchelli's superb technique to the local tropical fish which are increasingly available, both fresh and frozen, everywhere.

CAPITAINE SEYCHELLOISE

2 *capitaines rouges* or *blancs*, each
weighing 1½-2¾ lb
3 large mild onions
4 tomatoes
4 cloves of garlic
2 tablespoons butter
4-5 sprigs of herb fennel
2 limes
1 tablespoon olive oil
scant 1 cup fresh coconut milk or light
white wine

SERVES 4
PREPARATION TIME: 40 MINUTES
COOKING TIME: 20-25 MINUTES

PHOTOGRAPH ON PAGE 74

Capitain rouge *and* blanc *can be found under that name in some specialty shops; otherwise, substitute porgy or scup.*

Scale the fish and wipe with a damp cloth. Make three slashes across them.

Finely slice the onions and the tomatoes. Crush 3 cloves of garlic without peeling them. Peel and finely chop the remaining clove of garlic, and combine with the butter. Oil an ovenproof dish. Cover the bottom with onion rings, slices of tomato and the unpeeled garlic. Add the fennel.

Preheat the oven to 400°F.

Place the fish on the bed of vegetables and fill the slashes with the garlic butter and slices of lime. Pour on the oil and the coconut milk (or wine). Season to taste and bake for 20 to 25 minutes, basting from time to time with the aromatic juices in the dish – a combination of the oil, the coconut milk and the fish juices. Serve piping hot with a chilled white wine.

RAW FISH IN LIME JUICE
Job praslinoise

1 job (gris or jaune), weighing
2 lb 2 oz-2¾ lb – must be very fresh
9 limes
1 teaspoon chili oil★
salt and freshly ground black pepper

For the sauce:
4 tomatoes
1 tablespoon chili oil★
6 cloves of garlic
pinch of sugar
pinch of curry powder

SERVES 3-4
PREPARATION TIME: 25 MINUTES + 10
HOURS TO MARINATE AND TIME TO
COOL
COOKING TIME: 15 MINUTES

It is far more important to make this delicious dish with a spankingly fresh, delicately flavored white fish than with an authentically tropical variety. Job is similar to snapper, which is widely available in American fish markets. Fresh tuna, preferably albacore, would be good. The fish must be no more than 2 days old.

Fillet the fish and discard the bones. Cut each fillet into 4 pieces and arrange them in a dish. Squeeze 8 limes and pour the juice over the fish. Marinate for 10 hours in a cool place.

Drain the fish and arrange the pieces in a dish. Brush with the chili oil. (Jean Minchelli keeps a

brush specially for this purpose. In this way he ensures he uses a minimum of oil.) Season and refrigerate again.

Prepare the sauce by peeling, deseeding and crushing the tomatoes. Put the chili oil in a skillet with the minced garlic and sauté without letting it brown. Add the tomatoes, and cook until they disintegrate and excess juice has evaporated. Add the sugar, curry powder and seasoning to taste, stir and leave to cool.

Serve the fish and the sauce separately, with lime wedges.

RAW FISH IN LIME JUICE▶

SALTED AND SMOKED FISH

Lightly poached smoked haddock and kippers, two of Britain's stronger culinary points, are regarded as something of a delicacy in France. In contrast, salted fish have been cooked in all kinds of different ways in France for centuries.

In the south, anchovies and sardines used to be left with salt and herbs and crushed to make a paste called *pissalat*, which was the original topping for *pissaladière*. In former times, before refrigeration and rapid transport, salt cod was essential winter food: it keeps for years, and is also quite inexpensive (in places where it is regularly consumed). Then as now, it was imported along with stockfish, a gamey-tasting hake dried without salt. The tradition of eating salt cod has endured despite the excellent distribution system for fresh fish today – not least because there are so many good recipes for it. If you are not able to find salt cod in a specialty store, you could always adapt the recipes to fresh cod.

SMOKED HADDOCK *TARTARE* ON A BED OF FRESH SPINACH
Tartare de haddock aux épinards frais

1 lb fresh bulk spinach
1¼ lb smoked haddock fillets (finnan haddie), skinned
1 egg yolk from a large egg
2 teaspoons Dijon-style mustard
a few drops of hot pepper sauce
juice of 1 lemon
5 tablespoons olive oil
freshly ground black pepper
1 tablespoon pink peppercorns
salt
a little chives or flat-leafed parsley
1 teaspoon sherry vinegar⋆

SERVES 4
PREPARATION TIME: 35 MINUTES

Since it may be hard to find salmon, sea bass and the like with the freshness and quality on which a good tartare *depends, smoked haddock is a more reliable candidate. How finely you chop the fish depends on your own taste, but do try and leave some texture.*

Wash and trim the spinach, selecting only the young, tender whole leaves. Dry them. Coarsely chop the haddock fillets with a knife, or put them through a meat grinder using the disk with the largest holes.

Make the sauce by mixing the egg yolk with the mustard, pepper sauce, half the lemon juice and 3 tablespoons olive oil. Do not add salt because the haddock is already very salty. Pour the sauce over the haddock and sprinkle with pepper to taste. Add the pink peppercorns and chopped chives and mix well. Refrigerate while you prepare the dressing for the spinach.

Make a vinaigrette by mixing a pinch of salt, the vinegar, the remaining lemon juice and the remaining olive oil. Pour over the spinach and sprinkle with pepper. Either make a bed of spinach on a large serving dish and mound the tartare in the center, or divide the

leaves and haddock between four small plates. The rich yellow and dark green look wonderful set against each other.

SALT COD CASSEROLE WITH LEEKS AND OLIVES (see page 94)

SOAKING AND POACHING SALT COD

However you cook salt cod, it should always be desalted in water, preferably running water. A trickle is enough. Allow ½ lb salt cod per person. Cut the salt cod into two or three pieces to make the salt come out more readily. Put the fish skin side up in a salad shaker, colander or pressure cooker basket in a bowl, so that it does not touch the bottom of the bowl. Change the water frequently at first (even if it is running), and then every 4 hours. Allow 24 hours for new, pliable salt cod in fillets, and 36 to 48 hours if it is old and rigid or in one very large piece. For some recipes you need to poach the cod before using it; in others it can be used right away. If it has been well soaked, it will need salting during cooking. Bring the liquid to a simmer over a medium heat without letting it boil at all; otherwise the fish will take on a tough, matted texture. As soon as the surface of the liquid begins to tremble, either turn the heat down to a minimum, cover and leave the fish to simmer for 12 minutes, or remove from the heat, cover and leave to poach for 12 to 15 minutes. The second method preserves the firmness of the fish. Discard the skin and bones.

SALT COD CASSEROLE WITH LEEKS AND OLIVES
Estouffade aux poireaux et aux olives

1 clove of garlic
salt
4 whites of leek
1 fennel bulb
2 medium onions
handful of olives
scant 1 cup dry white wine
2 tablespoons olive oil
salt and freshly ground black pepper
1¾ lb salt cod in a thick piece,
    desalted (see page 93)
bunch of herbs: fresh chervil, flat-
    leafed parsley or chives
2 tablespoons fresh bread crumbs
a little butter

SERVES 4
PREPARATION TIME (NOT INCLUDING
TIME TO SOAK COD): 35 MINUTES
COOKING TIME: 35-38 MINUTES

PHOTOGRAPH ON PAGE 93

An estouffade or estouffot, is a dish, usually meat, that is braised very slowly and gently. It is a good way to treat salt cod, with its rather meaty texture and strong flavor.

For this dish you will require a deep flameproof casserole that can be transferred from oven to burner, and a thick slice of salt cod cut from the center of a fillet.

Crush the garlic completely with a little salt, using a pestle and mortar. Spread this purée over the bottom of the pot.

Finely slice all the vegetables and arrange over the garlic paste. Pit the olives, scatter them over the vegetables and pour on the white wine and half of the oil. Add pepper to taste and a little salt, and cook for 20 minutes over a low heat, keeping the pan almost covered. (Some cooks cover the vegetables with thin rounds of potato, which keeps in the delicious juice. It's a suggestion.) After 20 minutes, the vegetables should have softened and released their moisture. Preheat the oven to 400°F. If the casserole does not have a lid, cut a piece of baking parchment or aluminum foil large enough to seal it tightly. Remove the skin and as many of the bones as possible from the soaked salt cod. Hollow out a place for it among the vegetables, and bury it carefully. Pour on the remaining oil and sprinkle with the chopped herbs. Put on the lid or cover the pot and bake for 15 to 18 minutes.

Halfway through, spoon the juices over the fish; 5 minutes before the end, sprinkle with the bread crumbs and a few slivers of butter or a trickle of oil and do not replace the cover. Serve in the casserole with a chilled white wine.

SALT COD IN CIDER CREAM SAUCE
Morue à la mode d'Honfleur

2¼ lb salt cod
3 tablespoons butter
2 onions
1 shallot
1¾ lb small, firm potatoes
small bunch of fresh chervil
salt and freshly ground white pepper
1 *bouquet garni*★
1½ cups hard cider or dry white wine
½ cup *crème fraîche*★
1 teaspoon mild mustard
1 egg yolk from a large egg
grated nutmeg
brown bread

SERVES 4
PREPARATION TIME: 25 MINUTES +
24-48 HOURS SOAKING
COOKING TIME: 50 MINUTES

Honfleur is one of the main fishing ports of Normandy. Salt cod, brought back from Newfoundland, was once a staple food here, and rich cream and cider sauces are still found throughout Norman cooking.

Cut the salt cod into large chunks and soak as described in the introduction to these recipes (page 93). After this, the flesh should be rehydrated and bland. It will require some salt. Discard the skin and bones from the cod, and flake the fish.

Grease the bottom of a casserole with half the butter. Finely chop the onions and shallot. Quarter the potatoes. Chop the chervil and mix this, the fish and the vegetables with seasoning to taste. Put the mixture into the casserole with the *bouquet garni* in the middle. Pour on the cider (or wine), dot with the rest of the butter divided into pieces, cover tightly and cook over a gentle heat for 50 minutes.

Just before serving, remove a tablespoon of the juices from the pot and beat in a bowl with the *crème fraîche*, mustard, egg yolk and a little nutmeg. Pour into the casserole after removing the *bouquet garni*, and serve on hot plates accompanied by toasted brown bread and the same cider or wine as used in the cooking.
Variation: if you are feeling in an extravagant mood, you can give the cooking juices a kick by adding a little Calvados with the mustard, egg and cream.

FISH PÂTÉS AND TERRINES

Terrines and pâtés are some of the few fish dishes which do not need attention at the last minute and are easy to serve for large numbers of people. In these three recipes, the texture as well as the flavor of the fish is used, by keeping it in whole pieces.

TERRINE OF SKATE WITH FRESH MINT
Terrine de raie à la menthe fraîche

8 sprigs of fresh mint
6½ lb skate wings
3 limes
4 egg whites from large eggs
1 envelope unflavored gelatin

For the court bouillon:
2 carrots
1 large onion
2 shallots
1 *bouquet garni*★
salt
crushed black peppercorns
1 pint (2½ cups) dry white wine, such
as Graves

For the sauce:
scant 1 cup *crème fraîche*★
chopped fresh mint leaves
salt and freshly ground black pepper

SERVES AT LEAST 12
PREPARATION TIME: 1 HOUR + TIME
FOR STOCK TO COOL AND AT LEAST 5
HOURS REFRIGERATION
COOKING TIME: ABOUT 50 MINUTES

Christian de Leyssac and his brother together set up Le Grand Hôtel de la Muse et du Rozier, an old inn spectacularly sited on the banks of the River Tarn. The style of cooking – light with striking new ideas – was matched by the bold modern decor in the restaurant. Christian de Leyssac is also chef at Le Grand Galop in Marly le Roi. This recipe can be prepared 24 hours in advance and kept in the refrigerator. Or the stock can be cooked in advance and reheated the next day.

Separate the mint leaves from the stems and reserve the leaves in a cool place. The stems are used for the court bouillon. Put them in a pan with the sliced carrots, onion and shallots, *bouquet garni*, seasoning, white wine and enough water to cover the fish. Cover and cook over a gentle heat for 40 minutes. Leave the stock to cool at room temperature, then refrigerate until required.

Before starting to make the pâté, refrigerate an earthenware terrine. Bring the court bouillon to a boil with fish in it. Skim, then turn the heat down to the minimum. Poach the fish without boiling for 8 minutes. Remove the fish and drain. Leave the court bouillon to carry on simmering, uncovered.

Skin the fish while still hot. The skin, the dark, fatty parts and the cartilage should come away easily. Return them to the court bouillon.

Peel the limes, removing the white pith, throw the peel into the stock and whisk in the egg whites; these will collect all the impurities. Turn off the heat and strain the stock. Leave to cool. Dissolve the gelatin in a little warm water and add to the stock. As it cools, it will begin to set. Quickly coat the sides of the cold terrine with a layer of this jelly. It will start to set immediately. Put back in the refrigerator for a few seconds. Take it out as soon as the jelly has set firmly.

Line the bottom of the terrine with lime slices and mint leaves. Make a layer of skate flesh and pour on a little of the still liquid jelly. Put the terrine back in the refrigerator for a couple of minutes, until the jelly is set.

Repeat the layering until the terrine is full, refrigerating between each layer. Reserve a little mint. End with a layer of jelly and refrigerate until the next day, or for at least 5 hours. Slice the pâté before serving, and accompany with a sauce made from whipped *crème fraîche* flavored with chopped mint, salt and pepper.

FISH PÂTÉ WITH FRESH HERBS
Terrine de poisson aux herbes fraîches

10 oz salmon fillet, skinned
10 oz turbot fillet, skinned
2 envelopes unflavored gelatin
dissolved in 4 cups hot fish fumet (see
page 33)
1 tablespoon chopped fresh chervil
1 tablespoon chopped fresh tarragon
1 tablespoon chopped fresh basil
10 oz peeled cooked shrimps
1 tablespoon olive oil
1 tablespoon lemon juice
salt and pepper

To serve:
herb mayonnaise or whipped cream
with lemon juice

SERVES 6-8 AS AN APPETIZER
PREPARATION TIME: 20 MINUTES + AT
LEAST 2 HOURS COOLING AND
REFRIGERATION
COOKING TIME: 3 MINUTES

This recipe comes from Les Ambassadeurs, in the historic Hôtel de Crillon in Paris. The restaurant is known for its light modern cooking style and luscious desserts (see page 212).

Cut the salmon and turbot fillets into matchsticks. Quickly fry in a nonstick pan without any oil for 1 minute. Place in a deep flameproof pot or saucepan.

Pour on the hot fish fumet mixture or fish stock and gelatin mixture, and simmer for 2 minutes. Leave to cool.

Drain the fillets, reserving the fish fumet, and mix with the shrimp. Season with olive oil, lemon juice, salt and pepper. Place the mixture in a terrine or a glass salad bowl. Sprinkle with the chopped herbs. Pour over the almost cold fish fumet. Leave to set in the refrigerator.

Serve cut into slices with a herb mayonnaise or with whipped cream to which a little lemon juice has been added.

QUICK MONKFISH PÂTÉ
Pâté de lotte

2¾ lb boneless monkfish
4 lemons
1 small can tomato paste
12 large eggs
salt
a few green peppercorns

For the mayonnaise:
1 egg yolk from an extra large egg
1 teaspoon mustard powder
up to ⅔ cup peanut oil
juice of ½ lemon
handful of chervil and chives

PREPARATION TIME: 20 MINUTES +
TIME TO MAKE MAYONNAISE
COOKING TIME: 1 HOUR

This very quick, easy pâté with a chunky texture, comes from a recipe contributed by Anouk Lautier, a home cook with a large family who comes from the south of France.

Make sure the membrane has been removed from the monkfish so that it does not curl up. Squeeze the lemons. Cook the monkfish for 30 minutes in a large pan of simmering water to which the juice of the lemons has been added.

Put the tomato paste into a bowl, break in the eggs one at a time and stir them together. Add salt to taste and the whole green peppercorns. Preheat the oven to 375°C.

Drain the fish, cut it into cubes and wipe with paper towels. Mix it carefully with the egg mixture.

Pour into a buttered loaf pan. Put in a pan of hot water and bake for 30 minutes. Allow to cool completely before unmolding.

Meanwhile, make the mayonnaise. Beat the egg yolk with the mustard powder and whisk in the oil, at first adding it drop by drop and then, once the mayonnaise has caught, pouring it in as a smooth thin trickle. When it is thick and glossy, stir in the lemon juice and the chopped herbs.

Serve with a strong white or light red wine.

QUICK MONKFISH PÂTÉ▶

POULTRY

PHEASANT ON A BED OF
CABBAGE (see page 116)

STUFFED STEWING CHICKEN WITH
EGG VINAIGRETTE (see page 104)

BUYING CHICKEN

Fifty years ago chicken was a treat, a luxury. Then, with factory farming, prices fell. So, too, did chicken's reputation since more often than not it was flavorless or tasted of the artificial feeds on which it was fattened. Recently things have improved, thanks both to consumer pressure and the efforts of smaller producers. In France the habit of labeling chicken has spread so that it is possible to pick out grain-fed or free-range chicken at a glance. But it is still worth trying to buy from a good butcher whom you can trust.

Good chicken should be smooth and plump, but not excessively so, without too much apparent fat. Color depends on breed and feeding. There should be no blemishes or damage to the bird. A flexible beak and sternum and shiny skin on the feet are signs of quality.

It is important to choose the appropriate kind of chicken for the dish to be cooked. Six-week-old chicks and young corn-fed chickens – *poussins* and *poulets* – are ideal for grilling, roasting or sautéeing. They are spoiled by overcooking. Free-range chickens are good for roasting. Factory-farmed hens should be used only for rapid cooking with sauces to help give flavor. Stewing chicken and mature cocks should be reserved for prolonged braising, poaching or making stock.

CONCENTRATED WHITE CHICKEN STOCK
Fond blanc de volaille

Many recipes call for a *fond*, a concentrated chicken stock. It may be made either with a carcass and giblets as in the Bresse sauté of chicken with vinegar on page 106, or with a whole bird, preferably a stewing chicken with plenty of flavor, plus flavoring vegetables. The *fond* should simmer rather than boil so that the grease remains on the surface and does not cloud the finished stock. After skimming off the fat (see page 106), the *fond* may be further reduced to strengthen the flavor. Once degreased, it will keep in the refrigerator for 3 days; in the freezer for several weeks.

CUTTING UP RAW CHICKEN

To divide chicken for cooking in individual portions, cut down one side of the breast bone, then for each half cut off the leg and the wing with some breast. Finally cut out the backbone. If you wish, remove the skin. Finally, cut off any excess fat. Poultry shears are ideal for this job.

BAKED OR GRILLED CHICKEN WITH MUSTARD
Poulet grillé à la moutarde

6 large chicken pieces
6 tablespoons Dijon-style mustard
a few sage leaves
12 thick slices of smoked bacon*

SERVES 6
PREPARATION TIME: 5 MINUTES
COOKING TIME: 25 MINUTES

This recipe originally appeared as part of an article on meals that could be cooked in less than half an hour. Most supermarkets sell chicken already cut into quarters.

Preheat the oven to 425°F. Spread the mustard over the chicken pieces. Place a sage leaf on each one and cover with two slices of bacon. Bake for 25 minutes.
Variation: chicken with mustard may also be broiled or barbecued. To broil it whole, in the way the French call *à la crapaudine* – literally like a frog (see right) – cut along one side of the backbone, and flatten the bird.

GRILLED CHICKEN WITH CITRUS FRUITS
Poulet grillé aux agrumes

1 roasting chicken, weighing
about 3½ lb
scant 2 cups chicken stock (page 100)
4 oranges
1 lemon★
½ teaspoon ground mace
salt and coarsely ground white pepper
2½ tablespoons butter
1 teaspoon Curaçao liqueur
8 thick slices of smoked bacon★

SERVES 6
PREPARATION TIME (NOT COUNTING
MAKING STOCK): 25 MINUTES +
2 HOURS TO MARINATE
COOKING TIME: ABOUT 30 MINUTES

The classic French sauce for duck is
bigarade, *made with bitter oranges,
which originally came from Spain, like
many French recipes. Some recipes for
bigarade include lemon juice and alcohol
– Madeira, port or Curaçao – for a kick.
Here the idea is adapted for broiled
chicken pieces.*

Prepare the chicken stock as on
page 100, but make it more
concentrated than usual by using
less water or cooking it for longer.
The stock should be thick, like a
sugar syrup.
   Cut the chicken into 6 pieces.
Squeeze 3 oranges and the lemon.
Reserve the lemon peel. Add the
mace and seasoning to the juices
and leave the chicken to marinate
in it for 2 hours or longer.
   Put the chicken and the
marinade in a heavy stainless steel
saucepan. Add 2 tablespoons
butter and the concentrated
chicken stock. Set over a medium
heat and three-quarters cover the
pan. After 25 minutes, the chicken
will be cooked but not falling

apart.
   Turn off the heat and leave to
stand while you peel the last
orange. Pare the zest off the
orange and lemon peel and slice
into julienne strips. Slice the
orange. Take out the chicken
pieces and drain them. Arrange
them on a hot serving dish. Add
the Curaçao to the juices. Divide
the rest of the butter into tiny
pieces and whisk these into the
juices. Add the strips of orange
and lemon zest.
   Preheat the broiler. Place a slice
of orange on each chicken piece
and surround it with a slice of
bacon. Coat with the reduced
sauce and broil for 1 minute on the
underside and 2 minutes on the
other. As soon as the sauce
caramelizes, transfer to a very hot
dish and garnish with peeled
orange wedges and the remaining
sauce. Serve immediately. A white
(navy) bean purée, snow peas and
wild rice would go well with this,
as would a fruity white wine.

WHOLE STUFFED POULTRY

French roast chicken is often stuffed only with a peeled onion, a few sprigs of herbs – tarragon is the classic match – and a pat of butter. But chicken casseroled like *poule-au-pot*, as wished by Henry IV on his citizens as a Sunday treat, are often cooked with substantial stuffings involving bread crumbs, chopped liver and port, spinach or sorrel, perhaps some prunes or even truffles. As in the United States roast stuffed turkey or goose would usually be the *plat de résistance* of the main Christmas meal, in France called *le réveillon* and eaten in the early hours of the morning after midnight mass. The distinctive flavor of goose fat is marvelous in many regional dishes from the south-west and Alsace, and since it is difficult to buy, a roast goose is the best source (see page 9 for the method). For a crisp, golden skin it is a good idea to hang the goose in a cool, dry place the evening before cooking it.

BRAISED BALLOTTINE OF TURKEY WITH CHESTNUTS
Dinde farcie avec marrons

1 boned turkey, weighing 6½ lb, with carcass, giblets and turkey
1 *couenne*★ (piece of pork skin with fat) to cover bottom of casserole
1 carrot
1 onion stuck with 2 cloves
2 cups stock made from the turkey carcass and giblets
1 calf's foot split in half
1 *bouquet garni*★

For the stuffing:
½ lb chicken livers
1 tablespoon goose fat★ or butter
2 shallots
½ lb boned shoulder of veal
5 oz unsmoked slab bacon★
small bunch of flat-leafed parsley
blade of lemon grass★, or tiny pinch of lemon grass powder★
pinch of thyme
pinch of grated nutmeg
3 tablespoons brandy or *eau-de-vie*★
salt and freshly ground black pepper
10 chestnuts, fresh or canned

SERVES 8-10
PREPARATION TIME: 50 MINUTES (LESS IF USING CANNED CHESTNUTS)
COOKING TIME: ABOUT 3 HOURS

This is a Christmas turkey with a difference. By boning, stuffing and rolling into a ballottine, *it can be pot-roasted like a chicken, making it juicier and reducing the cooking smells.*

Ask the butcher to bone the turkey. Keep the bones and giblets to make the stock for the dish.

To make the stuffing, heat the chicken and turkey livers in half the fat until they harden. Finely chop them with the shallots and mix with the ground veal and bacon, chopped herbs, nutmeg, brandy and seasoning in a bowl. Cover and leave the flavors to mingle while you peel and chop the chestnuts if using fresh ones.

Prepare a trussing needle and thread. Open out the turkey on a board, skin side down. Spread over it a first layer of stuffing. Align the chestnuts from the neck to the "Pope's nose" (some French chefs like to add a chopped truffle, and a few chopped "horn-of-plenty" mushrooms★). Make a second layer of stuffing and carefully fold over the meat to enclose it. Sew up the turkey with small stitches. It is important for the bird to be completely sealed to keep the stuffing and the meat soft.

Preheat the oven to 350°F. Place the bird, seam down, on the bed of the *couenne* (skin side up), sliced carrot, onion and turkey bones.

Pour over the stock, which should come 1½ inches above the bed of vegetables and fat. Add the calf's foot and *bouquet garni*. Seal the pot, making sure it is airtight, and put in the oven to cook for 1¾ to 2¼ hours (count about 20 minutes per pound).

Turn off the oven, open the door and let the bird sit inside for about 15 minutes without uncovering the pot. Then transfer it to a heated serving dish. Strain the sauce and serve separately.

This would be good accompanied by celeriac and whole chestnuts. In France, it would probably be served after *boudin blanc* (see page 118), another traditional dish for *le réveillon*.

You could drink a number of wines with this: a full red or a medium-dry white, for example. It should be good, especially if you are toasting in the New Year.

ORCHARD GOOSE
L'oie du verger

1 goose, weighing 6½ lb, with giblets
3 tablespoons raisins
2 onions
8 medium slices of stale bread
scant ½ cup chopped hazelnuts
(filberts)
2 tart sweet apples
1 tablespoon chopped flat-leafed
parsley
a few sprigs of marjoram
10 juniper berries
¼ cup Calvados (optional)
salt and freshly ground black pepper
6 small tart apples for baking

SERVES 6
PREPARATION TIME: 30 MINUTES +
(OPTIONAL) OVERNIGHT
COOKING TIME: ABOUT 2¾ HOURS

Many French families still follow the custom of eating stuffed roast goose on the feast of St Martin on November 11. Here is an old recipe with a spicy apple stuffing. You can put a whole apple in above the stuffing to help blot up some of the fat from the bird.

Boil the gizzard together with the heart for 30 minutes in a little salted water.

Make the stuffing by chopping the gizzard, liver and heart together. Soak the raisins in hot water. Coarsely chop the onions and soften them gently in a little of the goose fat. Crumble the stale bread; peel, core and dice the apples; chop the herbs and crush the juniper berries. Mix all these ingredients with the Calvados and season generously.

Preheat the oven to 350°F. Prick the goose skin all over with a needle to allow the fat to escape. Spread the stuffing inside. Sew up the opening. Place the goose, breast up, on a rack over a roasting pan. Do not add fat. Allow just under 20 minutes cooking time per pound. Baste once or twice, especially the legs, which tend to get dry.

When the goose is cooked, turn off the oven and leave the bird to "rest" for 15 minutes with the oven door open. Accompany this substantial dish with tart apples, baked for 20 minutes.

STUFFED STEWING CHICKEN WITH EGG VINAIGRETTE
Poule farcie avec vinaigrette de Sorges

1 stewing chicken, weighing 4½ lb
12 cups chicken stock (see page 39)
1 *bouquet garni**
1 onion
3-4 cloves of garlic
1 lb 2 oz each of carrots, leeks and
turnips
salt and freshly ground black pepper

For the stuffing:
2 thin slices of bread, crusts removed
2 large eggs
2 shallots
1 tablespoon chopped parsley
4-5 chicken livers
1 clove of garlic

For the egg vinaigrette:
3 large eggs
2 shallots
⅓ cup wine vinegar
½ cup walnut oil
½ cup peanut oil
a little flat-leafed parsley

SERVES 6
PREPARATION TIME: 30 MINUTES
COOKING TIME: 15-20 MINUTES
(OPTIONAL) + 2½-3 HOURS

PHOTOGRAPH ON PAGE 99

In Périgord the broth for this chicken, cooked as for a pot-au-feu, would be poured over toasted bread in deep plates as a soupe *to start the meal.*

Prepare the stuffing by softening the bread with the eggs. Add the chopped shallots, parsley, chicken livers, minced garlic and seasoning, and mash together well. Stuff the chicken. Secure the openings firmly.

If you think your chicken is fatty, cook it in a moderate oven at 350°F for 15 to 20 minutes for some of the fat to drip on to a tray.

Put the chicken in a casserole containing the boiling stock, the *bouquet garni*, onion and garlic. Cook over a low heat for at least 2½ hours, or even 3. Prick with a skewer to see if it is tender.

Prepare the vegetables and cook them in boiling water for 30 minutes.

Meanwhile, make the vinaigrette. Soft-cook the eggs so that the yolks are still runny (see page 52). Put them in cold water and, when it begins to simmer, remove the eggs. Break the eggs and separate the yolks from the whites. Put the yolks in a bowl with the chopped shallots and vinegar. Whisk, then add the oils in a trickle as for mayonnaise. (The proportions of oil can be varied.)

Cook the egg whites in a little stock. Crush them with a fork and add to the vinaigrette with the chopped parsley and seasoning to taste.

Carve the chicken and serve on a hot dish surrounded by the drained vegetables. Serve the egg vinaigrette separately in a sauceboat.

REGIONAL DISHES

Because chicken and other farmyard poultry are such a common denominator in regional cooking, they offer the possibility of a quick *tour de France*. This small selection of popular recipes, which takes a zig-zag route from north to south, presents a quick tasting of regional produce and a general feel of the range and depth of local traditions. In some cases the recipes have been lightened, or given a new twist, for today's tastes.

BRAISED GUINEA FOWL WITH RED CABBAGE
Pintade au chou rouge

1 large guinea fowl
2 shallots
2 tablespoons butter
1 medium red cabbage
5 oz smoked slab bacon★
½ cup golden raisins
⅓ cup white wine
salt and freshly ground black pepper
sprig of thyme
2 tablespoons sherry vinegar★

SERVES 4
PREPARATION TIME: 20 MINUTES
COOKING TIME: 1¼-1¾ HOURS

Red cabbage is cooked with poultry and game in several regions of France – notably the Auvergne and Limousin areas of the Massif Central and French Flanders – but Alsace remains the real home of cabbage culture. Try to find a fruity Alsace-style wine for the sauce.

Chop the shallots and fry in the butter in a skillet. Put in the guinea fowl and brown it all over.

Meanwhile, preheat the oven to 400°F. Cut the cabbage into thin strips and finely dice the bacon.

Mix with the raisins and place in a heavy earthenware or cast iron casserole. Put the guinea fowl in the middle. Deglaze the skillet with the white wine, and pour this liquid over the guinea fowl on its cabbage bed. Season to taste and add the thyme. Cover and put in the oven to cook for 1 to 1½ hours. Carve the guinea fowl. Pour the vinegar over the cabbage, mix well and correct the seasoning.

DUCK FROM NANTES WITH OLIVES
Canard Nantais aux olives

1 roaster duck, weighing about 4½ lb
2¼ lb (about 6 cups) green olives in brine
2-3 tablespoons chicken fat
4 chicken necks
5-6 chicken wings
a few gizzards or red meat trimmings
½ lb onions
3 tablespoons flour
2 cups dry white wine
about 12 cups veal or chicken stock (see page 39)
1 *bouquet garni*★
scant 1 cup thick tomato purée (see page 26)
salt and freshly ground black pepper
2 tablespoons butter

SERVES 4
PREPARATION TIME: 4-5 MINUTES + 12 HOURS SOAKING
COOKING TIME: ABOUT 4½ HOURS

Duck from Nantes in southern Brittany is almost as renowned as chicken from Bresse in the Franche-Comté. This dish is a specialty of Chez Allard, one of the best known Parisian bistros (see page 138).

Pit the olives and, if necessary, soak them in a bowl of cold water for 12 hours to remove excess salt.

Preheat the oven to 300°F.

Melt the chicken fat in a casserole and lightly brown the chicken necks, wings and gizzards or meat trimmings over a high heat. As soon as they are golden all over, add the finely chopped onions and cook until brown. Sprinkle in the flour and mix without letting it brown. Pour in the white wine and 8 cups of the stock. Add the *bouquet garni*, tomato purée and seasoning. Mix and cook slowly in the oven for 4 hours, strain.

At the same time, prepare the olives. Drain them and put them in a medium-sized saucepan with nearly all the remaining stock. The liquid should come almost up to the brim of the pan. Simmer for 2 hours over a gentle heat, uncovered, so that the liquid reduces. Then add the wine stock, and continue cooking until reduced to a thick consistency.

Meanwhile, rub the duck with salt. About 45 minutes before the olives are cooked, place the duck in a casserole. Roast it for 40 to 45 minutes, first in a gentle oven to melt the fat, and then at a high temperature in the butter, basting with a little stock. The flesh should remain pinkish.

Carve the duck into thin slices and put it back together again on a heated serving dish. Pour over the olive sauce. Serve at once.

BLANQUETTE OF CHICKEN WITH TURNIP SAUCE AND LEEKS
Blanquette de volaille aux poireaux et navets

1 roaster chicken, weighing 4 lb
2¼ lb small leeks
scant ½ cup *crème fraîche*★
1 egg yolk from a large egg
few drops of lemon juice, or same
wine as in the stock
sprig of fresh chervil
sprig of fresh tarragon

For the stock:
3 turnips
1 carrot
1 stalk of celery
1 onion stuck with a clove
leek greens (see above)
1 *bouquet garni*★
pinch of *quatre-épices*★
salt and freshly ground white pepper
scant 1 cup white wine

SERVES 6
PREPARATION TIME: 40 MINUTES
COOKING TIME: ABOUT 1½ HOURS

Creamy blanquettes *made with any young white meat – rabbit, chicken, even kid as well as veal – are found everywhere in France, but especially in Normandy and the Ile-de-France. In this recipe the chicken is steamed, which keeps the dish white and makes it less rich. The original recipe suggests* morels, *a delicious but expensive woodland mushroom (see page 10), but dried mushrooms would be another good and more economical proposition.*

Cut the chicken into 6 pieces. Make a fairly concentrated stock from the carcass, the vegetables (including the green parts of the leeks), the *bouquet garni*, spice, seasoning and wine. When this is well cooked and aromatic, season the chicken pieces and put them on a steaming rack in the pot. The stock should not touch the chicken on the rack. Cover and seal by wrapping a damp dishcloth around the pot. Cook over a low heat for about 1 hour.
Remove the rack and keep the chicken hot. Strain the stock and reserve the turnips. Poach the chopped white of the leeks for 12 minutes in scant 1 cup of the stock. Add the rest of the stock to the turnips, and purée in a blender to a thick sauce.

In a small saucepan, whisk together the *crème fraîche* and egg yolk. Add a little turnip purée and, whisking continuously, cook over a gentle heat. Still whisking, add the rest of the purée in a thin trickle. The sauce will thicken as it cooks. Take care not to let it boil. Dilute with lemon juice or wine, remove from the heat and stir to a very smooth sauce.

Pour the sauce over the chicken on a piping hot serving dish and sprinkle with chopped chervil and tarragon. Arrange the leeks around the chicken. Give it 2 to 3 turns of the pepper mill. You can also add a few carrots and extra turnips, cooked separately, for a colorful touch.

BRESSE SAUTÉ OF CHICKEN WITH VINEGAR
Poulet de Bresse sautée au vinaigre

1 Bresse chicken, weighing 3¼ lb
7 tablespoons butter, at room
temperature
5 shallots
1¼ cups vinegar
1 clove of garlic (optional)
2 tablespoons capers or samphire★

For the stock:
1 carrot
1 onion stuck with a clove
1 clove of garlic
1 *bouquet garni*★
salt and freshly ground black pepper
¾ cup dry white wine

SERVES 6
PREPARATION TIME: 30 MINUTES
COOKING TIME: 60 MINUTES

Bresse and its surrounding area, on the borders of Burgundy and Franche-Comté, is known for its creamy blue cheese but most of all for its blue-footed Bressane chicken, considered the best in France. Locally this dish would be eaten with cardoons, a thistle with a stalk like celery, or scorzonera, a root vegetable like salsify with a black skin. See page 11 for a note on samphire.
This is also a great favorite with chefs. Paul Bocuse uses shallots and no tomatoes: Gerard Nandeau uses shallots, tomatoes and white wine; the two Troisgros brothers leave out the wine and the shallots but add garlic and tomatoes! But they do agree on one thing – the best chicken to use for it is Bressane.

Cut the chicken into 6 pieces and reserve the carcass, the wing tips, giblets, neck and the feet (singe and skin these) for the stock. Put these in a saucepan with the vegetables, unpeeled garlic clove, *bouquet garni* and seasoning. Pour on the wine and add water to cover. Put on a lid and simmer for 30 minutes over a low heat. Skim and discard the fat, then strain the stock.

Preheat the oven to 425°F. Choose a casserole large enough for all the chicken pieces to fit in without overlapping. Melt about 1½ tablespoons butter in the dish, add the chicken pieces skin side down and brown lightly. Turn over and brown the other side, then season to taste. Cover, and put in the oven to cook for 20 minutes. ▷

BLANQUETTE OF CHICKEN▶

BRESSE SAUTÉ OF CHICKEN WITH VINEGAR

◁While the chicken is cooking, finely chop the shallots. Soften them in juices from the chicken over a gentle heat, without letting them brown. As soon as they become translucent, drain off the chicken fat. Add the vinegar all at once and reduce it by half. (At this point, the Troisgros add 2 crushed fresh tomatoes and about 10 cloves of garlic, unpeeled – less traditional but very tasty.) Add the very concentrated chicken stock and simmer until there is just enough sauce left to pour over the chicken. Add the rest of the butter and whisk to obtain a light, frothy sauce. If you want to use garlic, now is the time to crush it and add to the sauce.

Pour the sauce over the chicken and sprinkle with capers or samphire.

Serve with a good white wine.

CHICKEN IN CHANTURGUES WINE SAUCE
Coq au vin de chanturgues

1 chicken with giblets, weighing about
3¼ lb, cut into eight pieces
salt and black pepper
about 20 pearl onions
5 tablespoons butter
pinch of sugar
¼ lb button mushrooms, trimmed and
quartered
juice of ½ lemon
5 oz unsmoked slab bacon, cut into
small strips
¼ cup *eau-de-vie*★
scant 1 cup Chanturgues, fruity
Bourgueil or solid red Burgundy wine
2 cups chicken stock (see page 39)
1 *bouquet garni*
1 clove
pinch of grated nutmeg

SERVES 4-6
PREPARATION TIME: 50 MINUTES
COOKING TIME: ABOUT 1¾ HOURS

*Chanturgues is a full-flavored wine, once
esteemed but then almost extinct; now
growers are reviving it. This is* coq au
vin *made properly – with good stock and
wine.*

Season the chicken and set aside. Put the peeled onions in a single layer in a small saucepan. Add 1 tablespoon butter, salt to taste and a pinch of sugar, and just cover with cold water. Bring to a fast boil, then turn the heat down, cover and cook until all the water has gone. Uncover the pan and cook to color them lightly.

Put the quartered mushrooms in a saucepan with the lemon juice and 1 tablespoon butter. Season to taste, cover and cook over a very low heat. Cook the meat gently in a large flameproof casserole to render the fat. Remove it. Now brown the pieces of chicken all over in the bacon fat in the casserole. Reduce the heat, cover and cook gently for 20 minutes. Pour on the *eau-de-vie* and flame it. When the flames die down, take out the chicken.

Preheat the oven to 425°F. Pour the wine and the stock into the casserole. Bring to a fast boil, then turn down the heat. Put in the chicken, bacon and onions. Add the *bouquet garni* and the clove, cover and put in the oven. Turn the heat down to 375°F and leave to cook for 45 minutes. Chop the cleaned gizzard and liver; add to the casserole after 15 or 20 minutes. After another 15 minutes, add the drained mushrooms. Sprinkle with nutmeg.

The exact cooking time depends on the age of the bird, it should be tender but not falling to pieces. Use a slotted spoon to transfer the chicken, bacon and vegetables to a warmed serving dish. Keep hot.

Reduce the cooking liquid – without the *bouquet garni* and the clove – if it is watery. Whisk the remaining butter into the liquid in small pieces, pour the sauce over the chicken and serve.

CHICKEN WITH FENNEL
Fondu du poulet et fenouil

1 roaster chicken, weighing 3½ lb
2 onions
1 clove of garlic
¼ lb unsmoked slab bacon★
¼ cup olive oil
1 teaspoon fennel seeds
salt and freshly ground black pepper
scant 1 cup concentrated chicken
stock (see page 100)
a few leaves of basil
4 very fresh young fennel bulbs
1 lb 2 oz tomatoes
2 tablespoons olive oil
1 teaspoon red wine vinegar
pinch of sugar
a few leaves of basil

SERVES 6
PREPARATION TIME: 45 MINUTES
COOKING TIME: 2¼ HOURS

*An old Provençal recipe dating back to
the relatively recent days when the region
was part of Italy.*

Cut the chicken into 6 pieces. Finely chop the onions, and crush the garlic without peeling it. Dice the bacon.

Heat the oil in a flameproof casserole and put in the diced bacon; remove as soon as the fat becomes translucent. Then sauté the onions and garlic until golden. Push them to the sides and put in the chicken pieces. Cook for a minute on each side, to brown. Put the diced bacon back in the casserole, add the fennel seeds, season to taste, then pour on the hot stock. Cover and simmer for 50 minutes over a gentle heat. Five minutes before the end, sprinkle with the basil leaves and cover again.

Meanwhile, trim the fennel bulbs and blanch them for 5 minutes in boiling salted water. Drain immediately, upsidedown, and reserve the cooking liquid.

Blanch the tomatoes in boiling water and peel them. Cut in half, deseed and drain them. Purée them and whisk in the olive oil, vinegar, sugar and basil.

When the fennel has cooled slightly, cut the bulbs in half and add them to the pan with the chicken. Pour on some of the fennel cooking liquid. Cover and cook for a further 6 to 8 minutes. Heat a deep serving dish. Arrange the fennel in a ring on the dish and pile the chicken pieces in the center. Moisten with the cooking juices. Serve the cold sauce separately.

THREE MODERN DISHES

The cooking of the former French colonies – especially Algerian, Moroccan, Caribbean and Vietnamese-Chinese – is one of the most obvious influences on French cuisine today. Together they have brought a new range of spices into everyday use and made dishes like cous-cous national favorites. A second influence and major talking point has been *nouvelle cuisine* which, since the mid-seventies, has revolutionized the classic French restaurant menu. Its lasting legacies have been a tendency towards light and quickly cooked dishes without so many embellishments, sauces with a strong concentration of flavor usually based on reduction, an emphasis on local seasonal and natural flavors, a freer spirit of invention and the revival of certain old dishes like warm salads and fruit *soupes*.

STEAMED DUMPLINGS FILLED WITH CHICKEN AND VEGETABLES
Petits pâtes farcis de volaille et légumes

½ lb smoked slab bacon★
1 clove of garlic
2 scallions
3-4 flat open mushrooms
1 tablespoon peanut oil
1 teaspoon cornstarch
1 tablespoon grated fresh gingerroot
1 tablespoon soy sauce
handful of snow peas or green beans
white of 1 leek
2 carrots
1 turnip
1 half chicken breast
salt and freshly ground black pepper
1½ lb very slightly sweetened bread dough, or ready-made Chinese pancakes or won-ton skins★
2-3 leaves of mint or coriander (cilantro)
1 Ceylon tea bag

MAKES 20-25
PREPARATION TIME: 45 MINUTES
COOKING TIME: 40-45 MINUTES

Cut the bacon into very small dice. Very finely chop the garlic and the scallions with their green tops, and cut the mushrooms into matchsticks. Gently heat the oil in the bottom of a steamer and put in the bacon, garlic and scallions. As soon as they begin to color, add the mushrooms and cook until the juice runs out. Then stir in the cornstarch, ginger and soy sauce. Cover and cook for another minute over a very gentle heat. Turn off the heat and leave the pan covered.

Chop the snow peas or beans, and finely chop the leek, including a little of the green top, the carrots and the turnip to make very fine julienne strips. Chop the chicken breast. Add all these ingredients to the pot and season. Cover and leave to stand. Divide the dough into at least 20 little balls and flatten out each one into a disk measuring about 5 inches in diameter.

(These can be prepared in advance and refrigerated, separated by wax paper. Chinese pancakes and won-ton skins come already shaped.)

Remove the ingredients from the pan and put them in a dish. Cut up the mint leaves and add to the filling. To stuff the dumplings, hold a disk of dough in one hand and place a spoonful of filling in the center. Close your hand a little and, with the other, crimp the edges together at the top in untidy pleats, just as they happen to fold. Press them firmly closed. Put the dumplings in the top of the steamer. Heat water with the tea bag in the bottom of the steamer. Steam the dumplings for 25 to 30 minutes after the water boils. Serve immediately with spicy oriental sauces or melted butter with lemon. Accompany with Chinese jasmine or green tea or a robust white wine.

Dumpling skins: if you have no yeast and cannot find any of the various kinds of dumpling skins mentioned in the ingredients list, it is perfectly simple to make your own. Make a stiff dough with hard all-purpose flour, salt, and as much water as is necessary. Cover the bowl with a damp cloth and leave to rest in a cool place for a couple of hours. Then break it into small pieces and roll these out into paper-thin circles. Dust them with flour to stop them from sticking together, and stack until needed.

WARM SALAD OF CHICKEN LIVERS AND MIXED LEAVES
Salade tiède de verdures aux foies de volaille

5 oz young dandelion leaves*
¼ lb fresh bulk spinach
3 oz button mushrooms
juice of 1 lemon
4 chicken livers
salt and freshly ground black pepper
1 level teaspoon goose fat*, or chicken fat
2 tablespoons red wine vinegar
3 tablespoons brandy (optional)

Dressing:
2 large hard-cooked eggs
1 teaspoon mustard powder
1 tablespoon lemon juice
¼ cup olive oil

SERVES 4
PREPARATION TIME: 30 MINUTES
COOKING TIME: 3 MINUTES

This recipe was adapted from an idea of the great Troisgros brothers, Pierre and Michel, whose influence on the nouvelle generation of chefs – including Paul Bocuse, Frédy Girardet and Michel Guérard – is still being felt today. You can marinate the chicken livers in Cognac overnight. It is an old trick which makes them resemble foie gras.

Trim the dandelion leaves and the spinach. Finely slice the mushrooms and squeeze lemon juice over them. Clean the chicken livers and finely slice them about ¼ inch thick.

Separate the eggs. Crush the egg yolks in a bowl with some salt and pepper, the mustard and lemon juice. Put the egg whites through a vegetable mill or sieve to sprinkle over the salad. (This is optional, as the whites do not add much taste but are purely decorative.)

Whisking or stirring vigorously with a wooden spoon, gradually blend the oil into the yolks. Pour into a chilled sauceboat, but reserve a generous tablespoonful. Place the greens in a sturdy salad bowl. Drain the mushrooms and arrange them on the bed of green. Pour on the reserved dressing and mix carefully but thoroughly.

Heat the goose fat and brown the sliced chicken livers over a medium heat at first. Cook for 1 minute on each side, and then another minute, turning the heat down to minimum and turning them over, so that they remain faintly pink inside. Season, and arrange the livers on top of the salad.

Discard the excess fat but do not wipe the pan. Reheat the pan and deglaze it with the vinegar. Bring this to a boil, add brandy if you wish, and pour it over the salad. Sprinkle with the egg white if you wish, and serve on warmish plates. Serve the chilled dressing separately.

This salad is a good accompaniment for roast chicken, of course, but also for crayfish cooked in a court bouillon (see page 62) or for crab.

STEAMED DUCK WITH PEACHES
Canard aux pêches

2 ducks, with livers and blood (or add 2 chicken livers and, if possible, scant 1 cup chicken blood)
1 tablespoon butter
1 shallot
1 teaspoon green peppercorns
1 tablespoon white wine vinegar
2 tablespoons Armagnac
1 lb can of peaches in syrup
scant 1 cup concentrated chicken stock (see page 100)
1 teaspoon cornstarch
½ cup dry white wine
salt and freshly ground white pepper

SERVES 4
PREPARATION TIME: 1 HOUR
COOKING TIME: ABOUT 40 MINUTES

Jacques Manière's recipes for game are good examples of modern French cuisine. Steaming is an especially good way of cooking duck, partly because it avoids the meat drying out and partly because it lessens the risk of overcooking, which kills the flavor. This recipe was originally written for wild duck, which is smaller than domesticated birds, but it works just as well for farmyard duck.

If preparing the ducks from scratch, reserve the blood and livers. Carefully discard the gall and the part of the livers that is stained green. If you have dressed ducks, use a couple of chicken livers, and see if you can get some chicken blood from a poulterer. Precook the birds for 10 minutes on the rack of a steamer, then take them out and cut in half with a large knife. Cut out fillets from the breast with the adjoining fleshy part, and from the leg (despite what some people say, it is a good piece, a little tough but tasty). Keep these warm between two plates.

You will have the lower part of the carcass left, the neck and the wings. Bone the drumstick, and crush all this meat and the bones.

To make the sauce, melt the butter in a large saucepan, and soften the finely chopped shallot▷

WARM SALAD OF CHICKEN LIVERS AND MIXED LEAVES ▶

and the green peppercorns. After a few minutes, put in the carcass and the bones. Leave to cook for 5 minutes, then deglaze with the vinegar. Let it boil for a few seconds, then add the Armagnac and set it alight. Allow the flames to die down. Add the peach syrup and the skimmed stock. Without covering the pan, reduce to 1 cup.

While the sauce is reducing, mix the livers, blood and cornstarch in a blender. Add this and the white wine to the sauce, and continue reducing.

Arrange each disjointed half duck on a piece of baking parchment, and surround it with peach quarters. Season to taste. Wrap up each parcel carefully and steam for 9 to 10 minutes. Take out of the steamer and leave to stand, still wrapped, until the sauce reduces to a good consistency.

Remove the bones from the sauce, then blend and whisk it. Return it to the pan and simmer for 2 to 3 minutes, then strain it.

Place a duck parcel on each plate. People unwrap their own parcel and help themselves to the sauce, served separately. ▷

STEAMED DUCK WITH PEACHES

GAME

The French love *la chasse*. By October hunters for rabbit and hare, pheasant, duck and pigeon, venison, even wild boar in some areas are out with their guns every weekend.

Real game from the wild always has certain characteristics. It has a very specific strong flavor, evoking all the herbs and berries of field and forest, and it is often quite tough. Hence the tradition of marinating in strongly flavored liquids, which have more or less the same tenderizing effect as hanging but which contribute additional flavor, and the many dishes are patiently cooked in large stewing pots with heavy lids to trap all the succulent flavors. Terrines have always been used as another good way of cooking tough game birds.

Recently, however, chefs have preferred the skillet or roasting pan to the casserole. This requires a different approach. Michel Guérard recommends wrapping both feathered and furred game for roasting in a *barde*, a strip of fat bacon, which should be removed before the end of cooking time to allow the meat to brown. This helps to keep the meat moist. If necessary, game can also be larded inside by threading *lardons*, small pieces of fat bacon, into the meat with a special needle. After roasting, game should be kept hot but left to rest for at least 40 minutes to make it more tender for carving.

STEAMED PHEASANT WITH GREEN PEPPERCORNS AND RUM
Papillotes de faisan au poivre vert et au rhum

1 hen pheasant
1 small can of green peppercorns in brine
5 tablespoons softened butter
salt and freshly ground white pepper
1 lime
4 baking apples
¼ teaspoon ground cinnamon
4 cloves
½ cup white rum
2 tablespoons *crème fraîche*★

SERVES 4
PREPARATION TIME: 1 HOUR
COOKING TIME: 30 MINUTES

This recipe comes from the Grand Livre de la Cuisine Vapeur *by Jacques Manière. See also his recipe for duck, left. Manière, who went into the restaurant trade only at the age of 30, blends modern and traditional.*

Quarter the pheasant. Drain the can of green peppercorns in a sieve and rinse under the cold tap. Leave to drain. Prepare 8 sheets of aluminum foil, 4 measuring 6 inches square and 4 measuring 4 inches square.

Mix 3 tablespoons of the butter and the peppercorns together to make a paste and spread this over the pheasant portions. Salt both sides. Cut 4 slices of lime and place one on top of each pheasant quarter. Place the pheasant on the larger foil squares. Wrap them up carefully, folding the seams to seal.

Peel the apples, quarter them and remove the core. Arrange the apple quarters on the smaller foil squares. Sprinkle with salt, pepper and cinnamon, add a few slivers of butter and a clove to each quarter, and wrap in foil.

If you have a steamer with tiers, use both levels. Fill the base with boiling water. Arrange the pheasant parcels on the lower tier, and steam with the lid on for 20 minutes. Then put the apple parcels in the next compartment, placing it on top of the first. Cover, and steam for another 10 minutes. If you do not have a tiered steamer, just make space for the apple parcels next to the pheasant parcels and stop cooking after the pheasant has steamed for 30 minutes.

Open the parcels, pour the rum over the pheasant and set it alight. Then add ½ tablespoon *crème fraîche* to each piece of pheasant. Place 1 pheasant and 1 apple parcel on each plate, and serve at once.

PHEASANT ON A BED OF CABBAGE
Faisan sur un lit de choux

1 hen pheasant
1-2 tablespoons olive oil
salt and freshly ground black pepper
pinch of thyme
20 juniper berries
1 small head white or Savoy cabbage
1 apple (optional)
3 tablespoons butter

SERVES 3-4
PREPARATION TIME: 15 MINUTES
COOKING TIME: 1 HOUR

PHOTOGRAPH ON PAGE 98

Preheat the oven to 425°F. Prepare the pheasant by cutting it down one side of the backbone, opening it out and flattening it. Put the pheasant in a roasting pan, brush the skin with a little oil and rub the inside with salt, pepper, thyme, and five of the crushed juniper berries.

Roast the pheasant, skin side down, for 20 minutes, then turn it over and roast for a further 20 minutes. Remove from the oven and leave to rest. Wash, drain and shred the cabbage. If you are using the apple, peel it and cut into thin strips or dice. Mix the remaining crushed juniper berries with the butter, salt and pepper. Melt the butter mixture in a heavy-based saucepan with a tightly fitting lid, add the cabbage and braise it for 8 minutes, shaking the pan occasionally (and adding the apple halfway through if you wish). Make a bed of the cabbage on a serving plate, place the pheasant on top and heat through in the oven for a minute before serving.

FRICASSÉE OF WILD RABBIT WITH THYME
Fricassée de lapin de Garenne au thyme

1 wild rabbit, weighing about 2¾ lb
2 leeks
2 carrots
1 tablespoon olive oil
3 sprigs of thyme
1 bay leaf
spring of rosemary
salt and freshly ground black pepper
4 cloves of garlic
¾ cup dry white wine

SERVES 4
PREPARATION TIME: 20 MINUTES
COOKING TIME: 45 MINUTES

Adrienne Biasin (see page 141), from whom this recipe comes, recommends rubbing domestic rabbit with herbs and crushed garlic and marinating them in oil and white wine. Carefully drain the rabbit and keep the white wine and oil mixture to add to the fricassée. This will taste nearly as good as wild rabbit.

Cut up the rabbit to make 8 pieces: the legs, then the saddle and breast each cut in half. Cut the leeks into thin slices and the carrots into thick ones.

Heat the oil in a casserole and brown the rabbit pieces with the thyme, bay leaf and rosemary. Remove the meat and put in the vegetables, keeping the herbs in the pot. When brown, season to taste and put back the rabbit pieces on top of the vegetables. Add the garlic without peeling it. Pour on the white wine, and simmer over a low to medium heat for 30 minutes. Stir occasionally, and if the liquid reduces too much, turn down the heat and three-quarters cover the pot.

RABBIT FLAMED IN PASTIS
Lapin flambé au pastis

1 large rabbit
4½ oz strong Dijon-style mustard
a few fennel seeds
handful of fresh basil
olive oil
salt and freshly ground black pepper
½ cup pastis*

SERVES 6
PREPARATION TIME: 10 MINUTES
COOKING TIME: 1 HOUR

Pastis, the licorice flavored aperitif, pops up in the most unexpected places in Provençal cooking. Sea bass with fennel flamed in pastis is a well-known dish. This one comes from Anouk Laitier, from the south, who describes her cooking as neither cuisine nouvelle *nor* cuisine bourgeoise, *but rather* cuisine latine – *in other words, latin cooking. For other recipes by her see pages 96, 136 and 188.*

Preheat the oven to 325°F. Cut the rabbit into 10 to 12 pieces. Coat the rabbit pieces generously with mustard. Put them in a gratin dish. Sprinkle with fennel seeds and finely chopped basil. Pour on a little olive oil. Season moderately. Cover with foil. Bake for 1 hour. Just before serving, pour on the pastis and flame it. Serve with boiled potatoes.

Flaming is not just a restaurant performance. Burning a spirit removes most of the alcohol and gives a mellow taste to the remaining liquid. Stand well back when you light it.

RABBIT WITH PRUNES
Lapin aux pruneaux

1 lb prunes
1 bottle (750 ml) of red Côtes du
Rhône or similar red wine
1 rabbit
2 tablespoons olive oil
salt and freshly ground black pepper
1 onion
2 cloves of garlic
6 thick slices of unsmoked bacon★
1 *bouquet garni*★
½ teaspoon *quatre-épices*★

SERVES 4-6, DEPENDING ON SIZE OF
RABBIT
PREPARATION TIME: 15 MINUTES + 2
HOURS SOAKING
COOKING TIME: 2¼ HOURS

*The French do not regard prunes with
the suspicion of the Americans and use
them in all kinds of savory dishes (see
also the recipe for pork with prunes, page
135). Lapin aux pruneaux is probably
the best known of the sweet and savory
combinations. Sometimes golden raisins
and red currant jelly are also added.
This is another dish that needs long slow
cooking in a heavy casserole.*

Soak the prunes in the wine for 2
hours without pitting them.
Preheat the oven to 350°F. In a
skillet, brown the rabbit in the oil.
Season to taste and transfer to an

earthenware casserole.
Chop the onion and garlic and
brown them in the oil left in the
skillet. Add to the casserole. Cut
the bacon into small pieces, brown
and add to the casserole.
Pour excess fat from the skillet,
then add the wine from the prunes
and deglaze the cooking juices.
Pour these into the casserole and
add the prunes, *bouquet garni* and
spice. Cover, and cook in the oven
or on a heat diffuser over low heat
for at least 2 hours.

PÂTÉS AND TERRINES

The Club de la Terrine in Quercy, south of Périgord, produced small quantities of handmade terrines, pâtés, mousses and confits that were sold in gourmet shops around France. Dominique Claudine painstakingly researched old recipes, then slowly refined them by trial and error before arriving at her final formulae. Here are two of her recipes for poultry: one for a duck terrine and a mousse for chicken or duck livers. Sadly the Club de la Terrine is no longer in existence.

Boudin blanc is a delicious light chicken and veal sausage traditionally eaten at *le réveillon*, the celebratory meals for Christmas and the New Year. This is a light recipe with no pork meat or fat.

TRADITIONAL WHITE SAUSAGE
Boudin blanc à l'ancienne

1 pork *crépine*★ (caul fat), or some large sausage casing (in which case you will also need some beaten egg)
scant ¾ cup flour
⅓ cup water
1 large mild onion
1 teaspoon lard or butter
¼ lb chicken meat (about ¾ cup)
2 oz fresh *foie gras*★
3 oz unsmoked slab bacon★, or chicken livers fried in butter and puréed
pinch of grated nutmeg
salt and freshly ground black pepper
1 large egg
fine fresh white bread crumbs
melted butter

SERVES 2
PREPARATION TIME: 45 MINUTES + 2 HOURS SOAKING
COOKING TIME: 10 MINUTES

Boudin blanc is very often made with pork fat and pork, which gives you a rather rich and fatty poaching sausage. This is a lean grilling sausage, the chicken enriched only with a little bacon and liver. Since it is food for a special occasion, it includes foie gras, *which is very expensive, but you could replace this with chicken livers marinated in Cognac. Do not forget that sausages may be left in the refrigerator to ripen for 3 or 4 days and so mature in flavor.*

Unfold the *crépine* carefully and soak it in cold water for 2 hours. (As *crépine* is usually preserved in brine these days, taste the water and, if it is noticeably salty, change it as many times as necessary; this also applies to sausage casing.) Drain and dry it.

Next, make what is known as a *panade*, (a flour, bread or similar paste for binding minced meat and fish mixtures). Dissolve the flour in the water and stir over a gentle heat until the mixture comes away from the sides of the pan. (For an even simpler *panade*, use a small brioche soaked in milk.)

Finely chop the onion, and soften it in the lard over a low heat. Finely grind the chicken meat, the *foie gras* and bacon, add the nutmeg and seasoning to taste, and work in the egg and then the *panade*. If you like a very smooth white sausage, work the mixture in a food processor; this tends to dry out the ingredients slightly, so add a little milk, *crème fleurette*★ or alcohol of your choice (hard cider, white wine or beer are good).

Spread out the *crépine* on a board, without tearing it. If there is a tear, cut off a piece from the end and put it on top of the hole so that the patch will be inside. Cut the *crépine* into rectangles 5¼×3 inches.

Make sausages 3½ inches long and 1¼ inches thick by rolling the mixture between your hands, which should be dipped in water. Place each sausage on a rectangle of *crépine* and wrap carefully. Roll them in bread crumbs. (If using sausage casings, stuff it loosely with a funnel or a special machine as for ordinary sausages, twist into links and dip the sausages in beaten egg before rolling in bread crumbs.) Broil or fry the sausages gently for 10 minutes, turning them and basting them from time to time with melted butter. Serve with a few pear or apple slices broiled or, even better, cooked in butter.

In France *boudin blanc* is often made as one long sausage, coiled into a spiral and fried.

118

TERRINE OF DUCK WITH ORANGE
Terrine de canard à l'orange

1 duck, weighing 3¼-3¾ lb
½ lb boned shoulder of veal
½ lb boned loin of pork
2 teaspoons *quatre-épices*★
2 teaspoons chopped thyme
pinch of rosemary
2 teaspoons salt
1 teaspoon freshly ground black
pepper
2 small shallots
1½ cups dry white wine
5 teaspoons brandy
2 large eggs
2 oranges
4 large, thin slices of unsmoked
bacon★, or more smaller slices
a little liquid aspic★, or stock thick
enough to form a jelly (see page 40)

SERVES 8-10 AS AN APPETIZER
PREPARATION TIME: 1 HOUR + 3
HOURS TO MARINATE AND 1 DAY IN
REFRIGERATOR
COOKING TIME: 1 HOUR 25 MINUTES

Cut the meat off the duck, keeping the breasts whole. Cut these into thin slivers and reserve. Cut the rest of the meat into small pieces, along with the veal and pork. Place in a mixing bowl, together with the *quatre-épices*, thyme and rosemary, salt, pepper, finely chopped shallots, white wine and brandy. Mix well with your hands, press down and cover. Leave to marinate for at least 3 hours.

Preheat the oven to 400°F. Put the meat mixture through a meat grinder and return to the bowl. Beat the eggs and add to the bowl with the grated zest of 1 orange. Mix well to blend smoothly.

Line a 1 quart ovenproof terrine with three of the slices of bacon (the French term for this is *barder*, and the strips are called *bardes*), and distribute the filling inside as follows: 1 layer of filling, a layer of duck breast cut into slivers, a layer of filling, a layer of breast, and so on, ending with a layer of filling and placing the last bacon slices on top. Cover with a lid. Seal around the edge of the lid with a flour and water paste. Put the terrine in a fairly deep roasting pan, pour in water to come most of the way up the sides and cook in the oven for 1½ hours. Turn off the heat and leave to cool in the oven.

When the terrine is cool, refrigerate to harden the fat – this will take a few hours. Remove the top layer of bacon. Slice the second orange and decorate the terrine with 2 or 3 slices. Coat with aspic (it will take several thin applications to make a good coating; let each layer set before applying the next) and refrigerate for another 24 hours.

SMOOTH CHICKEN LIVER PÂTÉ
Mousse de foie de volaille

2¼ lb chicken livers
½ lb good quality bulk sausagemeat
⅓ cup milk
4 large eggs
2 teaspoons salt
1 teaspoon freshly ground black
pepper
1 teaspoon *quatre-épices*★
2 tablespoons brandy
3 large, thin slices of unsmoked
bacon★, or more smaller slices

SERVES 10-12 AS AN APPETIZER
PREPARATION TIME: 20 MINUTES
COOKING TIME: 1¼ HOURS

Work the chicken livers and sausagemeat in a blender or food processor to a semiliquid purée. Add the milk, the beaten eggs, salt, pepper, spice and brandy. Whisk to obtain a light, frothy, perfectly blended mixture.

Preheat the oven to 400°F. Choose an ovenproof terrine with a capacity of 1½ quarts. Line it with the bacon slices and pour in the mixture. Place it in a roasting or baking pan in the oven and pour in water to come halfway up the sides of the terrine. Cook for 1¼ hours. Leave to cool.

If you want to keep the pâté, melt a little extra butter – enough to cover the surface of the pâté to seal it. A sealed pâté will keep for 2 to 3 months, but once broken must be eaten within a week.

Alternative cooking method: use 8 little glass canning jars, each with a capacity of 1 cup. Fill them with the mixture. Fit the rubber seals and close the lids. Boil in a deep pan of water, which must cover the jars completely at all times, for 1½ hours.

MEAT

BREAST OF VEAL WITH LEEKS
AND CELERY HEARTS (see page
129)

HOT VEAL PAUPIETTES (see page
132)

ROASTING MEAT

The cooking of a roast of meat – whether spit, oven or pot-roasted – should begin with sealing and browning. The high temperature hardens the fatty outside, sealing in the juices and blood and forcing it along the blood vessels to the center of the roast. Then the temperature needs to be lowered: too much heat causes toughness because it makes protein coagulate to a hard, shrunken texture. If the meat begins to burn, wrap it in aluminum foil.

Roast meat has to be left to rest before carving. If you carve it immediately, you will find a very well cooked layer on the outside, then another layer which is less well cooked and the inside rare. If you remove the roast from the oven and keep it warm on a covered dish or wrapped in foil, it continues cooking very gently, becoming firmer, easier to carve and a more uniform pinkish color. At the same time, the muscle fibers contracted by the heat relax and become more tender.

The French are also fond of pot-roasting in a covered casserole, or *cocotte*, particularly for very lean cuts of meat. For the basic method see the recipe for pot-roast veal on page 129.

MICHEL GUÉRARD'S ROAST AND GRILLED BEEF

POT-ROASTING EN COCOTTE

Roasting a joint of beef, according to Michel Guérard, a butcher's son depends on a few simple but essential rules. Preheat the oven at maximum temperature, 500°F. Keep the oven very hot for 10 minutes after the meat has been put in to allow it to brown.

Then turn the oven down a little to 425°F. Salt the meat, but do not prick it with a fork during cooking. Baste frequently, but the roast should be set on a rack above the roasting pan, so that it is not swimming in juice. Adding potatoes to roast in the same pan will make the meat damp and less tender.

Cooking should finish at least 10 minutes in advance. Then the door should be opened and the meat left in the hot oven. "Roast beef has an outer shell which imprisons the juices and the fat in the center of the joint," explains Michel Guérard. "Leaving it in a hot oven makes the juices run outwards." Salt the meat on each slice as it is carved, adding a twist of the pepper mill.

For broiled meat, the piece of meat should never be pierced, because that would let the juices escape. A good broiled steak must be thick; otherwise it will be like a piece of old leather.

See page 16 for advice on deglazing the pan and an idea for *les jus de rôti* or sauces made with roasting juices.

SKIMMING MEAT JUICES

In many braised meat and poultry recipes the fat needs to be skimmed off the cooking juice to keep the finished dish from being greasy or indigestible.

To do this, remove the meat and any vegetables after cooking and keep them hot on a serving dish. Pour the juices through a strainer lined with a cloth, paper towel or a coffee filter soaked in iced water so that the grease sets and is trapped. Then pour the juices into a pitcher or bowl; the remaining fat will float to the surface and can be skimmed or brushed off.

Degreasing can be done more easily if a dish has been prepared a day ahead and left to cool. (This often improves the taste anyway.) When the fat has set on the surface, scrape it off with a spoon.

TOURNEDOS

Lean and tender tournedo steaks or filet mignons, cut from the tenderloin of beef and tied into a neat round in a dog-collar of fat, are favorites of chefs since they can be cooked to order in a matter of minutes. Here are two ideas from young French chefs without rich sauces or extravagant garnishes. Both dishes would be good served with sautéed potatoes or a potato purée (see page 156), followed by a green salad.

FILET MIGNON WITH JULIENNE VEGETABLES
Tournedos au parfum du pot-au-feu

1 large or 2 small carrots
2 stalks of celery
2 whites of leek
2 turnips
1 large onion
1 clove
2 sprigs of thyme
sea salt and freshly ground black pepper
8 filet mignons, 2½-3 oz each
scant 1 cup beef stock (see page 39)
4½ tablespoons butter

SERVES 4
PREPARATION TIME: 15 MINUTES
COOKING TIME: 8 MINUTES

Pierre Larapidie, the young chef at the Clovis in the Frantel Windsor, began to develop a very pure, simple style of cooking, using fats as a finishing touch rather than a cooking medium, after his own long illness. He emphasizes that this requires top-quality produce.

Cut the carrots, celery, leeks and turnips into fine julienne strips, and finely chop the onion. In a dish, mix the vegetables with the crushed clove, chopped thyme and seasoning to taste. Cover both sides of the steaks with this mixture, pressing lightly to make it adhere.

Cook in a nonstick skillet over a medium heat, allowing 4 minutes for each side. As you turn the steaks over, make sure that the vegetables do not come away. They should cook without burning.

Meanwhile, heat the stock and whisk in the butter. Serve the steaks hot from the pan, with the sauce poured over.

FILET MIGNON WITH HERBS FROM THE CURÉ'S GARDEN
Tournedos aux herbes du jardin de monsieur le curé

4 filet mignons, about 5 oz each
salt and freshly ground black pepper
1 tablespoon peanut oil
1 cup mixed herbs: flat-leafed parsley, chives, tarragon, chervil, basil
½ cup warm water
¼ cup *crème fraîche**
2 tablespoons strong Dijon-style mustard
1 tablespoon mild mustard
1 teaspoon butter

SERVES 4
PREPARATION TIME: 10 MINUTES
COOKING TIME: 15 MINUTES

Christian Ignace, who helped Raymond Oliver make the table *at the Grand Phoenix one of the most inventive and refined in Paris, is now on his own at Le Petit Bedon. He uses very little butter in the cooking itself, but often adds it at the end to a sauce to bring out the flavors.*
"Speedy and simple cooking does not have to be at the cost of quality," he commented on today's home cooking. "Quick cooking methods, which leave natural flavors undiluted and allow ingredients to release some of their juices, using lighter stocks or wines, lemon juice and a little butter – never cooked – are in any case my own preference."

Season the steaks. Heat the oil in a skillet over a fairly brisk heat. When the oil is very hot, put in the steaks and brown them for 4 minutes on each side.

Meanwhile, finely chop the herbs. Transfer the steaks to a hot serving dish and discard the cooking oil. Pour the warm water into the skillet and reduce it by three-quarters. Add the *crème fraîche* and reduce by half.

Combine the two mustards and stir into the sauce along with the herbs. Turn down the heat. Put the steaks back into the pan and add the butter. Heat each side for a few seconds, and serve.

123

DAUBES

A good *daube* is a regal dish. A *ragoût* of meat braised in stock and a wine marinade, it takes its name from the *daubière* – a tall, fat-bellied earthenware casserole with a concave lid. When cooking was still done on an open fire, *daubes* were simmered slowly overnight in the hot ashes with more hot ashes or embers placed in the hollow lid to give heat from above as well as below. Now the lid is used for water to keep the temperature down. Although especially associated with Provence, *daubes* have become something of a national dish.

The three main elements – the meat, the wine marinade and the finished sauce – vary from recipe to recipe. In a classic *daube*, the meat is beef, but it may be lamb; the marinade may be red or white wine, or wine vinegar; the sauce may be left clear or thickened with the flavoring vegetables rubbed through a sieve. Walnuts, chestnuts and olives may turn up in the delicious rich juices, which are mopped up with boiled or mashed potatoes, macaroni or rice.

Although a *daubière* is not essential, a good *daube* does depend on the cooking pot. It should be heavy and thick to cook the food slowly and evenly, with a tight-fitting lid to prevent the liquid from evaporating. If it is not a good fit, the pot can be sealed by wrapping a strip of paper around the rim of the lid and sticking it down with flour and water paste. The pot should also be of the right capacity; if it is too big, evaporation will be too rapid and the result less tender.

A PERFECT *DAUBE*

There are a few important principles to be observed to ensure the success of a *daube*. These are: the choice of meat, the choice of liquid, the method of cooking and, finally, the sauce.

The meat should be tender and a little fatty, though not too much. If it is not, the *lardons* or *bardes* (strips of fat bacon) will keep it from drying during cooking. The best cuts are fresh brisket, chuck, flank steak and bottom round: the tougher the cut, the tastier the sauce. You can use two different cuts. The meat should be cut into 1½ to 2 inch cubes. If they are too small, the meat will become tough and less tasty. You will also require a *couenne* (the skin and underlying fat from a roast of pork) and a calf's foot for added smoothness. The best fat to use is lard, which does not turn black or spit.

The liquid dictates the general tone of the *daube*. Traditionally, a good but not vintage red wine is used. For slightly fattier meats it might be better to use a white wine. Its acidity towards the end of cooking produces a pleasant feeling of lightness which balances the texture of the meat. Ideally, choose a simple local wine and serve a better quality wine from the same region with the meal. For a traditional *daube* it is best to marinate the meat for 12 hours, but that depends on the choice of meat and the time available.

The marinade and all of its ingredients are then used in the cooking. You can buy an enameled cast iron pot of the same shape as a *daubière* (including the concave lid); this is sold under the North African name for such a pot, *doufeu*. Otherwise, make sure the pot is airtight. It is best to cook the *daube* in the oven for an even, regular heat.

To keep the *daube* from being indigestible, skim off the fat before serving either by straining the juices or by allowing the *daube* to cool and scraping off the fat, following the instructions on page 122.

The sauce should be clear, translucent and smooth. It should not need thickening with flour or starch. Three ways of thickening are to purée the vegetables in a blender or food mill (or by pressing them through a sieve with the back of a spoon to extract all the juices) and to add them to the *daube*; to add a few chestnuts, cooked in the sauce and crushed; or to add the puréed meat from the calf's foot.

A *daube* can be kept in the refrigerator for 4 days.

Serve with a complementary wine, either good red or white.

BEEF *DAUBE*
Daube de boeuf

10 oz fatty pork belly (side pork)
¼ cup Armagnac
sprig of flat-leafed parsley
pinch of chopped savory
freshly ground black pepper
1¾ lb beef bottom round
1 lb 2 oz beef chuck
about ½ lb *couenne*★ (fresh pork skin
with fat)
3 shallots
1 calf's foot
1 tablespoon lard
2 cups chicken stock
salt
3 canned anchovy fillets in oil

For the marinade:
1 carrot
1 shallot
2 cloves of garlic
1 *bouquet garni*★ (sprig of thyme, bay
leaf, sprig of celery leaves, few stalks
from flat-leafed parsley, 3 small strips
of green leek leaves, piece of dried
orange zest★)
1 tablespoon peanut oil
2 tablespoons good red wine vinegar
1 level tablespoon crushed black
peppercorns
6-8 coriander seeds
1 onion stuck with a clove
3 cups good red wine

SERVES 8-10
PREPARATION TIME: 1½ HOURS + AT
LEAST 13 HOURS TO MARINATE
COOKING TIME: 3¾ HOURS

Cut the belly of pork into
matchsticks about ½ inch thick
and leave to marinate in the
Armagnac, seasoned with the
chopped parsley, savory and
pepper to taste, for about 1 hour in
a fairly cool place.

Cut the beef into regular cubes
measuring about 2 inches. Then
lard the beef cubes: that is, use a
big larding needle to thread strips
(*lardons*) of pork into the beef
parallel to the grain. Place them in
a mixing bowl as they are ready.

Now prepare the marinade.
Finely slice the carrot and the
shallot, and crush the unpeeled
garlic. Put these and the *bouquet
garni* in with the meat, and add
the peanut oil, vinegar, pepper,
crushed coriander, onion stuck
with the clove and lastly the red
wine. Cover and leave to marinate
in a cool place for 12 hours,

stirring frequently.

Remove the meat and put it in a
strainer over the bowl to catch the
juices.

Cut the *couenne* to fit the bottom
of a large casserole. Peel the
shallots and leave them whole. Cut
the calf's foot in two.

Heat the lard in the casserole.
Wipe each of the meat cubes with
paper towels to remove excess
moisture, then brown them on all
sides and set aside on a plate.
Discard half the cooking fat. Sauté
the shallots in the rest of the fat
until golden, then remove them.

Preheat the oven to 400°F.
Wipe out the casserole. Place the
couenne in the bottom, fatty side
down. Then put in the calf's foot
halves and all the ingredients of
the marinade, including the
bouquet garni. Arrange the meat
cubes on this aromatic bed, add
the shallots and moisten with the
marinade liquid. The liquid
should cover the meat with ½ inch
to spare; add chicken stock if
necessary. Salt lightly, as the
reduction of the liquid tends to
make the salt more concentrated.

Cover the casserole and put cold
water in the lid if appropriate (see
opposite). Put it in the oven, turn
the temperature down to 325°F,
and cook for 3½ hours.

Remove the meat, shallots and
calf's foot and place them on a
heated serving dish. Discard the
bouquet garni and the *couenne*.
Remove the garlic (peel it) and
onion (remove the clove). Crush
with the anchovies using a pestle
and mortar, or purée them in the
blender. Skim the fat off the
cooking juices (see page 122) and
put them into a saucepan. Add the
anchovy purée, bring the sauce to
a simmer and pour over the meat.
Serve immediately.

125

WHITE WINE BEEF CASSEROLE FROM THE PÉRIGORD
Daube du Périgord

DAUBIÈRE WITH CONCAVE LID

½ lb unsmoked slab bacon★
small bunch of flat-leafed parsley
2 cloves of garlic
1 onion
2 shallots
salt and freshly ground black pepper
pinch of *quatre-épices*★
1 *couenne*★ (piece of fresh pork skin with fat)
3¼ lb boneless beef sirloin
1 *bouquet garni*★
1 large, thin slice of unsmoked bacon★, or several smaller slices
1 bottle (750 ml) of dry white wine

SERVES 8
PREPARATION TIME: 30 MINUTES
COOKING TIME: 6-7 HOURS

Charles Reynal of La Cremaillère restaurant in Brive-la-Gaillarde, in the Corrèze on the eastern edge of the Dordogne, recommends eating this dish, thickened only by the gelatin of a calf's foot or pig's foot, sliced like a pâté when it is cold.

Chop the piece of bacon, the parsley, garlic, onion and shallots fairly finely. Season, and add the *quatre-épices*. Line the bottom of a stewing pot with the *couenne*, skin side up. Preheat the oven to 350°F. Thinly slice the beef and lay one slice on top of the *couenne*. Cover with a thin layer of the chopped mixture, and then another layer of beef. When half the ingredients have been used, put in the *bouquet garni*, then continue with layers as before ending with the chopped onion mixture and placing the thin slice of bacon, or *barde*, on top. Tuck in the ends. Pour in the wine, or more, to cover the ingredients. Add more if necessary. Cook for 6 to 7 hours. Remove the *barde* and skim off as much fat as possible (see page 122).

To eat this light daube cold, cool to room temperature and then chill until set.

FRENCH COTTAGE PIE
Hachis Parmentier

1 lb 2 oz cooked stewing beef
2 onions
4 shallots
½ lb (2 sticks) butter
2 sprigs of flat-leafed parsley
1 very small clove of garlic
salt and finely ground black pepper
3¼ lb potatoes
milk as required
fresh bread crumbs (optional)

SERVES 4-6
PREPARATION TIME: 40 MINUTES
COOKING TIME: 50 MINUTES

Hachis Parmentier is a dish of French childhood memories which, like its American cousin, hash, can inspire horror or delight. This recipe comes from Adrienne Biasin, whose recipes represent traditional French cooking at its very best (see page 141).

Finely chop the onions and shallots and soften them gently in 2 tablespoons of the butter. Meanwhile, chop up the cooked meat with the parsley and garlic, and season. Mix in the cooked onions and shallots, and set aside.

Cut the potatoes into large pieces and boil in a mixture of half milk and half water, just enough to cover the potatoes. Add a pinch of coarse salt. When cooked, drain well and mash in a bowl, adding half of the butter in small pieces.

Beat well with a little salt and pepper.

Preheat the oven to 425°F. Butter an ovenproof dish. Put in a layer of mashed potato, then one of meat. Make several layers of meat and potato, ending with potato. Sprinkle with pieces of the remaining butter, and top with bread crumbs if you like, although this is not essential. Bake for 20 minutes.

Halfway through, turn down the oven temperature to 375°F. If the top is browning too quickly, cover with buttered baking parchment.

DAUBE: THE RAW MATERIALS▶

STEAK TARTARE
Steak tartare

6 oz lean steak, such as tenderloin or
top sirloin
1 egg yolk from a large egg
2 tablespoons lemon juice
1 onion
1 shallot
1 teaspoon Dijon-style mustard
1 teaspoon hot pepper sauce
salt and freshly ground black pepper
1 tablespoon hazelnut oil*
1 tablespoon capers
2 tablespoons chopped herbs (flat-
leafed parsley, chervil, thyme,
marjoram etc.)

SERVES I
PREPARATION TIME: 15 MINUTES

*It is possible to weave all sorts of ideas
around this basic steak tartare. Jean
Moussié from Bistro 121 suggested
binding the meat with one or two peppery
mayonnaises, either flavored with
cracked green peppe;rcorns, chopped
chervil and tarragon, or generously laced
with hot paprika.*

*Steak tartare really is a dish invented
by the Tartars. From the late Middle
Ages on, ships from the Hanseatic ports
of Germany and Scandinavia sailed into
Russian ports, where the sailors
discovered these little patties of raw
meat. The idea spread from northern
Europe to France, where the recipe
became rather more sophisticated. Other
recipes from Bistro 121 appear on pages
23 and 194.*

Grind the steak fairly coarsely so
as to preserve the flavor and
texture. Some chefs prefer to cut it
up with a knife. In a bowl, mix
the egg yolk, lemon juice, finely
chopped onion and shallot, the
mustard, pepper sauce, salt and
pepper to taste and a dash of oil.
Mix well, then add the capers, half
the herbs, and the rest of the oil.

Lastly mix in the meat. When
prepared in this way, the steak
will remain firm and tender.

Turn the mixture on to a
serving plate, hollow out the
center and sprinkle in the rest of
the herbs. Serve rather cool.

MOROCCAN SPICED MEATBALLS IN VINEGAR SAUCE
Boungigaz

2¼ lb ground beef
2 eggs
2 tablespoons paprika
½ tablespoon ground cumin
tiny pinch of ground cinnamon
handful of coriander (cilantro) leaves
1 tablespoon dried marjoram
2 tablespoons fresh bread crumbs
2 tablespoons peanut oil

For the sauce:
1 tablespoon olive oil
1½ cups water
tiny pinch of powdered chili
1 chicken bouillon cube
2 eggs
3 tablespoons white vinegar

SERVES 4
PREPARATION TIME: 30 MINUTES + 30
MINUTES WAIT
COOKING TIME: 6 MINUTES

*A North African recipe from a
Moroccan-born Parisian, Perla Danan,
who gave a selection of her mother's
recipes for an article on traditional
Moroccan cuisine adapted to the lifestyle
of the modern working woman who does
not have hours to spend preparing
elaborate dishes. The meatballs would be
good eaten either with a salad and rice
or, better still, with other Moroccan
dishes. The eggplant salad (page 174),
tomato and sweet pepper purée and spicy
lentils (page 167) would all be good
partners. If you are feeding eight people
or more, you could cook the Algerian
sardines (page 86) as a second main
dish.*

Put the ground beef in a bowl and
combine with the eggs, spices,
finely chopped coriander, dried
marjoram, bread crumbs and
peanut oil. Add a few
tablespoonfuls of cold water, and
knead like a bread dough to form
a smooth, firm mixture. Leave to
stand for 30 minutes.

To make the meatballs, have a
bowl of cold water in which to
rinse your fingers after rolling each
ball. Roll the meat quickly into
balls no bigger than ¾ inch in
diameter.

Heat the olive oil, water and
powdered chili in a saucepan,
adding a chicken bouillon cube for
extra flavor. Put in the meatballs
as soon as they are shaped, cover
and cook for 5 minutes over a
fairly high heat.

Transfer the meatballs to a
plate. Whisk the eggs with the
vinegar, turn the heat down to
minimum and pour the mixture
into the cooking juices. Cook,
stirring continuously, for 1
minute. Put the meatballs back in
the pan, shake to distribute evenly
in the sauce, and serve. The sauce
has a delicious piquancy and
contrasts beautifully with a fresh
salad.

If you have problems with the
meatballs falling apart, try
refrigerating them before cooking
and adding another 2 tablespoons
of bread crumbs.

VEAL

The more expensive lean cuts of veal like loin and scallops or cutlets are well known and easily found, but the French also appreciate and make use of cheaper and often under-used cuts. Breast of veal can be boned, but will always be tastier cooked on the bone. Veal shank, especially cut from the hind leg, is a gelatinous cut, rich in meat and marrow, with lots of flavor. The qualities of both the dishes here, a hot one for winter and a cold one for summer, are brought out by slow, moist cooking.

POT-ROAST VEAL
Rôti de veau à la cocotte

2 tablespoons oil
1 boned veal roast such as loin, round or rump, weighing about 2¾ lb
½ lb onions
2 shallots
2 cloves of garlic
salt and freshly ground black pepper
scant 1 cup dry white wine
pinch of thyme
1 bay leaf
pinch of rosemary or savory
pinch of grated nutmeg
small piece of fresh gingerroot
1 tomato

SERVES 6
PREPARATION TIME: 15 MINUTES
COOKING TIME: 1½-2 HOURS

A French butcher usually wraps a lean boned and rolled roast in a barde *– a thin piece of bacon – to keep it juicy. But this is not strictly necessary and many of today's chefs prefer to use only enough narrow strips of fat to protect the joint when it touches the casserole so that the roasting meats are less greasy. This is a basic method for pot-roasting to be varied to suit the meat – see, for example the marinated roast pork on page 135.*

Pour the oil into a heavy casserole. Heat it over a fairly high heat, and brown the meat for 5 minutes on each side.

Coarsely chop the onions, shallots and garlic, and distribute them around the meat. Shake the pan. When the veal is golden brown and the onions well browned, turn down the heat. Season and add the white wine, herbs, the thyme, bay leaf and rosemary or savory together with the nutmeg and ginger. Cover the casserole and, if it has a concave lid, pour a little cold water into it. Cook for 1 to 1½ hours, depending on the size of the roast.

Halfway through, add the tomato cut into quarters. If there is too much juice, remove the lid and turn up the heat to reduce.

BREAST OF VEAL WITH LEEKS AND CELERY HEARTS
Tendrons de veau d'Adrienne

1¼ lb veal breast
2 tablespoons butter
1 tablespoon oil
1 *bouquet garni*★
3 large tomatoes
24 small white onions
salt and freshly ground black pepper
3 celery hearts
2½ cups sweet wine
6 whites of leek
3 tablespoons *crème fraîche*★
1 lime
pat of softened butter

SERVES 2
PREPARATION TIME: 25 MINUTES
COOKING TIME: 1-1¼ HOURS

PHOTOGRAPH ON PAGE 120

Another delicious recipe from Adrienne Biasin, recently published in La Table d'Adrienne *(see page 141). Robert Courtine, better known as La Reynière of* Le Monde *chose it for his book* Le Grand Jeu de la Cuisine. *Riblets of veal with the bone left in will have more flavor than boned veal.*

Cut the breast of veal into 6 pieces and brown them on all sides in the mixed butter and oil. Put in the *bouquet garni,* the tomatoes, peeled, deseeded and coarsely chopped, and the onions, peeled and left whole. Season and leave to simmer, uncovered, for 45 minutes. Meanwhile, blanch the celery hearts for 10 minutes.

Transfer the cooked meat to a heated serving dish. Pour the wine into the pan. Cut the leeks in half lengthwise and poach them and the celery in the sauce. Drain, and arrange around the veal.

Reduce the sauce for 10 minutes or so. Remove the *bouquet garni.* Thicken with the *crème fraîche.* Reduce for another 2 minutes. Add thin slices of lime. Remove from the heat, stir in the butter and strain the sauce over the meat.

VEAL SHANK WITH FENNEL
Jarret de veau au fenouil

2 onions
2 tablespoons olive oil
4 slices of veal shank
½ cup peanut oil
2¼ lb fennel bulbs
1 lime
salt and freshly ground black pepper
½ cup dry white wine
¼ cup capers
20 small ripe olives

SERVES 4
PREPARATION TIME: 10 MINUTES
COOKING TIME: ABOUT 2 HOURS

This is a delicious, warming dish full of the flavors of Provence, good served with a potato purée and salad.

Chop the onions, and gently brown them in the olive oil in a heavy casserole. Meanwhile, brown the veal in the peanut oil in a skillet.

Preheat the oven to 400°F. Cut the fennel bulbs in half and make a layer of half of them in the bottom of the casserole on top of the onion. Then make a layer of meat and one of lime slices. Cover with another layer of fennel, and season. Pour on the white wine. Cover the casserole dish and cook in the oven for 1½ hours.

Five minutes before serving, put in the capers and olives.

VEAL SHANK IN GREEN ASPIC
Jarret de veau en gelée verte

1 veal shank, weighing about 2¼ lb
1 calf's foot, boned and cut in half
1 large *bouquet garni*★
1 stalk of celery
4 small leeks
small bunch of flat-leafed parsley
1 onion studded with 2 cloves
3 large cloves of garlic
salt
white peppercorns
1 fennel bulb
2 celery hearts
¼ lb (about 2 cups) mixed greens:
chervil, spinach etc.
juice of ½ lemon

SERVES 4
PREPARATION TIME: 30 MINUTES +
TIME TO COOL
COOKING TIME: 4½ HOURS

Put the veal shank and the meat and bones from the calf's foot in a casserole just large enough to hold them. Pour in cold water to cover the meat with 2 inches to spare. Heat gently to delay boiling for as long as possible.

Skim off the froth as it forms. When the water begins to boil, pour in a ladleful of cold water so that the froth continues to form, and go on skimming. Repeat this cold water and skimming operation until the liquid is almost clear.

Then put in the *bouquet garni*, the celery, the green part of the leeks and the parsley stems tied together. Add the onion studded with cloves and the garlic, crushed but not peeled. Bring back to a boil, and if more froth forms, skim it off as it appears.

Add salt to taste and the peppercorns, and turn down the heat to a gentle simmer. Cover the pot with the lid slightly ajar, so that the steam can escape. Cook for 3½ hours, skimming occasionally with a spoon.

Cut the fennel bulb in half and add this together with the leek whites, tied together, and the celery hearts. Cook gently for another 30 minutes.

Remove and drain the meat, the bones, the fennel, leek whites and celery hearts. Strain the stock and leave to cool in a bowl.

Make a coloring for the stock by puréeing the parsley, chervil and spinach and straining off the juice. Decant the stock, leaving behind the deposit; give it a last skim and add the green juice and lemon juice. The stock will turn a wonderful green color.

Remove the meat from the veal shank. Place it in a bowl or mold with the meat from the calf's foot. As soon as the stock begins to set, pour it over the boned meat. Chill until firm, then serve with the vegetables and a mustard vinaigrette (see page 15).

VEAL SHANK IN GREEN ASPIC▶

HOT VEAL PAUPIETTES
Paupiettes d'Adrienne

1 oz dried *cèpes**
1 slice of stale bread
scant ½ cup milk
½ lb Swiss chard leaves
4 sprigs of flat-leafed parsley
4 sprigs of chervil
6 leaves of basil
3 oz calf's liver
2½ oz prosciutto
¼ lb cooked ham
salt and freshly ground black pepper
grated nutmeg
1 large egg
½ cup port wine
1 piece *crépine** (caul fat)
4 veal cutlets, pounded thin (or 3 for a
single roll)
12 small onions
4 carrots
2 tablespoons butter
1 bay leaf
small sprig of thyme
sprig of rosemary
scant 1 cup white wine

SERVES 4
PREPARATION TIME: 30 MINUTES + 2
HOURS SOAKING
COOKING TIME: ABOUT 45 MINUTES

PHOTOGRAPH ON PAGE 133

At Chez La Vieille Adrienne Biasin (see page 141) makes this roll as individual paupiettes, also known as alouettes sans têtes – *literally birds without heads – but she adapted it for* Marie Claire *to a more practical, less fiddly and time-consuming large* roulé *to make for eating at home. Cheesecloth or aluminum foil will replace the* crépine *very well.*

Soak the dried *cèpes* in a little water, covered, for 2 hours. Drain, reserving the mushroom-flavored water to add to the sauce.

Soak the bread in the milk, squeeze dry and put in a bowl. Blanch the chard leaves for a few seconds, drain and dry them, then coarsely chop them and add to the bread. Chop the parsley, chervil and basil and add these too.

Coarsely mince the calf's liver, the drained *cèpes*, the ham and the prosciutto and add all these to the bowl. Season with salt, pepper and nutmeg. Add the lightly beaten egg and the port wine, mix well and adjust the seasoning if necessary.

Rinse the *crépine* under warm water and then under cold. This is essential if it has been preserved in brine. Lay it on a board and cut it into four pieces, or into a large rectangle, according to whether you are preparing a single roll or four smaller ones.

Place the veal cutlets on top of the *crépine*, either each to its own piece or, for one large roll, two pieces slightly overlapping with the third straddling both of them. Spread the filling to within ¾ inch of the edges, pressing it down well. Roll up the veal and tuck in the ends. Wrap the veal roll in the *crépine*. It can be tied up to secure it better.

Peel the onions. Cut the carrots into a few large pieces. In a casserole the size of the roll (or rolls), brown the vegetables in butter. Put the roll (or rolls) in the casserole and brown on all sides over a medium heat for 10 minutes. Then put in the bay leaf, thyme and rosemary and moisten with the white wine and the strained mushroom juice. Cover and simmer over a low heat for 35 minutes, or 25 minutes for individual rolls.

132

ROULADE OF VEAL AND HERB OMELETTES
Roulade de veau aux herbes

piece of veal top round, measuring
8×12 inches and ½ inch thick
salt and freshly ground black pepper
thin slices of cooked ham
6 extra large eggs
flat-leafed parsley, chervil, chives and
tarragon
olive oil
a few shallots
diced bacon★
oregano

SERVES 4
PREPARATION TIME: 45 MINUTES
COOKING TIME: 1¼ HOUR

*Cold stuffed rolled veal is excellent as
long as the filling is lean. Since it is best
served at room temperature rather than
chilled and is easily transportable, it is
good for picnics as well as meals at
home.*

Ask your butcher to prepare the
veal for you. Season it with salt
and pepper and cover with thin
slices of ham.

Separately, make three 2-egg
omelettes, flavoring them with a
mixture of chopped parsley,
chervil, chives and tarragon. Place
the omelettes on top of the ham,
covering the entire surface. Roll
up the meat from a long side and
tie up. Put it in a casserole with
olive oil, a few chopped shallots
and a little diced bacon. Season.
Add a little oregano.

Sauté the meat gently to brown
it, then gradually turn it, browning it as you do so.

Cover and cook for about 1¼
hour, adding liquid if necessary.
Leave to cool, slice and serve.

BLANQUETTE OF VEAL
Blanquette de veau

3¼ lb veal pieces (shoulder, breast,
loin)
1 large carrot
1 stalk of celery
1 leek white
2 cloves of garlic
2 onions each stuck with 1 clove
1 *bouquet garni*★
pared zest of 1 lemon★
salt and freshly ground white pepper
5 cups water
1 cup dry white wine
20 pickling onions
10 oz button mushrooms
3 egg yolks from large eggs
scant 1 cup *crème fraîche*★
juice of ½ lemon
generous dash of good port wine
(optional)

SERVES 6
PREPARATION TIME: 40 MINUTES
COOKING TIME: ABOUT 2 HOURS

*The characteristic, creamy whiteness of a
blanquette comes from the long, gentle
simmering of the meat, without any
browning first, and the liaison of cream
and eggs. Most chefs recommend
blanching the meat before the main
cooking. Put the veal in cold water,
bring it to a boil and leave it for just one
minute; then rinse the meat before the
main cooking.*

*Providing you are not mean with the
egg and cream for the liaison, there will
be no need for flour to thicken the sauce.*

*Choose the meat carefully. Don't ask
the butcher for veal to make a stew, or
you may get gristly veal stew meat. Look
at what is on offer: first try shoulder or
breast. If they are too fatty, ask for
loin. Choose an assortment of cuts. Keep
the bones: blanquette, like all stews, is
better cooked with the bones.*

Finely chop the carrot, celery,
leek and garlic and put into a large
casserole. Add the meat, onions,
bouquet garni and lemon zest. Add
salt and plenty of pepper: the
flavor of the stock should be
brought out. Cover with water and

white wine. Do not overdo the
wine thinking that it will make the
sauce better: it should be about
one fifth of the amount of water.
Bring to a boil. Skim, cover and
simmer for 1½ hours.

Check that the meat is cooked.
If not, simmer for another 30
minutes. Remove the meat and set
aside. Skim off the fat (page 122).

Strain the stock into a clean
pan. Peel the pearl onions and add
them to the stock with the
mushrooms. Simmer for 15
minutes. Check the seasoning.

Whisk the egg yolks and *crème
fraîche* with the lemon juice. Add a
dash of port wine if you like – the
sweetness and taste go well with
the rest. Pour into the hot stock,
whisking well. Taste: a little more
pepper is often needed. Add the
meat. Leave over a very gentle
heat for a few seconds to reheat
and make sure the sauce thickens,
but do not allow it to boil. Serve
with white rice or potatoes.

SALAD OF WARM VEAL KIDNEYS AND CABBAGE

Salade de rognons de veau tièdes au chou croquant

1 medium head of green cabbage
1 carrot
1 small zucchini
salt
2 shallots
1 sprig of chervil
1 chive
⅔ cup vinaigrette,
made with walnut oil and sherry
vinegar*
1 teaspoon light oil
1 whole veal kidney, fat trimmed off
1 tablespoon butter
⅔ cup red Côtes de Buzet, or other
good, light fruity red wine
freshly ground black pepper

SERVES 4
PREPARATION TIME: 45 MINUTES
COOKING TIME: 30 MINUTES

This recipe comes from Michel Trama, of the L'Aubergade restaurant, not far from Agens. He is one of the most inventive young chefs working in the southwest. He began cooking after training as a lawyer. For him there are a few basic principles which never vary. "First, quality ingredients and then, after carefully thinking about what you are going to do with them, giving free rein to your inspiration and imagination. Absolute freshness, minimum cooking (not to be confused with undercooking) and boldness balanced with restraint are fundamental. No overcooked fat – it is a crime against taste and health – no heavy sauces or sauce bases which overwhelm the other ingredients. The flavor and the texture of the product should not only be discernible but actually brought out. For example, I fry almost without oil, keeping my eye on the pan constantly. I only add the seasoning or the fat which will emphasize its flavor afterward."

Côtes de Buzet, a wine from south-west France, is an easily varied regional suggestion.

Cut the cabbage into thin strips, except for two leaves which should be reserved. Finely dice the carrot or cut it into thin strips. Do likewise with the zucchini without peeling it. Cook the carrot and zucchini together in boiling salted water, 3 minutes for the carrot and 2 minutes for the zucchini. Cook the strips of cabbage in the same way for 3 minutes without covering the pan. Drain the vegetables, cool in iced water and drain. Chop one shallot and the herbs.

Put the cabbage, carrots, zucchini, shallots and herbs into a salad bowl. Mix carefully and pour on the vinaigrette. Keep at room temperature. Preheat the oven to 425°F. Heat the oil in a skillet and brown the kidney over a high heat, 2 minutes on one side and 1 minute on the other. Put the kidney in a strainer and let the juices run out for 5 minutes at room temperature. Wrap the kidney in the two reserved cabbage leaves and place in a flameproof casserole. Cook in the oven for 7 minutes, turning over halfway through.

When cooked, discard the cabbage leaves and leave to drain in a colander while you prepare the shallot sauce.

Discard the fat from the casserole but do not wash it. Melt half the butter in it and add the second shallot, finely chopped. As soon as it begins to brown, deglaze with the wine and season. Turn up the heat and reduce the sauce to about 3 tablespoons. Whisk in the rest of the butter.

Transfer the kidney to a board and slice it. Divide it between four plates, and place the salad next to the kidney. Pour the sauce over the kidney. Serve immediately.

PORK

MARINATED ROAST PORK WITH HERBS
Rôti de porc à la sauge

3¼ lb boned pork loin roast
1¾ cups dry white wine
4 tablespoons olive oil
1 large onion
3 sprigs of thyme
1 bay leaf
4 cloves
4 sprigs of sage
salt and freshly ground black pepper

SERVES 6
PREPARATION TIME: 20 MINUTES + 2
HOURS TO MARINATE
COOKING TIME: 1¾-2 HOURS

In the Alpes-Maritimes region, pork is usually marinated before cooking, in white wine and olive oil with herbs and seasonings.

Remove any skin with most of the underlying fat from the pork (you can save this for use as a *couenne* in a *daube*; see page 124). Put the meat in a deep dish and add the white wine, 2 tablespoons olive oil, the sliced onion, the thyme, bay leaf, cloves and sage. Marinate for 2 hours, turning the pork every 30 minutes so that the flavor penetrates it evenly all over. Drain.
Preheat the oven to 325°F.

Place the pork in a roasting pan with the sage. Add the remaining olive oil and roast for 1¾ to 2 hours, turning the meat occasionally and adding water so that it does not dry out. Season when cooking is complete. Serve with a light young red or white wine.
Variation: another idea for roast pork, from Alain Senderens' *La Grande Cuisine à petits prix*, is to add ½ cup of white rum mixed with the juice of four oranges to the pan to baste the meat while it roasts. At the end of the roasting time, 3 tablespoons of *crème fraîche* and the blanched zest of an orange are added to the cooking juices.

STUFFED BRAISED SHOULDER OF PORK
Epaule de porc farcie et braisée

3¼ lb Boston butt roast, with skin and fat
2-3 prunes
2 tart-sweet apples
pinch of ground cinnamon
small pinch of grated nutmeg
1 onion
2 cloves of garlic
bunch of herbs: flat-leafed parsley, chervil, chives, tarragon, mint, Swiss chard leaves
4 juniper berries
1 level teaspoon chopped lemon verbena leaves (optional)
salt and coarsely ground black pepper
2 cups chicken stock (see page 39), with a little Banyuls (fortified sweet brown wine), Madeira or port wine
1 tablespoon butter

SERVES 4
PREPARATION TIME: 40 MINUTES + A
FEW HOURS WAIT
COOKING TIME: I HOUR 5 MINUTES

Savory dishes with prunes are associated with Touraine, which was once famous for its plum orchards. Now Agen, in the Périgord, has the reputation for the best prunes in France. Their heavy sweetness goes well with tart apples in stuffings for goose, pork and veal. See also the recipe for lapin aux pruneaux on page 117.
This dish can be eaten either hot or cold and is good accompanied by a young red wine.

Bone the pork and reserve the bone. Remove the skin with the underlying fat (this is known as *couenne★*) and reserve this too. Pit the prunes, and peel and finely dice the apples. Spread out the meat and sprinkle with the spices, chopped onion and garlic, chopped herbs, juniper, verbena, salt and pepper to taste, apples and prunes. Add any meat adhering to the bone. Fold over the meat to enclose the stuffing. Truss, and leave for a few hours.
Preheat the oven to 425°F.

Cover the bottom of a casserole with the *couenne*, skin side up, and place the pork on it. Lay the bones around the meat and roast for 15 minutes, turning the meat once. Then pour in the stock. Cover the dish, turn the oven down to 350°F and cook for 40 minutes, turning the meat from time to time. To glaze the meat properly, turn up the oven to 425°F for the final 10 minutes and baste frequently.

Transfer the meat to a carving dish and return it to the switched-off oven to keep hot. Remove the bones from the cooking juices, skim them as thoroughly as possible and reduce over a high heat. Whisk in the butter.

Slice the meat and serve the sauce separately.

135

QUICK *POTÉE*
Potée express

1 green cabbage
1 smoked pork butt, weighing about
3 lb
10 oz leeks
10 oz turnips
10 oz carrots
1 onion stuck with a clove
a few black peppercorns
2 large boiling sausages
10 oz potatoes

SERVES 8
PREPARATION TIME: 15 MINUTES +
OVERNIGHT SOAKING
COOKING TIME: 1 HOUR

The original recipe for this speedy simplified potée *(see page 144 for a more traditional version) specifies Morteau sausage, a meaty sausage sold only in autumn and early winter, but any large, meaty boiling sausage will do well. The recipe for this* potée *comes from Anouk Lautier. For other recipes by her see pages 96, 116 and 188.*

Cut the cabbage into 6 pieces. Put them in the bottom of a large casserole and place the pork butt on top. Arrange the leeks, turnips, carrots and onion in the pot. Cover all the vegetables with cold water. Add a few peppercorns but no salt. Bring to a boil, but gently.

After 30 minutes simmering, prick the sausages and put them into the pot.

Fifteen minutes later, add the potatoes. After 1 hour the *potée* is ready. The aroma is marvelous.

Serve the sliced meat and sausages on the vegetables on a large platter. Suggested accompaniments are gherkins, pickled onions, mustards, and coarse salt mixed with chopped parsley, perhaps with a bowl of walnut oil with red wine vinegar.

ALAIN SENDERENS' CARAMELIZED HAM
Jarret de porc caramelisé

4½ lb smoked ham, shank half
2 tablespoons groundnut oil
¼ cup sugar
¼ lb carrots
¼ lb onions
2 large stalks of celery
3 whites of leek
¾ lb tomatoes
3 cloves of garlic
1½ tablespoons butter
1 *bouquet garni*★ (sprig of thyme, bay leaf, 4 stems of flat-leafed parsley)
1 chicken bouillon cube
2 young heads of green cabbage, about 1½ lb each

SERVES 4
PREPARATION TIME: 30 MINUTES +
12-15 HOURS SOAKING
COOKING TIME: I HOUR 25 MINUTES

Alain Senderens is one of the most prestigious of the nouvelle cuisine chefs. *Unexpected marriages of flavors, often researched and retrieved from antiquity, yet with a surprisingly modern feel, are one of his trademarks. When he wrote* La Cuisine réussie, *his wife cooked all the recipes at home to check they were adapted to the everyday kitchen.*

If necessary, soak the ham for 12 to 15 hours to remove excess salt, changing the water several times. Before cooking, dry it carefully. Preheat the oven to 425°.

Place a fairly large, heavy casserole over a medium heat and put in 1 tablespoon oil. When this is hot, put in the ham, sprinkle it with sugar, and put the dish in the oven. Allow the meat to bake for 30 minutes, turning it as soon as one side is brown, to obtain an even color all over. Meanwhile, finely dice the vegetables (except the cabbage) and garlic.

When the meat is golden brown, remove it from the oven and turn the heat down to 400°F. Place the meat on a plate. Wash and dry the casserole and put it over a medium heat with the remaining oil and the butter. As

soon as the fat is hot, put in the *bouquet garni*, diced vegetables and garlic, mix and gently brown for about 10 minutes.

Put the ham back in the casserole on the bed of vegetables and return it to the oven to cook for 15 minutes. Turn the meat over and cook for a further 7 minutes. Dissolve the bouillon cube in a glass of hot water, pour this over the ham and cook for another 25 minutes, basting with the juices a couple of times.

While the ham is cooking, cut the cabbages into strips. Blanch these for 3 minutes in boiling water. Cool with cold water and drain.

Remove the ham from the oven and strain the juices into another casserole, pressing the vegetables with the back of a spoon to extract all the flavor. Spread the cabbage over the bottom of the second casserole, place the ham on top and put back in the oven to cook for 20 minutes.

Carve the meat before presenting it on a bed of cabbage on a hot serving dish. Serve with a red wine such as Côtes du Rhône.

STEAMED LETTUCE LEAVES WITH PORK FILLING
Crépinettes de porc en feuilles vertes

5 oz boned pork shoulder
1 large egg
pinch of curry powder
1 tablespoon chopped chervil
1 tablespoon chopped flat-leafed parsley
2 leaves of sage
salt and freshly ground black pepper
8 lettuce leaves

SERVES 4
PREPARATION TIME: 20 MINUTES
COOKING TIME: 30 MINUTES

Crépinettes are grilled or fried flat patties or sausages made with ground meat or poultry. They take their name from crépine, *the web-like pork caul (see page 9) in which they are wrapped. Here Jacques Manière (see page 115) played with the idea to produce a less fatty* crépinette *wrapped in lettuce leaves. He suggests serving them with pasta and melted lemon butter or firm rice with a fresh tomato purée (see page 26).*

Grind the pork. In a bowl, beat the egg and add the curry powder and meat. Add the chopped herbs

to the bowl, season to taste and stir all the ingredients together. Leave to meld for a few moments.

Meanwhile, steam the lettuce leaves to soften them.

Divide the pork mixture into 4 portions and put each portion in the center of a lettuce leaf. Fold the lettuce over and wrap with another leaf. Put the four "parcels" in the top of a steamer. Steam for 20 minutes, then leave for 5 minutes with the heat turned off before serving.

SMOKED PORK WITH RED KIDNEY BEANS
Petit salé aux haricots rouges

2⅔ cups dried red kidney beans
2-3 tablespoons oil
a few chicken giblets or meat trimmings
4 onions
⅓ cup flour
2 cups dry white wine
12 cups "white" (veal and chicken) stock (see page 39)
1 small can tomato paste
large *bouquet garnis*★
salt and freshly ground black pepper
smoked pork butt, weighing about 2½ lb
2 level tablespoons chicken fat
2 cups red wine, preferably Beaujolais, or another cheaper light red wine
3 cloves of garlic

SERVES 6
PREPARATION TIME: 45 MINUTES + 12 HOURS SOAKING
COOKING TIME: 3-3½ HOURS

Petit salé *is the name given to lightly salted cuts of pork. It is one of the specialties of Chez Allard, a Parisian bistro in the rue Saint-André-des Arts. It is no longer entirely a family concern, as it was for over forty years, but the menu remains the same. This recipe and another (page 105) come from La Cuisine de Chez Allard.*

Soak the beans in cold water for 12 hours. For the cooking liquor heat the oil in a pot and brown the chicken giblets or meat trimmings with 2 onions cut into quarters. Sprinkle in the flour, mix and pour in the white wine and 8 cups of stock. Add the tomato paste, half the *bouquet garni*, and salt and pepper to taste, and mix well.

Simmer gently for 1½ to 2 hours on top of the stove, or in a low oven at 300°F. Strain the liquid and reserve. Put the smoked pork butt in a pot and pour on the cooking liquor. Simmer for about 2 hours.

Meanwhile, drain the beans and put them in another pan with cold water, a quartered onion and a *bouquet garni*. Bring to a boil and boil for 10 minutes, then cook more gently until tender. Do not add salt until at least half-time.

When the meat is cooked, prepare the sauce for the beans. Chop the last onion and fry it in the chicken fat until soft. Add the red wine and bring to a boil. Add the rest of the stock, two generous spoonfuls of the cooking liquor, the minced cloves of garlic, and salt and pepper to taste. Reduce for an hour.

Drain the beans carefully and mix them with the sauce. Simmer for 2 minutes. Drain the bacon and serve on the bed of beans.

FARMHOUSE PORK PÂTÉ WITH JUNIPER BERRIES
Terrine de porcelet aux baies de genièvre

¾ lb boned pork shoulder
¾ lb lean boned pork loin
3 tablespoons juniper-flavored *eau-de-vie*★, or Dutch gin
1 cup dry white wine
½ tablespoon juniper berries
1 teaspoon crushed thyme
1 teaspoon *quatre-épices*★
2 teaspoons salt
1 teaspoon freshly ground black pepper
3 tablespoons chopped flat-leafed parsley
2 teaspoons chopped chervil
1 large egg
4 large, thin slices of unsmoked bacon★
a little liquid aspic★

SERVES 8-12
PREPARATION TIME: 30 MINUTES + SEVERAL HOURS TO MARINATE AND 2 DAYS MATURING
COOKING TIME: 1¼ HOURS

Crushed juniper berries, used in the distillation of gin, are often added to marinades, braised game and pork terrines. This is a recipe from the Club de la Terrine (see page 118).

Grind the pork using the coarse disk. Pour the *eau-de-vie* and the white wine over the pork and mix in the lightly crushed juniper berries, thyme, *quatre-épices*, salt and pepper. Marinate for a few hours. Add the parsley, chervil and beaten egg. Mix well.

Preheat the oven to 400°F. Line the bottom and sides of a 1 quart capacity terrine with bacon slices (*bardes*) and fill with the pork mixture. Place the last slice of bacon on top and cover the terrine, sealing the lid with flour and water paste. Cook for 1¼ hours, turn off the oven and leave the terrine to cool inside. When it is cold, refrigerate it for a few hours, then remove the top slice of bacon. Make a small amount of aspic and pour it into the terrine. Leave to mature for 48 hours in the refrigerator.

If you want to keep the terrine for any longer in the refrigerator it must be completely dry, so scrape off all fat and jelly, put in a clean container and seal with lard.

Serve with good bread, butter and a dry white wine.

FARMHOUSE PORK PÂTÉ WITH JUNIPER BERRIES ▶

LAMB

ROAST LEG OF LAMB
Un simple gigot de rôti

1 Frenched leg of lamb, weighing about 4½ lb
1 peeled fat clove of garlic
salt and freshly ground black pepper
4-5 unpeeled cloves of garlic

SERVES 6-8
PREPARATION TIME: 15 MINUTES
COOKING TIME: 40 MINUTES

The Ambassade d'Auvergne in Paris (see page 156) is known for its succulent, juicy gigot served, as in the Auvergne, with baked sliced potatoes. Ask the butcher to remove the skin around the roast and to take out the bone.

Preheat the oven to about 400°F. Quickly rub the roast all over with garlic and brush with butter. Lightly sprinkle the top with salt. Put it in a roasting pan surrounded by the unpeeled cloves of garlic, and place in the oven. At once turn the heat up to 450°F. Count 8½ minutes per pound. Season *after* cooking.

MARINATED SHOULDER OF LAMB WITH HONEY AND FRESH MINT
Epaule d'agneau marinée sauce menthe

1 shoulder of lamb, weighing about 4½ lb
2 tablespoons runny honey
1 tablespoon wine vinegar
juice of ½ lemon, or ½ cup wine or wine vinegar
6 leaves of mint

For the marinade:
2 sprigs of thyme
6 sprigs of rosemary
2 bay leaves
1 sage leaf
10 black peppercorns
8-10 juniper berries
2 cloves
8 cloves of garlic
1 teaspoon sea salt
½ cup *eau-de-vie*
large piece of dried orange zest*
2 cups red wine
1 cup red wine vinegar

SERVES 6
PREPARATION TIME: 35 MINUTES + 4-5 HOURS MARINATING
COOKING TIME: 50 MINUTES

This is a superb shepherds' recipe for tough old mountain sheep. The same method of preparation and cooking is used in the Auvergne, the Languedoc and in the Alps. Only the herbs, spices and wines vary slightly from one region to another.

Accompaniments could be white (navy) beans cooked with a mutton or lamb bone and a piece of pork fat to give a smooth texture, as in Provence, or fennel bulbs braised with two mint leaves, the juice of a lemon and a pinch of brown sugar.

Strip the marinade herbs from their stems, reserving 4 sprigs of rosemary to insert in the meat. Blend or crush with the spices, orange rind, two garlic cloves and the salt to a thickish paste. Moisten with the *eau-de-vie*.

Use a sharp knife to make criss-cross slashes over the fat, penetrating ¼ inch into the meat. Rub the herb paste all over the shoulder, and into the cuts. Place the meat in a deep bowl with the zest and pour on the wine and vinegar. Cover and leave to marinate for 4-5 hours at room temperature, basting and turning from time to time.

Preheat the oven to 350°F. Divide the reserved rosemary into small sprigs, and cut the remaining 6 cloves of garlic into slivers. Insert the garlic and rosemary alternately in the criss-crosses. Dilute the honey with the vinegar and brush the surface of the meat with it, making sure it penetrates the slashes. Set the meat on a rack above a roasting pan filled with ½ inch water and put it in the oven. As soon as the surface caramelizes slightly you can begin to baste. After 20 minutes, turn the meat over and brush with vinegar and honey again. Reduce the heat to 325°F. When a light crust has formed, baste again.

Keep basting at first with the marinade and then with the roasting juices. Add more water if the level of liquid falls. Allow about 45 minutes in all for a 4½ lb shoulder. The juice which runs out of the thickest part of the meat should be pale pink, but not red. Turn off the heat and let the shoulder rest in the oven while you prepare the sauce.

Remove the juices from the roasting pan, skim and strain (see page 122) into a saucepan. You will need about 1¾ cups of liquid. If you have less, you can add the lemon juice or wine or wine vinegar. Bring to a boil and add the mint leaves, cut up with scissors. Adjust the seasoning and serve immediately with the lamb.

LAMB LOIN CHOPS IN BATTER
Côtelettes d'agneau de lait en beignets

2 lamb loin roasts
1 teaspoon peanut oil
salt and freshly ground black pepper
oil for deep frying

For the batter:
1 cup flour
1 tablespoon water
pinch of salt
3 large eggs
few drops of peanut oil
1 tablespoon butter

SERVES 4
PREPARATION TIME: 25 MINUTES
COOKING TIME: 25 MINUTES

James de Coquet is a columnist for Le Figaro. *Now aged ninety, he is one of France's most respected food writers. His two books are as much about his travels as food. This is his recipe.*

Preheat the broiler. Brush both sides of the lamb with oil. Make a few slashes in the fat without cutting into the meat and sprinkle with pepper. Broil for 6 minutes on each side, then broil each side for another minute. Keep an eye on the heat, as the melted fat can catch fire and blacken the meat.

Place the broiled lamb on a board and divide it into chops. The less-cooked chops in the center should be fried first and for longer, or reserved for those who prefer the meat to be quite pink. Sprinkle with a little salt.

Prepare the batter by mixing the flour with the water, salt and eggs, reserving one of the whites which should be beaten until stiff and folded in to make the batter lighter. Add the oil and melted butter, and lastly the beaten egg white. Heat the frying oil and check that it is hot enough by throwing in a small piece of bread; this should rise immediately and brown within a minute.

Dry each chop with paper towels and dip it in the batter, holding it by the bone. Fry both sides until golden brown.

LAMB CHOPS BAKED WITH POTATOES AND ONION
Côtes d'agneau découvertes au four

2¼ lb potatoes
3 large onions
6 tablespoons softened butter
salt and freshly ground black pepper
grated nutmeg
3 tablespoons olive oil
4 lamb rib chops, about 6 oz each
2-3 cloves of garlic
few sprigs of flat-leafed parsley

SERVES 4
PREPARATION TIME: 25 MINUTES
COOKING TIME: 45 MINUTES

Adrienne Biasin is a name to conjure with in French culinary circles. For thirty years she has been cooking plats de la bonne femme with loving care in her small restaurant, Chez la Vieille, on rue de l'Arbre Sec near les Halles. During that time, she has built up a devoted and discriminating clientele which includes both professional gourmets, like Robert Courtine, the food writer for Le Monde, and fellow chefs like Paul Bocuse. Her recipes rarely use spectacular ingredients, they have little emphasis on stylish presentation and they make few concessions to food fashions. But they are finely tuned and superbly cooked.

This recipe is a version of côtes Champvallon, a great favorite among the nineteenth-century bourgeoisie; there are other recipes by Adrienne Biasin on pages 116, 126 and 155.

Peel the potatoes, cut them into not too thin rounds and leave them in cold water while you slice the onions. Butter a large ovenproof dish. Drain and carefully dry the potato rounds. Mix with the onions in a bowl, add the rest of the butter and season with salt, pepper and nutmeg. Mix so that the vegetables are coated with butter. Preheat the oven to 400°F.

In a lightly oiled skillet, quickly brown the chops on all sides. Spread half the vegetables over the bottom of the dish, place the chops on this bed and cover with the rest of the potato and onion mixture. Crush the garlic without peeling it and add this. Pour on the remaining olive oil and bake for 40 minutes. If the vegetables brown too quickly, cover with baking parchment.

When the potatoes and onions are cooked, they will become very soft. Sprinkle with chopped parsley and serve in the same dish.

Follow with a green salad or green beans sautéed in garlic butter, and accompany with a robust red wine.

141

NAVARIN

A *navarin* is a ragoût of lamb. Originally it was intended for mutton in need of long, slow simmering, but now, of course, that is hard to find. It becomes a *navarin printanière* when young spring vegetables like baby carrots, peas, and green beans are added.

A PERFECT *NAVARIN*

The liquid should cover the other ingredients with ½ inch to spare, and by the end of cooking much of it should have evaporated. If it is still watery, remove the meat and vegetables and reduce over a high heat.

Traditionally the cooking juices from a *navarin* are thickened with a sprinkling of flour before adding the liquid. But for a more refined, lighter effect this can be replaced by other ingredients. Back in 1880, *La Cuisinière provençale* suggested cooking with a handful of dried white beans that were then rubbed through a sieve to remove the skins. Adrienne Biasin of Chez la Vieille restaurant mashes one or two well-cooked potatoes with a fork. Other cooks add a roll of well-secured *couenne*★ (pork skin and fat) as soon as the stock has been added, or a calf's foot split into four pieces. These add a delicate smoothness and, unlike flour, do not tend to separate from the rest of the liquid. Skimming is vital (see page 122). Reheat the sauce before pouring it over the *navarin*.

NAVARIN WITH YOUNG SPRING VEGETABLES
Navarin printanière légère

1½ lb shoulder of lamb (blade or arm bone steak); boned
1 lb breast of lamb, boned
1½ lb lamb sirloin chops, boned
pinch of sugar
1 tablespoon goose fat★
1 large onion
2 cloves of garlic
1 teaspoon savory leaves
pinch of dried rosemary
bunch each of small white onions, new carrots, new turnips, green asparagus
5 small new potatoes
2 sprigs of chervil
2 sprigs of flat-leafed parsley

For the stock:
14 oz chicken giblets
1 calf's foot
a few lamb bones
2 carrots
green part of 3 leeks
1 onion stuck with a clove
1 *bouquet garni*★
1 clove of garlic
2 cups dry white wine
6 cups water
sea salt
black peppercorns

SERVES 4-6
PREPARATION TIME: I HOUR
COOKING TIME: 5 HOURS

Use young lamb, with tender, pale meat and thick, white fat, tasty without being overpowering. It is important to mix fatty pieces, with or without bones, and lean cuts.

Prepare the stock the day before, or in the morning to use in the evening. Put the giblets, halved calf's foot, bones, vegetables, *bouquet garni*, garlic, wine and water in a pot. Start off over a high heat and when it begins to boil, turn the heat down to minimum and skim carefully. When the liquid is clear add a little salt and the peppercorns. Cover, and simmer for 2½ hours.

Leave to cool, then remove the vegetables and the calf's foot. Strain and refrigerate.

Cut the meat into chunks. Sprinkle with a pinch of sugar. Heat the goose fat in a casserole and brown the meat. Chop the onion, and add to the meat. When the meat and onions are well browned, remove them with a slotted spoon and put them on a dish. Discard the fat and, without either washing or wiping the casserole, put back the meat and onions with the chopped garlic.

Sprinkle with the savory and rosemary, mix and wait for 1 minute before adding enough hot stock to nearly cover the meat. Add a little white wine if it is necessary. Bring to a simmer over a medium heat, then turn the heat down to minimum, cover and cook for 1 hour 20 minutes; or, better, put the casserole in a preheated oven at 350°F to cook.

Meanwhile, prepare the vegetables, leaving them whole if they are small. Keep the green shoots on the onions and the small leaves on the turnips. Add the vegetables to the casserole in this order: onions, carrots, turnips, then potatoes. After a further 12 minutes add the asparagus cut into halves or thirds. Add a little stock so that the vegetables are covered. Cook for about 10 minutes more.

Sprinkle with a mixture of chopped chervil and parsley, and serve immediately.

NAVARIN WITH YOUNG VEGETABLES ▶

POTS-AU-FEU

A *pot-au-feu* could be described simply as a one-pot meal: a piece of beef simmered with flavoring vegetables and, sometimes other meats, in a broth. The broth becomes a soup, followed by a main course of the meat and vegetables.

But a *pot-au-feu* is far more than that. It describes a whole range of one-pot meals which are fundamental both to provincial cooking and *grande cuisine*. There are *potées* of fresh and cured pork, sausage and cabbage; there are *poules-au-pot*, or casseroled whole chickens, and similar dishes made with rabbit and other game; then there are the regional variations like hochepot and the other dishes for which a *pot-au-feu* is the starting point: *Hachis Parmentier* (see page 126) and soups, for example. The rich bouillon can be used as a base for sauces.

A PERFECT *POTÉE*

The cooking instructions for *potée* need to be rigorously followed. **The meat:** heavily salted meats should be blanched in advance. Put the meat into cold water which is brought to simmering point, and simmer for 2 to 3 minutes. After this it should be drained and rinsed under the hot tap, then put into fresh water for the rest of the cooking.

The froth that forms during cooking should be skimmed off frequently. To make the meat tender, it is important that the liquid should never be more than barely simmering. The lid of the pot should be slightly open to allow some of the steam to escape, in order to keep the temperature constant.

The stock: if you want to keep the stock to serve as a soup, to cook other meats in or to use as a sauce base (you can, for example, cook a stronger flavored meat than pork, lamb or beef in it), do not put cabbage, turnips or potatoes to cook in the same pot, as these will turn the stock sour. These vegetables should be cooked separately in a little of the skimmed stock. Keep the stock in a covered container in the refrigerator. Once it has been strained, brought back to a boil and skimmed, it can be made into a delicious aspic flavored with herbs or citrus fruit zest. To obtain a more subtly flavored stock, it is advisable to blanch the cabbage first for a few seconds, which also makes it more digestible.

See page 136 for accompaniments.

NORMANDY *POTÉE*
Potée Normande

¾ lb piece uncooked country-style ham
1 fresh pig's foot, tail and ham hock
salt and freshly ground black pepper
1 *bouquet garni**
small sprig of sage
1-2 stalks of celery
piece of fennel (if available)
1 onion stuck with 2 cloves
2 cloves of garlic
piece of lemon zest*
1 *couenne** (fresh pork skin with fat), tied in a roll
5 oz smoked slab bacon* or pork butt
5 oz unsmoked slab bacon
vegetables: 1 parsnip or celeriac, 4 small turnips, 4 small carrots, 1 medium head green cabbage, 6 leeks

SERVES 6
PREPARATION TIME: 45 MINUTES + 8 HOURS SOAKING
COOKING TIME: 2 HOURS 20 MINUTES

Soak the ham in cold water for 8 hours, then drain. Split the pig's foot in half. Season all the fresh meats.

Tie up the *bouquet garni*, including the sage, celery and, if possible, fennel, which will discreetly flavor the meats. In the bottom of the cooking pot place the *bouquet garni*, the onion, garlic, lemon zest, pig's tail and foot, the *couenne* and the green part of the leeks tied together. Arrange the ham and the bacon on top, cover with plenty of water, place over a high heat, and half cover the pot. When it begins to boil, turn down the heat to minimum and skim.

After about 30 minutes, the liquid should be almost clear. Heat the oven to 425°F and as soon as it is hot, transfer the pot, three quarters covered, to the oven. Turn down to 375°F; cook for 50 minutes.

Peel and trim the vegetables. Quarter the cabbage and blanch for 5 minutes in boiling water. Add the root vegetables, and 15 minutes later the leeks. Gently simmer for another 20 minutes. Remove the onion, *bouquet garni*, leek leaves, *couenne*, tail and foot from the pot. Arrange the other meats in the center of a heated serving dish surrounded by the drained vegetables.

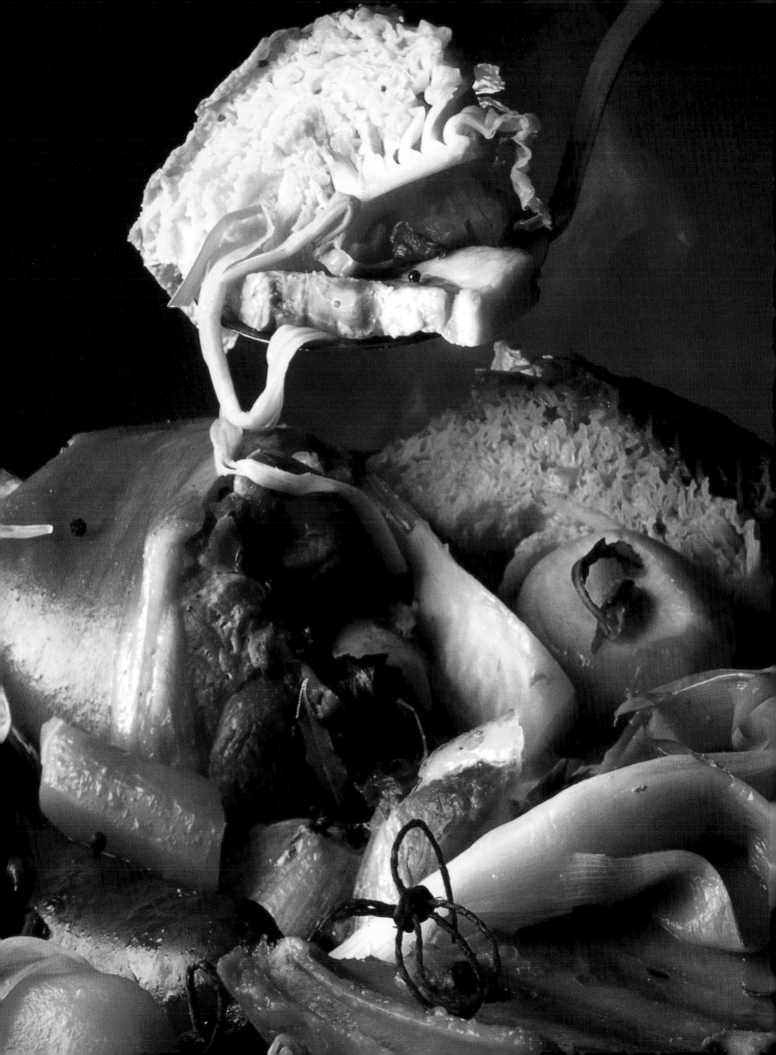

FARMHOUSE STEW WITH MIXED VEGETABLES
Pot-au-feu campagnard

3¼ lb beef chuck pot-roast (cross-rib)
4½ lb beef shank cross-cuts
1 veal shank
1 smoked ham hock
⅔ cup sea salt
1 onion stuck with 2 cloves
1 *bouquet garni*★
1 stalk of celery
4 carrots
4 turnips
1 firm celeriac
8-10 leeks
8 potatoes
1 marrow bone
several kinds of mustard, to serve

SERVES 8-10
PREPARATION TIME: 25 MINUTES + 1
DAY TO MARINATE
COOKING TIME: ABOUT 4 HOURS

Another marvelous recipe from Adrienne de Biasin (see page 141).

Rub all the meats with the salt and put them in a large, nonmetallic container. Refrigerate for 24 hours.

The next day, half fill a very big stew pot with cold water. Put in the onion and the *bouquet garni*. Do not add salt. Shake the meat and wipe it to remove as much salt as possible. Put the beef chuck into the stew pot first, then the beef shank. Gently bring to a boil and skim carefully. As soon as there is no more froth, add the vegetable trimmings, except the potato peel, tied up in a cheesecloth bag. The chuck will cook faster than the shank; remove it when done and keep it hot with a little of the stock. Rub the ends of the marrow bone with salt, add to the pot, cook for 30 minutes and remove.

After 2½ hours, add the veal shank and the ham hock. In a separate pan of boiling water, cook the celery, carrots, turnips and quartered celeriac; 15 minutes later, put in the leeks, tied together, and the potatoes. Salt lightly. Cook till tender.

When the veal and ham are tender, put the marrow bone back in the pot and turn off the heat. Serve the meat surrounded by the vegetables on a very large, heated platter. Serve with two or three different types of mustard, sea salt and the pepper mill. The delicious stock can be kept in the refrigerator and used for cooking pasta or vegetables.

MARINATED MEAT AND POTATO CASSEROLE
Baeckenoffe

1 lb 2 oz pork shoulder butt
1 lb 2 oz shoulder of mutton or lamb
1 lb 2 oz beef chuck
1 lb veal shank
1 pig's tail
1 calf's foot
2¾ lb potatoes
14 oz onions
salt and coarsely ground black pepper

For the marinade:
1 carrot
1 onion
1 clove of garlic
2 tablespoons lard
1 *bouquet garni*★
3 juniper berries
4 black peppercorns
1 bottle (750 ml) of Alsace Riesling
(tends to be dryer and more aromatic
than German Riesling)

SERVES 8-10
PREPARATION TIME: 35 MINUTES + 1
DAY TO MARINATE
COOKING TIME: 3 HOURS

This sumptuous dish from Alsace, known also as potée boulangère, *was traditionally prepared the evening before washing days or very long days of work in the fields and taken at dawn the following day to the baker's oven (in German the* Backofen) *to cook there slowly until lunchtime.*

Here is one made from several different meats, potatoes and onions cooked in Alsace white wine. The version of the Haeberlin brothers, who have revived the dish at the Auberge de l'Ill, their three star restaurant in Illhaeusern, includes leek whites, a single layer of the three meats, no veal and a pig's foot.

Ask the butcher to bone the meats and cut them into 1¾ inch cubes. Also, have the tail cut into 3 pieces and the calf's foot into small pieces.

For the marinade, slice the carrot and chop the onion and garlic. Grease a large ovenproof dish or casserole with the lard and put in the vegetables, *bouquet garni*, juniper berries, crushed peppercorns and the meats. Pour on enough wine to moisten well (reserve some), cover and leave overnight in a cool place.

The next day, cut the potatoes into fairly thin rounds. Finely slice the onions. Remove the meats from the marinade, but leave the marinade ingredients in the dish. (Purists tie them in cheesecloth.) Preheat the oven to 325°F.

Make a layer of onions in the dish, then a layer of potatoes, a layer of meats, a little seasoning, a layer of onions, then potatoes and so on until all the ingredients are used up, finishing with potatoes.

Pour on the rest of the wine, put on the lid and seal it with flour and water paste. Cook for 3 hours.

Serve in the dish with a green salad and strong-flavored dressing or sauerkraut. Accompany with Alsace Riesling.

TOULOUSE *CASSOULET*
Le cassoulet de Mamai

2¾ lb (about 7 cups) dried white (navy) beans, soaked overnight in cold water
1 pig's foot
¼ *couenne*★ (tied into a roll)
2 carrots, sliced into rounds
¼ lb unsmoked slab bacon★
2 cloves of garlic
1 *bouquet garni*★
sea salt
2 large onions
14 oz boned shoulder of mutton (if possible) or lamb
4 fair-sized pieces of *confit d'oie*★ (preserved goose)
1 small garlic sausage (type for boiling), or 2 Polish boiling rings
3 tomatoes
1¼ cups dry white Minervois wine or other dry white wine
2 sprigs of flat-leafed parsley
freshly ground black pepper
2 tablespoons fresh white bread crumbs

SERVES 6
PREPARATION TIME: I HOUR +
OVERNIGHT
COOKING TIME: ABOUT 3½ HOURS

What is an authentic cassoulet? *There are three: the oldest from Castelnaudary, originally made with pork but now with some* confit d'oie *added: a later version from Carcassonne, enriched with leg of mutton and, in the hunting season, partridge; and the more recent one from Toulouse, which combines the ingredients of the first two. There are also cassoulets from Montauban and Cominges. What makes a* cassoulet *authentic is the round white haricot bean called* coco – *though in Castelnaudary they prefer the elongated* lingot *bean – but you can make a first-class* cassoulet *with dried Great Northern or navy beans as long as the beans are not old and hard. This recipe, for Toulouse* cassoulet *as made by an old family cook, has the advantage of relative simplicity – although a properly made* cassoulet *is a dish which always requires enthusiasm and dedication.*

Blanch the pig's foot in boiling water. Rinse the beans in fresh cold water. Cut the pig's foot in half, bone it (leave the bones at the tip for now) and tie the bones up in a piece of cheesecloth.

Put the carrots into a large saucepan with the pig's foot and its bones, the *couenne*, the bacon, the whole garlic cloves and the *bouquet garni*. Add a little sea salt, cover with water 2 inches above the ingredients, and simmer gently for about 1¼ hours.

Meanwhile, finely chop the onions. Cut the mutton or lamb into large cubes. Remove all the fat from the *confit d'oie* and melt it in a heavy-based saucepan. Reserve 1 teaspoon of this. In the rest, soften the onions over a low heat, then add the mutton.

When the mutton cubes are browned on all sides, add the *confit d'oie*. Prick the sausage(s) with a fork and add them. Keeping the heat low, cook for 15 minutes, turning the pieces occasionally.

During this time, blanch the tomatoes in boiling water, peel them, remove the seeds and rub through a sieve. Spread the purée over the mutton and onions, and stir.

Remove the bacon from the pan of beans. Dry it, cut it into small pieces and add to the other pan. Also take out the pig's foot. Remove the remaining bones and cut the meat into small cubes.

By now the beans will be half-cooked. Discard the bag of bones and add the contents of the pan, including the cooking liquid, to the other pan. Add the white wine and simmer gently, uncovered, for 15 to 20 minutes.

Preheat the oven to 425°F. Use the reserved goose fat to grease the inside of an ovenproof earthenware casserole large enough to hold all the ingredients. Transfer all the meats to a dish.

Slice the *couenne* into thin strips and the sausage(s) into chunks. Put the four pieces of *confit d'oie* in the bottom of the casserole, then the sausage, the mutton, the *couenne* and the carrots.

The beans should still be cooking. Remove them with a slotted spoon and spread half of them over the meats. Sprinkle with chopped parsley and cover with the remaining beans. Grind on plenty of pepper, and taste to see if more salt is needed.

Hold a fine strainer over the casserole and pour on the cooking liquid from the beans until the contents are covered by ½ inch. Sprinkle with bread crumbs and put in the oven, uncovered.

When the surface of the *cassoulet* begins to bubble, baste any exposed parts with liquid. Turn down the oven to 300°F. The top will become brown and crusty; use a spatula to break it up and push it down below the surface. Add a little more cooking liquid.

When the crust has re-formed, push it down again and add more liquid. Repeat this several times until you run out of liquid – some enthusiasts insist on seven times! The total time in the oven should be 1½ to 2 hours for a really good *cassoulet*. Turn off the oven and leave the *cassoulet* in it for 15 minutes. A final crust, crunchy but pale, will form. Serve at once, in the casserole.

STUFFED CABBAGE

A stuffed cabbage is such a perfect whole – in shape as well as taste – that it is hard to remember it originated as a way of making a little meat go a long way. Stuffings can include good ground pork or sausage meat mixed with rice, bread crumbs, greens like spinach or sorrel or other more local ingredients – chestnuts, for example, in the Limousin.

French connoisseurs of *les choux farcis* insist that blanching the cabbage at least once, and preferably twice, makes all the difference to the way it lies in your stomach. If you do decide to blanch it, then it needs to be drained upside down, in a colander, for at least five minutes afterward. Aluminum foil will be as good to wrap the cabbage and hold it together as the more traditional cheesecloth bag. Any leftover cabbage is good eaten cut into slices, either cold or lightly fried in butter.

STUFFED RED CABBAGE
Chou rouge farci

1 largish, compact head red cabbage
1 tablespoon lemon juice or vinegar
10 oz best chuck eye
½ lb boned shank of veal
½ lb boned shoulder pork butt
¼ lb unsmoked slab bacon★
salt and freshly ground black pepper
pinch of grated nutmeg
small bunch of flat-leafed parsley
1 large onion
2 large eggs
20 chestnuts (or a small can chestnut purée)
1 large, thin slice of unsmoked bacon★, or several smaller slices
1 carrot
1 *bouquet garni*★
1 bottle (750 ml) of red Bordeaux wine
a little light stock, made fresh (see page 39) or from ½ bouillon cube
1 lb 2 oz fresh or canned chestnuts, to serve

SERVES 4
PREPARATION TIME: 30 MINUTES
COOKING TIME: 3½-4 HOURS

Soak the cabbage in cold water for 10 minutes then, with a pointed knife, cut out the center from the stem end, without cutting through the top of the cabbage. Reserve a little of the removed part, blanch it briefly in boiling water with the lemon juice or vinegar to stop it from discoloring, chop it and use it as part of the stuffing. Save the rest of the inside for another dish. Preheat the oven to 325°F.

Grind all the meats and combine them in a bowl with salt and pepper to taste, nutmeg, chopped parsley, chopped onion, eggs, blanched chopped cabbage and cooked, chopped chestnuts (or purée). Mix all the ingredients together and fill the cabbage, packing the mixture in well. Cut the strip of bacon (*barde*) in half lengthwise and make a cross. Place the cabbage on it, bring the ends up to the top of the cabbage and tie them together. Put the cabbage in a casserole with the carrot, *bouquet garni* and more salt, preferably sea salt, and pepper. Pour on the red wine, then fill up to the brim with water or light stock. (If making this with a cube, only use half – the flavor of the meats must not be drowned.) Cover the pot and cook in the oven for 3½ to 4 hours.

Half an hour before the end, remove a little of the juice and use it to simmer the peeled chestnuts (fresh or canned) to serve with the cabbage.

When the meat is cooked, if the sauce is not thick enough, take the meat out and reduce the sauce over a high heat. It should have a syrupy consistency.

Serve the cabbage on a hot dish surrounded by the chestnuts, and pour on the sauce. With it, drink the same Bordeaux wine as used in cooking.

In Auvergne, a piece of pork skin and fat (*couenne*★) is used to line the bottom of the pot, and a pig's tail or sliced feet are added for extra richness.

Farée charentaise: take one large head white cabbage, blanched if you wish. Reserve eight or ten good outer leaves. Cut away the rib of the stalk. Make a stuffing with a chopped bunch of sorrel or spinach, 14 oz ground pork, a minced clove of garlic, parsley, chives and seasoning. Mix with the finely chopped heart of the cabbage and wrap in the outer leaves. Simmer gently, covered with 2 cloves and 2 glasses of stock, for 2 hours.

STUFFED CABBAGE ▶

VEGETABLES

BROCCOLI AND CAULIFLOWER
TERRINE (see page 162)

SALADE NIÇOISE (see page 172)

GLOBE ARTICHOKES

Artichokes were brought to France by Catherine de Medici. The large ones are eaten boiled, braised, fried, stuffed, in soufflés and salads; smaller ones are excellent raw with dressings and sauces. Choose firm, green artichokes without brown tips; the stalks should snap cleanly. They can be kept for several days like flowers: put the stalks in a little water and change it every day.

PREPARING AND COOKING ARTICHOKES

Prepare the artichokes by breaking rather than cutting the stalks, thus detaching any tough filaments at the same time, and trimming the leaves with a stainless steel knife. As you prepare each artichoke, put it into water acidulated with a dash of vinegar, or rub it with lemon, to prevent discoloration. In water and vinegar, they will be tinged pink, and rubbed with lemon, white.

Large artichokes should have their leaves trimmed by 1½ inch and be cooked for about 35 minutes in boiling salted water with a lemon wedge or a spoonful of vinegar. A folded cloth placed over the artichokes prevents them from rising to the surface and sticking out of the water. Once one of the outer leaves comes away easily, the artichoke is cooked. When overcooked, they turn a blackish color. Turn upside down to drain.

Once cooked, artichokes should be eaten within 24 hours, even if kept in the refrigerator. After that, they spoil.

To remove artichoke flesh:
Pull off the leaves and use a small spoon to scrape off the flesh, which can be used to enrich purées and stuffings. You can also prepare the hearts and pour oil over everything to stop the air getting in.

STUFFED ARTICHOKE FROM ANGERS
Artichauts farcis à l'angevine

4 large globe artichokes
¼ lb mushrooms
1 shallot
5 tablespoons butter
juice of 1 lemon
5 oz veal (shoulder or shank), boned
¼ lb pork (shoulder butt or sirloin), boned
2 sprigs of flat-leafed parsley
1 sprig of tarragon or chervil
salt and freshly ground black pepper
pinch of grated nutmeg
1 large egg or ¾ cup fresh bread crumbs (optional)
scant 1 cup *crème fraîche*★
4 thick slices of bacon★ (optional)
½ bottle (1⅓ cups) of white Anjou wine
a little chicken stock (see page 39)
1 *bouquet garni*★

SERVES 4
PREPARATION TIME: 45 MINUTES
COOKING TIME: 15 + 45 MINUTES

This is an old family recipe from the Augereau family of the Restaurant Jeanne de Laval, in Les Rosiers near Angers. It can be served as a main course with a green salad in a walnut and peanut oil dressing.

Trim and blanch the artichokes (see above) for 15 minutes. Cut a cross in the base of the artichoke stem, as you would for a cauliflower. Drain, and when they have cooled a little remove the chokes and dry the insides with paper towels.

Coarsely chop the mushrooms and the shallot and sweat them in a little butter and the lemon juice until just wilted. Drain, and reserve the juice. Grind the meats and combine with the chopped herbs, salt and pepper to taste, nutmeg and the mushroom mixture. Grandmother Augereau always added an egg or bread crumbs to bind. Beat in a third of the *crème fraîche*, and stuff the artichokes with the mixture.

The old recipe recommends wrapping each artichoke in a strip of fat bacon (*barde*) to hold the stuffing in and add its fat, but unless you trim the leaves very short that is not necessary.

Place the artichokes in a pot, and pour on the white wine and the reserved mushroom juice. Add a little chicken stock – but there is no need to cover the artichokes. Add a small *bouquet garni* – without too much bay leaf – and cook over a gentle heat for 40 minutes.

Just before serving, thicken the juice, which should have reduced considerably, with the rest of the *crème fraîche*. Bring to a boil, whisk, then pour over the artichokes.

ASPARAGUS

Asparagus spears can be eaten all year round. Home-grown asparagus is in season from late February through June, with the peak in April and May. The delicate flavor of asparagus is at its best when freshly picked. Choose smooth asparagus that breaks cleanly; if you can, try breaking a spear at the base to check.

ASPARAGUS WITH SAUCES
Asperges aux sauces

For a generous serving for 4 people, allow 5½ lb asparagus. You may want to peel it, depending on its age and variety: start at the bottom and finish 1 to 1½ inches from the tips, which should be left unpeeled. Put each spear into cold water as you peel it, then tie them up in bunches of about 10, depending on their thickness.

Cook the bunches standing up in well-salted water: 2 teaspoons salt to 1 quart of water. The water should come about two-thirds of the way up but not cover the tips, which would then be overcooked. They should take no longer than 8 to 15 minutes to cook, depending on thickness. Asparagus should remain a tiny bit crunchy and always be drained well. To eliminate any bitter taste at the end of the season, rinse the asparagus in boiling salted water after cooking.

Alternatively, the Swiss boil the spears just covered with water, with salt and sugar, for 5 minutes in a covered pan, remove them from the heat and leave them to poach for about 11 minutes.

Hot asparagus is usually served with a hollandaise or mousseline sauce (see page 23), melted lemon butter and herbs; cold asparagus with a vinaigrette dressing or variously flavored mayonnaises (see pages 14 and 22).

CABBAGES

Cabbages are beautiful vegetables, whether smooth white spheres like new moons, curly Savoys with leaves like crinkly flower petals or dramatic crimson and deep purple globes. In the eighties they have made a long overdue comeback on the tables of three-star restaurants – look at Michel Trama's recipe for warm kidney and cabbage salad, for example. But the traditional recipes, such as *potée* and stuffed red cabbage, remain many of the best ones. See the index for recipes elsewhere in the book.

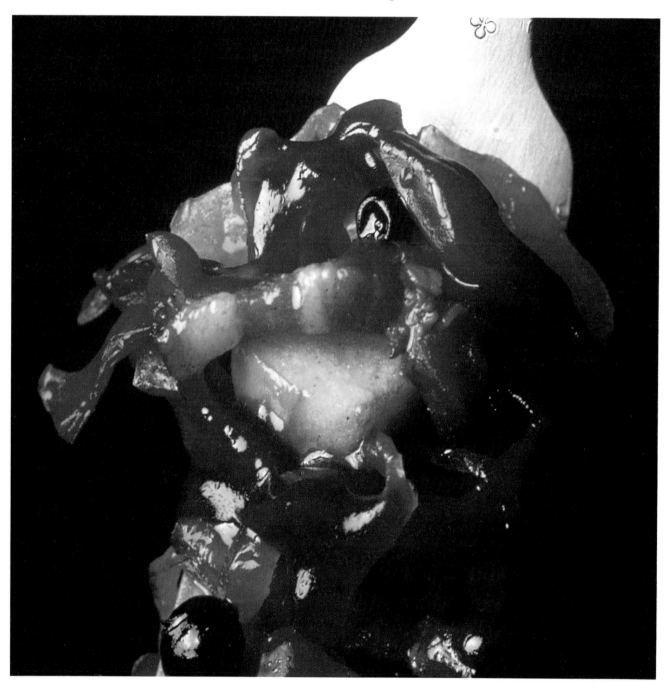

STEAMED OAT DUMPLINGS WRAPPED IN CABBAGE LEAVES
Galettes de céréals en chemise verte

2½ cups oat flakes
½ cup barley flakes
1-1¼ cup milk
1 onion
2 shallots
1 clove of garlic
1 tablespoon oil
4 sprigs of flat-leafed parsley
1 head green cabbage or lettuce
salt and freshly ground black pepper
pinch of grated nutmeg
1 level tablespoon ground hazelnuts
(filberts)

For the sauce:
½ cup *crème fraîche*★
1 egg yolk from a large egg
juice of 1 lime
½ teaspoon mustard seeds

MAKES 12
PREPARATION TIME: 35 MINUTES
COOKING TIME: 15-20 MINUTES

PHOTOGRAPH ON PAGE 148

Adrienne Biasin of Chez la Vieille (see page 141) contributed this recipe to an article on vegetarian cooking. It was originally published in La Table d'Adrienne. *The galettes or dumplings, like pancakes, can simply be fried, six or eight at a time, in oil or a mixture of oil and butter and served as an excellent and unusual accompaniment for fish, eggs or poultry.*

Put the oat and barley flakes in a bowl. Scald the milk and pour it over the cereals, which will puff up within 10 minutes. Chop the onion and shallots, and crush the garlic. Heat the oil and soften the onions, shallots and garlic, letting them color very slightly. Meanwhile, cut up the parsley and blanch the cabbage or lettuce leaves for 1 minute. Drain and place on a cloth to dry.

Mix the herbs with the cereals, which should now be nice and puffy. Season, and add no more than a pinch of nutmeg. Remove the onion mixture from the pan with a slotted spoon, and add to the cereal mixture. Mix, and leave for 10 to 15 minutes for the flavors to meld. Spread out the leaves and sprinkle them with the ground hazelnuts. Place a heaped tablespoonful of the cereal mixture in the center of each leaf, then secure the leaf around it. Wrap up well in a second leaf. Make 12 balls altogether, and place them in a steaming basket. Steam for 15 to 20 minutes.

Serve with a sauce made from the ingredients listed here, or with *tapenade*, tomato purée or vinaigrette (pages 164, 26 and 14).

ALSACE SWEET AND SOUR RED CABBAGE
Chou rouge à l'Alsacienne

1 compact head red cabbage
1 tablespoon lemon juice or vinegar
4 onions
2 tart-sweet apples
2 large carrots
5 oz lean fresh pork belly (side pork)
or boned country-style spare ribs
1 tablespoon goose fat★
2 tablespoons red wine vinegar★
1 bottle (750 ml) of light red wine
salt and freshly ground black pepper
1 tablespoon juniper berries
1 tablespoon brown sugar
2 tablespoons red currant jelly

SERVES 4
PREPARATION TIME: 20 MINUTES
COOKING TIME: ABOUT 1½ HOURS

◀ SWEET AND SOUR RED CABBAGE

This method of braising red cabbage is common in the north of France where brown sugar and red wine are often used in cooking, and makes a good accompaniment for game. Below is a recipe for braised green cabbage from the Loire.

Cut the cabbage into fine strips and cook it in boiling water for 15 minutes, with a little lemon juice or vinegar in the water to preserve its color. Drain well, and cover so that it does not go cold. Finely slice the onions, apples, carrots and pork. Drop the apple slices into salted water.

Melt the goose fat in a very heavy enamel pot (not aluminum, which would affect the cabbage) and, as soon as it begins to sizzle, put in the pork and the onions. When these begin to brown, add the carrots and the drained apples. Stir well, and put in the cabbage strips. Cook for 20 minutes, then add the vinegar and wine to cover the vegetables. Season to taste, and add the juniper berries and brown sugar. Cover and gently simmer for about 1 hour. Stir from time to time and taste. Turn off the heat as soon as the cabbage is cooked but still a little firm.

Transfer to a very hot dish, using a slotted spoon to leave behind the juices. Turn up the heat under the pot and add the red currant jelly, stirring to help the reduction of the sauce. When the sauce coats the spoon, pour it over the cabbage.

Chouée: cut 2 green cabbage hearts into quarters, dice ½ lb lean bacon and brown it with 2 sliced carrots and 3 sliced onions. Add the drained cabbage. Just cover with stock, then add a clove of garlic, a *bouquet garni* and a ham bone with a little meat on it. Season. Cover and braise for 2½ hours. Just before serving pour over ½ cup wine vinegar.

155

POTATOES

Although the French did not begin to cultivate the potato seriously until the end of the eighteenth century, when Parmentier wrote his famous book on the possibilities of the scorned root as a solution to famine and King Louis XVI backed his campaign, there is now a huge range of French dishes of all kinds, both humble and smart, built around the virtues of the potato. It is not hard to see why. As André Simon wrote, "The flavor of the potato is not aggressive and yet it holds its own against all comers, be it steam or boiling water, sizzling butter, olive oil or any kind of fat." Here are some recipes which show off this often overlooked talent.

THREE POTATO PURÉES
Trois purées de pommes de terre

There are three different schools of thought on potato purée (mashed potatoes). Each has its supporters.

The first is to cook the potatoes in milk instead of water. Once cooked, discard the milk (or give it to the cat). Then purée the potatoes and beat in the butter and cream. This is the best purée in the world, according to Paul Bocuse.

The second method was recommended by Modeste Magny, creator of the *petite marmite* and *tournedos Rossini*, who ran a restaurant where leading literary figures used to dine in the 1860s.

POTATO WITH HERB PURÉE

Bake the potatoes in their skins and peel them hot. Weigh them. In a bowl standing in a pan of hot water, mix the potatoes thoroughly with their own weight in good unsalted butter, and salt and pepper, and serve at once. This is a useful method to adapt to stuffing potatoes.

The third method, in which olive oil is beaten into the hot mashed potatoes, has won supporters recently thanks to Frédy Girardet, the superb Swiss chef. Allow scant 1 cup of very good olive oil to every pound of potatoes.

POTATO PURÉE WITH CHEESE AND CREAM
Aligot

2¼ lb potatoes
1 cup milk
⅓ cup *crème fraîche**
10 tablespoons butter
5 oz unsmoked bacon*
1 teaspoon finely chopped garlic
salt and freshly ground black pepper
1 lb 2 oz white Tomme or Cantal* cheese (or Port-Salut or Camembert), cut into slivers

SERVES 4-6
PREPARATION TIME: 20 MINUTES
COOKING TIME: 30 MINUTES

Aligot, a rich cheese and potato purée from the Auvergne, needs to be eaten immediately or carefully kept warm over a bowl of hot water so that it does not lose its texture. The recipe comes from the Ambassade d'Auvergne, an excellent restaurant in Paris which serves straightforward Auvergnat dishes (see also page 140). This is always on the menu.

Boil the potatoes and make a purée with the milk, *crème fraîche* and butter. Gently heat the diced bacon, and add the rendered fat to the potato purée but not the pieces of lean meat. Mix in the garlic and

salt and pepper to taste.

When the purée is still hot, but not too hot, fold in the slivers of cheese with a spatula, as if folding beaten egg whites into a soufflé. Put the mixture over a gentle heat, without stirring: the cheese will begin to melt. Lift and turn it with the spatula until all the cheese has been incorporated. Do not let it boil. Just before serving, lift and turn the mixture again to pull the melted cheese into strings.

POTATO PURÉE WITH CHEESE AND CREAM ▶

GRATED POTATO CAKE
Crêpe de pommes de terre

1¾ lb large potatoes
1 tablespoon peanut oil
5 tablespoons butter
salt and freshly ground black pepper
pinch of grated nutmeg

SERVES 4
PREPARATION TIME: 15 MINUTES
COOKING TIME: 35 MINUTES

Grate the potatoes. Rinse them and dry thoroughly. Heat the oil and half the butter in a fairly heavy skillet. Pour the grated potatoes into the hot fat, pressing down with your hand or a spatula to make them stick together. Turn down the heat, season and cook, half-covered, for 20 minutes.

Then cover with either the lid or a plate, and, with a sharp movement, turn out the potato cake. Put it back in the pan, browned side up, and spread the rest of the butter in slivers over it. Season again. Sprinkle with the nutmeg and serve with a crisp green salad.

LAYERED POTATO TERRINE WITH HERBS
Gâteau gratin

2¼ lb potatoes
2 egg yolks from large eggs
salt and freshly ground black pepper
a little cayenne pepper
bunch of chopped herbs (flat-leafed parsley, thyme, rosemary, etc.)
2 cups *crème fleurette*★
scant ½ cup grated Gruyère cheese
1 clove of garlic
3 tablespoons slightly salted butter

SERVES 4
PREPARATION TIME: 30 MINUTES
COOKING TIME: 1½ HOURS

Finely slice the potatoes. Beat the egg yolks and seasoning together in a bowl, and add the chopped herbs. Beat in the cream and a third of the grated cheese. Rub a cake pan or a deep ovenproof dish with the clove of garlic; discard the garlic. Generously butter the bottom and sides, not forgetting the corners, using 1 tablespoon butter.

Dip each potato slice in the cream mixture and place it in the dish, overlapping with the one before. Make several layers in this way, sprinkling a little cheese over each one. When the potatoes come halfway up the sides of the dish, press down with the back of a spoon. When the dish is full to within ½ inch of the edge (the gratin will become more compact during cooking) pour on the rest of the cream mixture and sprinkle with the remaining grated cheese and slivers of butter. Place in a pan of hot water with water reaching halfway up the sides. Cover the surface with baking parchment to prevent it from browning too quickly, then bake

for 1½ hours, as the cake is fairly thick.

Check to see if it is cooked by plunging a pointed knife into the heart of the cake. If it comes out covered in smooth, creamy potato, the cake is cooked. Turn off the oven and leave the cake in it for 15 minutes before unmolding it. You can put the cake back in the oven for a few minutes to brown and crisp the surface.

If you do not have time to dip each slice into the cream mixture, just pour some of the mixture over each layer.

Going back to roots: the potato arrived in Europe from America at the same time as the more attractive sweet potato (whose native name, *patata*, it borrowed) and the Jerusalem artichoke (launched in France with a fine flair for publicity under the name *topinambour*, after a group of Brazilian Tupi Tambo Indians who had just been brought to France). Both of these roots would also make a good terrine.

LAYERED POTATO TERRINE ▶

GRATIN DAUPHINOIS
Le vrai gratin Dauphinois

2¼ lb regular, unblemished, medium-
sized, waxy potatoes
1 small turnip
1 clove of garlic
3 tablespoons slightly salted butter
salt and freshly ground black pepper
pinch of grated nutmeg
2 cups cream

SERVES 4
PREPARATION TIME: 30 MINUTES
COOKING TIME: 1¼-1½ HOURS

A gratin Dauphinois may seem to be a simple dish, but it is not always easy to get right. The potatoes need to be waxy and firm; the cream fresh and of good quality. Once made, the gratin will sit happily in a warm oven for an hour without spoiling. But it will not take kindly to reheating.

Cut the potatoes into thin slices of even thickness. Wash and dry these. Choose a fairly large gratin dish, preferably big enough to take the slices in two layers. Quarter the turnip and rub the dish with it, and then with the garlic; discard the turnip and garlic. Butter the dish, using about 1 tablespoon butter. Preheat the oven to 350°F.

Arrange the potato slices in the dish with each one overlapping the last by a third. Season and grate a little nutmeg over them. Make a second layer in the same way. If necessary, make a third. Pour on the cream until it reaches the level of the potatoes, waiting for a few seconds while the cream seeps between the layers. Divide the remaining butter into slivers and sprinkle these over the surface. Bake for 1 hour if there are two layers, or 1¼ hours for three.

Fifteen minutes before the end, turn up the temperature to 425°F to brown the surface quickly without drying out the gratin. Check that the potatoes are cooked by sticking in the tip of a knife. When they are soft, turn off the oven and leave inside for 10 minutes with the door closed.

FLAKY PASTRY POTATO AND BACON PIE
Tourte "Maï Mimi"

4½ lb potatoes
½ lb smoked Canadian bacon★
3 shallots
1 clove of garlic
3 tablespoons chopped flat-leafed
parsley and chives
a few sprigs of thyme
1½ recipe quantities French pie pastry
without sugar (page 202) or about ⅔
recipe quantity puff pastry (page 203)
salt and freshly ground black pepper
1 egg yolk from a large egg
1 cup *crème fraîche*★

SERVES 6
PREPARATION TIME: 30 MINUTES
COOKING TIME: 1-1¼ HOURS

A surprising thing about this recipe is that the potatoes are put in the pie raw. French pies usually have a pottery "chimney" under the crust to let the steam out; this one is unusual in that the filling is completely sealed in.

Thinly slice the potatoes. Chop the bacon, shallots, garlic and herbs, and mix together.

Preheat the oven to 425°F. Use a 9 inch diameter cake pan with a removable base if possible, or a large deep pie dish or casserole. Roll out half of the pastry and use to line the dish, leaving plenty to spare at the rim. Put in a layer of potato slices, and sprinkle with the chopped mixture. Add salt, but not much because of the bacon, and pepper, and make another layer of potatoes, followed by the chopped mixture. You can make these layers quite thick.

Roll out the rest of the pastry and cover the pie. Turn over the edges and press them together well to seal. Using a plate as a guide, score a ring on the top with a knife, not cutting right through the pastry. Glaze with the beaten egg yolk, cover with a sheet of foil to keep the top from burning, and bake for at least 1 hour, preferably 1¼ hours.

Remove the pie from the oven. Carefully cut out the circle in the top, following the line drawn earlier. Remove it without cracking the pastry – this is difficult with really good pie pastry – and pour the *crème fraîche* over the steaming contents of the pie. Replace the lid, and leave the pie in the oven with the door open for 10 minutes before serving.

FLAKY PASTRY POTATO AND
BACON PIE ▶

160

NEW AND OLD

BROCCOLI AND CAULIFLOWER TERRINE
Terrine de chou brocoli et choufleur

1¾ lb broccoli, fresh or frozen, trimmed
7 oz cauliflower, trimmed
10 oz ham cooked on the bone, coarsely chopped
4 large eggs
5 oz brioche★, crusts removed, soaked in ½ cup chicken stock and squeezed dry
2 cups *crème fraîche*★
2 tablespoons sunflower oil
½ tablespoon mixed salt, freshly ground black and white pepper and a little ground nutmeg
leaves only from a large bunch of flat-leafed parsley and a large bunch of chervil
1 tablespoon crushed pink peppercorns

SERVES 8-12
PREPARATION TIME: I HOUR
COOKING TIME: ABOUT I HOUR

PHOTOGRAPH PAGE 150

Separate the broccoli and cauliflower florets from the stalks and cook separately in boiling salted water, 3 minutes for the florets and 10 minutes for the stalks. Drain.

Purée the ham with 2 eggs, half the brioche, a third of the *crème fraîche*, a third of the oil, and a third of the seasoning mixture.

Purée the cauliflower stalks with a third of the broccoli stalks and the less attractive florets from both, a third of the *crème fraîche*, a third of the oil, a quarter of the brioche, a quarter of the seasoning mixture and 1 egg. Add 2 tablespoons of the first mixture.

Finally, purée the herbs, remaining broccoli stalks, brioche, oil, *crème fraîche*, egg and seasoning mixture, and add 1 tablespoon of the first mixture.

Line a deep rectangular terrine or mold of 2-quart capacity with buttered wax paper, which should reach well above the rim. Preheat the oven to 325°F.

Now make the landscape. Make a layer of dark green, higher on the left side. That is the grass. Then stand up the cauliflower and broccoli florets to make "trees" and between the trees pack a layer of pink ham mixture, the earth. Bring the ham layer above the trees, then make a hill in the distance to the right with a long roll of the herb mixture. To the left, make a layer of little florets representing trees in the distance. Sprinkle unevenly with pink pepper and nutmeg. Make the "sky" with the broccoli and cauliflower cream and a "cloud" made from a cauliflower floret.

Pack the mixture down well. Bake in a pan of warm water for 50 minutes. If a knife plunged into the center of the terrine comes out clean, turn off the oven. Leave to cool in the oven with the door closed. Then chill. Serve with a cold or hot sauce of your choice.

STUFFED TOMATOES *BONNE FEMME*
Farce à la bonne femme

8 ripe but still firm tomatoes of medium and equal size
1 onion, peeled and chopped
2 cloves of garlic, peeled and chopped
2 tablespoons butter + a little extra
7 oz cooked beef or veal
2 tablespoons fresh bread crumbs
salt and freshly ground black pepper
pinch of *quatre-épices*★
3 sprigs of flat-leafed parsley
1 tablespoon peanut oil

SERVES 4
PREPARATION TIME: 40 MINUTES, ABOUT IO OF THESE WAITING
COOKING TIME: ABOUT 50 MINUTES

Cut off the top of each tomato to form a lid, discarding any calyces, and scoop out the seeds and pulp without damaging the walls. Lightly salt the insides and leave to drain upsidedown.

Soften the onion and garlic gently in 2 tablespoons butter while you finely grind the meat. When the onion and garlic are translucent, stir in the meat and cook over a very low heat for 10 to 12 minutes, stirring from time to time. Preheat the oven to 435°F. Meanwhile, put the tomatoes in an oiled ovenproof dish and cook them in the oven for 5 minutes,

remove them and turn the oven down to 400°F

Put half the bread crumbs in a bowl and mix in salt and pepper to taste and the *quatre-épices*. Chop the parsley. When the meat mixture is ready, add it and the parsley to the bowl and mix well.

Stuff the tomatoes with the mixture, sprinkle over the rest of the bread crumbs and top each with a dot of butter. Bake, without the lids, for 30 to 35 minutes, turning the temperature down to 350°F after 20 minutes and adding the lids to the dish so they will just cook through.

GARNISHES AND ACCOMPANIMENTS

DEEP-FRIED PARSLEY
Persil frit

large bunch of flat-leafed parsley
oil for deep frying
salt and freshly ground black pepper
1 extra large hard-cooked egg
fine-quality vinegar (see page 11)

PREPARATION TIME: 5 MINUTES
COOKING TIME: INSTANTANEOUS

Parsley is not only a first-class garnish, but is also rich in vitamins, minerals and fiber. Use it frequently in soups and sauces, in salads and in omelettes. One delicious snack is bread lightly rubbed with garlic and spread with parsley butter. This recipe comes from Paul Chêne, a chef in Paris.

Wash the parsley, drain and dry well. The drying is very important. Put the parsley in a frying basket and immerse for a few seconds in very hot oil.

Drain on paper towels, lightly salt and pepper and sprinkle with hard-cooked egg that has been put through a vegetable mill or sieve. Add a few drops of fine-quality vinegar. Toss carefully and serve at once. This is a good garnish for roast meat, fried fish or veal cutlets.

SHALLOT AND LEMON COMPOTE
Compôte d'échalotes au zeste de citron

4½ lb shallots
1 bottle (750 ml) of red wine
1¼ cups red wine vinegar
1¼ cup firmly packed brown sugar
2 tablespoons butter
1 *bouquet garni*★
1 onion stuck with a clove
pared zest of 1 lemon★

MAKES ABOUT 5½ LB
PREPARATION TIME: 15 MINUTES
COOKING TIME: 1¾-2¼ HOURS

The sweet intensity of an onion or shallot compote is wonderful with roast meat, game or fish. Some chefs replace the sugar with honey.
If you can find them, use what the French call échalotes grises. *Their drab exterior conceals an infinitely more delicate aroma than that of the common shallot. Use a fairly deep stainless steel pan so that the shallots can float in plenty of cooking liquid.*

Trim the base of the shallots and remove the first thick layer of skin to disclose the delicate color of the inside. Leave them whole. Put the shallots and all the other ingredients in a saucepan, and top up with water so that they are covered. Place over a very gentle heat, and cook as slowly as possible, placing a heat diffuser between the saucepan and the heat. Allow at least 1½, preferably 2, hours, stirring from time to time with a wooden spoon.

In the end you should have a thick, smooth mixture that coats the shallots like shiny Japanese lacquer. Remove the *bouquet garni* and the lemon zest.

GLAZED CARROTS
Carottes glacées

1 lb young carrots
3½ tablespoons butter
3 tablespoons brown sugar, or 1 tablespoon runny honey
salt and freshly ground white pepper

SERVES 4
PREPARATION TIME: 5 MINUTES
COOKING TIME: 15 MINUTES

These sweet, buttery carrots accompany meat, poultry or fish well.

Scrub the carrots. Leave the smallest ones whole, and cut slightly larger ones into two or three so that they will cook in the same time.

Choose a saucepan wide enough to take the carrots in a single layer. Just cover them with water, and dot with the butter in little pieces. Add the sugar or honey and salt and pepper to taste, and set the pan over a high heat.

As soon as it begins to boil, turn the heat right down, cover the carrots with a circle of baking parchment cut to fit the pan, put on the lid and cook very gently. By the time the carrots are tender the liquid should be reduced to a small amount of thick, shiny glaze. Tilt the pan so that the glaze coats the carrots. These are excellent with meat or fish.
Variations: you can replace some of the butter with cooking juices from roast meat or poultry, or add some *fines herbes*★ or cream, or even some chopped shallot.

MEDITERRANEAN VEGETABLE DISHES

FENNEL IN WINE AND TOMATO SAUCE
Fenouil à la Provençal

4 fennel bulbs
2 tablespoons olive oil
3 cloves of garlic
3 onions
2 tomatoes
1¼ cups Provençal rosé wine
sprig of thyme
sprig of marjoram
salt and freshly ground black pepper
pinch of cayenne

SERVES 4
PREPARATION TIME: 10 MINUTES
COOKING TIME: ABOUT 1 HOUR

Blanch the fennel for 5 minutes in boiling salted water, remove it and dry on paper towels. Heat the oil in a heavy pan and put in the garlic, crushed without peeling, and the chopped onions. As soon as they start to brown, add the fennel, then the tomatoes, peeled and coarsely chopped. Pour in the wine, which should be warm, add the herbs and season to taste.

Cover as soon as it begins to simmer. Cook over a gentle heat for 35 to 40 minutes.

OLIVE *TAPENADE*
Tapenade

1 lb (about 3 cups) ripe olives, pitted
1 clove of garlic
2 canned anchovy fillets
2 tablespoons capers
2-3 leaves of basil, mint or flat-leafed parsley
freshly ground black pepper
scant 1 cup olive oil

MAKES ABOUT 3 CUPS
PREPARATION TIME: 5 MINUTES

Combine the olives, garlic, anchovies, capers, herbs and pepper to taste in a blender, then work in the olive oil. This can be kept in the refrigerator for a month, to be served with crudités, lamb and eggs. *Tapenade* can be a milder sauce. For this whisk in two egg yolks, the juice of half a lemon and herbs.

The food and landscape of Mediterranean France are often described in the same way: earthy, robust, with glowing colors and pungent aromas. Certainly the food of Roussillon, Languedoc and Provence has a Latin sun-drenched sensuality, permeated with the flavors of wine, herbs, garlic, tomatoes and olives.

Along with the famous *primeurs*, the early spring vegetables that are rushed to Paris for sale at Rungis, the great wholesale market, *ratatouille, salade Niçoise* and, more recently, *tapenade* – are well known vegetable exports from the Midi. But there are other characteristic and less well known southern vegetable dishes using the extraordinary range of vegetables available in different seasons. *Tians* are Provençal gratins named after the shallow earthenware dish in which they are made. There are many braised vegetable dishes with wine sauces: cauliflower and celery hearts, for example, can be prepared like fennel in a light sauce of rosé wine. Other dishes, especially those of Nice and Corsica, show a marked Italian influence.

ZUCCHINI *TIAN*
Tian de zucchini

2¼ lb zucchini
2 tablespoons olive oil
1 clove of garlic
1 cup long-grain rice
salt and freshly ground black pepper
4 large eggs
1 cup *crème fraîche**
½ cup freshly grated Parmesan cheese

SERVES 6
PREPARATION TIME: 20 MINUTES
COOKING TIME: 1 HOUR

A tian may be made with all sorts of vegetables: Swiss chard, eggplant or artichoke, for example.

Cut the zucchini into rounds ½ inch thick. Heat the olive oil in a frying pan, and when it is hot put in the zucchini. Finely chop the garlic and add to the pan. Stir with a wooden spoon, and turn down the heat.

Rinse the rice in warm water to remove the excess starch, and add it to the zucchini. Season to taste and cook for 30 minutes over a gentle heat, stirring from time to time. The rice will cook in the liquid from the zucchini. Preheat the oven to 425°F.

When the rice is cooked – taste to check – remove the pan from the heat and add the eggs, the *crème fraîche* and the grated Parmesan cheese. Taste again, and correct the seasoning. Transfer to a gratin dish and bake for 20 minutes. This is good cold as well as warm.

MAURES RATATOUILLE
La véritable ratatouille

1 lb eggplants, thickly sliced
salt
½ lb onions (not mild ones)
1 lb tomatoes, peeled, quartered and deseeded
¾ lb mixed sweet green and red peppers, cored, deseeded and cut into strips
1 lb zucchini, peeled in lengthwise strips and cut into thick slices
6 tablespoons olive oil
3 cloves of garlic, skinned and minced
1 *bouquet garni**
pinch of sugar
freshly ground black pepper
small bunch of flat-leafed parsley
10 basil leaves

SERVES 6
PREPARATION TIME: 45 MINUTES
COOKING TIME: ABOUT 1 HOUR IF
VEGETABLES ARE COOKED
SIMULTANEOUSLY

Purists will accept as a genuine ratatouille only the maurenque *version, from the Maures mountains on the Mediterranean coast. The vegetables are cooked separately, to preserve their true flavors, and mixed only on your plate.*

In summer ratatouille is served cold, preferably after overnight refrigeration. But the Provençals like it hot, topped with a gratin of bread crumbs and grated Parmesan. Instead of the final 30 minutes cooking, they give it 1½ hours in a low oven to brown the top.

Sprinkle the eggplant slices with salt and leave to wilt for 30 minutes. Prepare the other vegetables.

Put 1 tablespoon of oil in a heavy-based flameproof casserole. Add the onions and cook gently, stirring, until they are just beginning to color. Add the quartered tomatoes, the minced garlic, the *bouquet garni* and the sugar. Add another dribble of oil. Cook, uncovered, on a low heat.

At the same time, heat 1 tablespoon of oil in a skillet and put in the strips of sweet pepper, skin side down. Cook over a low heat.

Heat 1 tablespoon of oil in another skillet and, when it is beginning to bubble, put in the zucchini slices. They will exude liquid, so a rather higher heat is needed to cook them. After 5 minutes add another spoonful of oil, sprinkle the slices with salt and turn them. Check that the sweet peppers and the tomato mixture are not drying out.

Drain the eggplant slices and wipe them with paper towels. Heat another spoonful of oil in a skillet or any wide pan, and sauté the eggplant slices until golden. Add another spoonful of oil, and raise the heat slightly to fry the second side.

Take out the zucchini, drain on paper towels and at once put them in a layer on top of the tomato mixture. Salt very lightly. Do the same with the sweet peppers, adding ground pepper as well as salt and sprinkling with chopped parsley. Arrange the drained eggplants on top. Leave on a low heat for 30 minutes, half covered and add the basil 5 minutes before the end.

165

EGGPLANT FANS
Aubergines en éventail

3 large onions
4 tablespoons olive oil
3 large eggplants
3 large, firm tomatoes
salt and black pepper
1 clove of garlic
sprig of thyme
pinch of dried oregano
⅔ cup small ripe olives
½ cup freshly grated Parmesan cheese

SERVES 6 AS AN APPETIZER OR SIDE
DISH
PREPARATION TIME: 15 MINUTES
COOKING TIME: 1 HOUR 10 MINUTES

Chop the onions and soften in 2 tablespoons of olive oil. Slice the eggplants into 4 or 5 lengthwise slices, stopping ¾ inch from either end. Slice the tomatoes into twice as many slices as there are cuts in all the eggplants.

Insert 2 tomato slices into each cut. Preheat the oven to 350°F. Transfer the onions to an ovenproof dish. Arrange the eggplants on top. Sprinkle with the seasonings, herbs and garlic; pour on the rest of the oil. Bake for 45 minutes. Add the olives. Sprinkle with the Parmesan. Return to the oven for 15 minutes.

CORSICAN PRESERVED MUSHROOMS
Conserve à la Corse

2¼ lb mushrooms
olive oil, as required to cover the mushrooms
scant 1 cup red wine vinegar
scant 1 cup water
1 large onion stuck with 3 cloves
2 cloves of garlic
sprig of marjoram
pinch of myrtle leaves (optional)
1 bay leaf
5 juniper berries
pinch of sea salt

SERVES 4-6
PREPARATION TIME: 15 MINUTES +
TIME TO COOL + 1 MONTH
COOKING TIME: 45 MINUTES

These mushrooms are delicious in salads or hors d'oeuvres *with an* aïoli *(see page 22) or sweet pepper purée (page 167). Only wipe the mushrooms. Myrtle, much used in Corsican cooking, adds a bitter, aromatic flavor.*

Blanch the mushrooms for 2 minutes in boiling salted water; drain. Put 1 tablespoon of olive oil in a pan, and add all the other ingredients. Three-quarters cover it, and cook over a gentle heat for 30 minutes.

Add the mushrooms. Cook for a further 10 minutes over a gentle heat. The liquid should have evaporated. Let the mushrooms cool. Transfer the mushrooms to a large jar. Pack them in without squashing them, and cover with olive oil. When filling with oil, pour it to ½ inch above the level of the mushrooms. Allow them to absorb the oil without moving the jar. Once the level has settled, replenish with more oil to the brim. In this way the mushrooms are sure to be protected from the air. Seal the jar and keep for 1 month in a cool, dark place before serving.

SPICY MOROCCAN LENTILS
Lentilles piquantes

5 cups green lentils
2 bay leaves
3 cloves of garlic
salt and freshly ground black pepper
3 onions
scant 1 cup olive oil
1 tablespoon coriander seeds
1 or more chili peppers, or up to 1
tablespoon chili paste (to taste)
juice of 1 lemon
bunch of fresh coriander (cilantro) or
flat-leafed parsley

SERVES 10
PREPARATION TIME: 10 MINUTES
COOKING TIME: ABOUT 45 MINUTES

Algerian, Moroccan and Tunisian cooking all have a strong French influence from their time as colonies, and, naturally, many North African dishes – above all cous-cous – are very popular in France. Here are a good pair to accompany the Moroccan meatballs (page 128), Algerian fish (page 86) or a méchoui – spicy roast whole lamb, as shown below.

Put the lentils in a saucepan with cold water to cover. Bring to a boil, then drain. Put the lentils back in the saucepan and cover with hot water. Add the bay leaves, garlic, and salt and pepper to taste and cook for 30 minutes. Drain, reserving a little of the cooking liquid.

Chop the onions and fry them in half the olive oil. Pour in the lentils and reserved cooking liquid, and add the coriander seeds and the deseeded chili peppers or chili paste. Simmer for a few minutes.

Before serving, add the lemon juice and the rest of the olive oil. Taste, and correct the seasoning. Sprinkle with chopped fresh coriander (cilantro). This dish is very good eaten cold.

TOMATO AND SWEET RED PEPPER PURÉE
Compôte de tomates et poivrons

9 lb firm tomatoes
2¼ lb sweet red peppers
1 lb sweet yellow peppers
1 lb sweet green peppers
1 lb onions
scant 1 cup olive oil
4 cloves of garlic

salt and freshly ground black pepper
1 sprig of thyme

SERVES 10
PREPARATION TIME: 40 MINUTES
COOKING TIME: ABOUT 1½ HOURS

Preheat the oven to 450°F. Arrange the sweet peppers on the oven rack, and cook them for 15 to 20 minutes, until the skin browns and comes away from the flesh. (Alternatively, char them under the broiler.) Wrap each pepper in a paper towel moistened with cold water. Leave to cool.

Peel and deseed the tomatoes, cut them into quarters and drain. Slice the onions, and brown them in half the olive oil in a cooking pot. Peel and deseed the peppers, cut them into largish pieces and add to the onions, together with the minced garlic and the tomatoes. Season to taste and mix all the ingredients together thoroughly. Add the thyme, and cook half covered over a gentle heat for 45 minutes.

Taste to check the seasoning, and add the remaining olive oil. Serve hot or cold; this dish is equally good either way.

◄ TOMATO AND SWEET RED PEPPER PURÉE, SPICY MOROCCAN LENTILS AND *MÉCHOUI*

SALADS

PRESERVED MIXED VEGETABLES IN OIL
Petites légumes dans l'huile

eggplants, zucchini, sweet peppers,
mushrooms and pearl onions, as
required
salt and freshly ground black pepper
fresh or dried oregano
olive oil
whole cloves of garlic
lemon juice

MAKES QUANTITIES DESIRED
PREPARATION TIME: ABOUT 1 HOUR
+ 2 HOURS WAIT FOR EGGPLANTS
COOKING TIME: 20-30 MINUTES
IF COOKING VEGETABLES

*Preserved vegetables have almost
disappeared from everyday cooking
because of the range of fresh and frozen
vegetables available. But they do stand
in their own right, to be eaten just as they
are – as an hors d'oeuvre or salad – or
to be given as presents, especially at
Christmas as reminders of the pleasures
of summer that have gone but will come
again.*

Basic preparations
Eggplants: wash and cut them into
rounds ⅝ inch thick. Sprinkle
with salt and leave to drain for 2
hours. Wipe with paper towels.
Put the slices on a rack in the
oven, pour over a little olive oil
and cook at 350°F for 20 minutes.
Leave to cool.
Zucchini: wash and scrub the
zucchini, cut them into quarters
lengthwise, sprinkle with salt,
pepper and oregano and brush
with olive oil. Dry them out in a
350°F oven for about 20 minutes.
Leave to cool.

Sweet peppers: put them into a
425°F oven for 20 minutes. When
the skin begins to blister, take
them out and wrap each pepper in
paper towels. Pour over cold water
and leave to cool. They should
then peel easily. Deseed the
peppers and cut into strips.
Onions: blanch the onions in very
hot water for 5 minutes, rinse in
cold water, peel and leave to cool.
Mushrooms: trim the mushrooms,
peel them if necessary and shake
them in a damp cloth. Blanch for
5 minutes with ½ tablespoon
lemon juice added to the water.
Drain and cool.
For vegetables in oil: Place the
vegetables in jars that have been
sterilized in boiling water, with 1
or 2 cloves of garlic and a little
oregano, salt and pepper in each
jar. Pour over boiling olive oil to
within ¼ inch of the rim. Shake
the jars to eliminate any bubbles,
then seal.

SPICY CARIBBEAN CRUDITÉS
Achards antillais

1 lb each of carrots, artichoke hearts,
sweet peppers, cauliflowers, green
beans
salt and freshly ground black pepper
1 lb small white onions
1 head of garlic, preferably new
1 small fresh chili pepper
small bunch of flat-leafed parsley
scant 1 cup olive oil
small piece of fresh gingerroot
1 teaspoon curry powder
pinch of powdered saffron

SERVES AT LEAST 15
PREPARATION TIME: 35 MINUTES + 2
HOURS WAIT AND 2 HOURS
REFRIGERATION
COOKING TIME: 10 MINUTES

*Achards are a kind of tropical crudités,
served with a hot sauce called* rougail.
*They should be made several hours in
advance.*

Cut the carrots, artichokes and
sweet peppers into small cubes.
Divide the cauliflower into small
florets. Chop the beans. Put each
vegetable into an individual bowl
of salted water. Leave for 2 hours.
Finely slice the onions, and
chop the garlic. Broil the chili
pepper to loosen the skin, peel it
and cut into thin strips. Chop the
parsley.
Heat the oil and put in the

onions and chili. Stir and season to
taste. Finely slice the ginger.
When the onions begin to brown,
add the ginger. Cook for 2 or 3
minutes, then sprinkle with the
curry powder and saffron. Remove
from the heat. Drain and dry the
vegetables thoroughly, and
arrange them separately on a
serving dish. Pour on the hot
dressing, sprinkle with chopped
parsley and refrigerate.
This can be prepared the day
before. If there is any left over,
put it into a container and cover
with oil. *Achards* will keep for
several days in the refrigerator.

MIXED GREEN LEAF SALAD
Le mesclun

A mesclun, *the Provençal word for mixture, varies according to the season and what is available in the shops or by the wayside: a leaf of this with a leaf of* that and a sprig of the other, as well as little known seeds, wild plants and rare condiments (for suggestions see the vinaigrettes on page 14).

The mesclun *above includes rocket, dandelion, savory, parsley, chervil, chicory, lettuce, Belgian endive, watercress, tarragon, chives and mustard seeds.*

WARM MIXED SALAD OF GARDEN VEGETABLES
Jardinière en salade tiède

1 sweet red or yellow pepper
1 tomato
¼ lb piece of pumpkin
4 white onions, with stalks (or add
scallion greens)
2 shallots
1 clove of garlic
1 eggplant
1 zucchini
2 tablespoons olive oil
salt and freshly ground black pepper
1 tablespoon capers
sprig of basil
sprig of flat-leafed parsley
2 tablespoons *crème fraîche*★
1 tablespoon white wine vinegar★

SERVES 4
PREPARATION TIME: 20 MINUTES
COOKING TIME: 35 MINUTES

The warmth of a salade tiède *releases the full aroma and flavor of the dressing and allows the vegetables to absorb it. See also the warm salads on pages 112 and 134.*

Broil the sweet pepper to char the skin, peel and deseed it. Blanch and peel the tomato. Discard the skin and seeds of the pumpkin. Dice these vegetables. Chop the onion and shallots. Mince the garlic. Peel the eggplant and zucchini in strips, leaving on strips of skin, and chop them.

Heat half the oil in a stainless-steel saucepan over a fairly gentle heat. When it is hot, put in the onions. When they begin to soften, put in the garlic and shallots. Stir, and after 5 minutes put in all the vegetables except the tomato and pumpkin.

Soften for 15 minutes, stirring all the while. Then add the tomato and pumpkin, stir and three-quarters cover. Cook for 10 minutes longer. Season to taste, and add the capers, the chopped herbs and the *crème fraîche*. Stir, and cook for another 2 or 3 minutes. Cover, remove from the heat and leave for 5 minutes.

Serve warm, with the vinegar and the rest of the oil poured over it. This salad can also be tossed in *tapenade* (see page 164), and is excellent cold.

SPECIAL LEAF SALAD WITH SESAME
Salade folle au sesame

1 turnip
2 small new carrots
6 pods of broad (fava) beans
2 oz fine green beans
2 oz snow peas
2 small stalks from a celery heart
1 fennel bulb
4 clumps of young dandelion leaves★
1 small zucchini
½ oz tender fresh spinach leaves
4 small white onions with stalks or
scallion greens
2 very young globe artichokes
juice of 1 lemon
2 cups light chicken stock, skimmed
and salted (see page 39)
1 egg yolk from a large egg
salt and white pepper
½ level teaspoon mild Dijon-style
mustard (optional)
pared zest and juice of ½ orange
3 tablespoons sesame oil
1 teaspoon blackberry vinegar★
sprig of flat-leafed parsley
sprig of chervil
1 teaspoon sesame seeds

SERVES 4
PREPARATION TIME: 1 HOUR
COOKING TIME: ABOUT 15 MINUTES

A salade folle *like this should always have character and imagination, so add or omit ingredients to suit yourself. The contrasting raw and cooked ingredients would be delicious served with steamed scallops, roast veal or poached eggs.*

Finely slice the turnip and the carrots. Hull the broad (fava) beans, then peel them (unless they are very young). Remove any strings from the green beans, the snow peas and the celery. Discard the outer layer of the fennel, reserving only the heart; finely slice this. Wash and trim the dandelion leaves without separating the clumps: cut each one into four. Peel the zucchini as thinly as possible. Cut into small cubes. Remove the spinach stalks. Remove the first layer of onion and half the tips of the stalks, then finely slice. Trim the ends of the artichokes and divide them into 8 or 10 sections. Squeeze lemon juice over the artichokes, carrots, turnip and fennel.

Heat the stock in a stainless steel saucepan. Put the snow peas into the boiling stock to cook for 6 minutes, and the green beans for 4 minutes, so that they remain crunchy. Remove immediately with a slotted spoon and set aside. Cook the carrots for 3 minutes, and the turnip for 2 minutes. Remove and reserve. Cook the zucchini for 1 minute, then leave to drain in a sieve.

Now prepare the dressing: mix the egg yolk with salt and pepper to taste, the mustard if you like, and a little of the orange juice. Whisk in the oil a little at a time until the mixture has the consistency of a mayonnaise. Dilute with more orange juice and the vinegar. Arrange the vegetables attractively in a salad bowl, and pour on the dressing. Sprinkle with chopped parsley and chervil, fine strips of orange zest, cut into strips, and sesame seeds.

SPECIAL LEAF SALAD WITH
SESAME ▶

170

SALADE NIÇOISE
Salade Niçoise

6 tomatoes
salt and freshly ground black pepper
1 cucumber
6 artichoke hearts
3 sweet green peppers
⅔ cup ripe olives
2 mild onions
2 cans of anchovy fillets or 11 oz
canned tuna
handful of fresh young broad (fava)
beans (when in season)
6 hard-cooked eggs
olive oil
a few sprigs of basil

SERVES 6
PREPARATION TIME: 20 MINUTES + 15
MINUTES TO MARINATE

PHOTOGRAPH PAGE 151

Here is a recipe for a proper salade Niçoise, *made only with young raw vegetables, anchovies or tuna, hard-cooked eggs and olive oil. Once you have tried it, you will never again add cooked potatoes, green beans – or any other leftovers lying in little dishes in the refrigerator.*

Good tomatoes, white or red onions and fruity olive oil are important.

Cut the tomatoes into quarters and sprinkle with salt. Peel and finely slice the cucumber. Salt the cucumber slices to drain them. Sprinkle the artichoke hearts with salt too.

Peel the green peppers by charring the skin under the broiler and wrapping them in wet paper towels to loosen it, then deseed and slice them. Pit the olives, slice the onions and cut the anchovy fillets into tiny pieces (or flake the tuna). Put all the vegetables and the fish in a large salad bowl. Quarter the hard-cooked eggs and arrange on top.

Make a dressing from olive oil, salt (only a little if using anchovies), pepper and chopped basil leaves. Serve chilled.

Drink a chilled light white or rosé wine with this.

CABBAGE SALADS

Just when other salad vegetables are disappearing, after the first frost, cabbages become sweeter and crispier than ever. So they are perfect winter salads. Eaten with thick slices of rye bread, cheese and a light red wine, they are a meal in themselves.

CABBAGE AND FRESH FRUIT SALAD
Salade de choux aux fruits

½ head green cabbage
2 oz white cabbage
1 pear
1 tart apple
salt
a little orange juice
juice of ½ lemon
1 dried fig

For the dressing:
1 teaspoon cider vinegar
orange and lemon juice (see above)
1 teaspoon *crème fraîche*★
1 tablespoon olive oil
salt and freshly ground pepper
1 tablespoon chopped herbs
(flat-leafed parsley, chervil or fennel)

SERVES 4
PREPARATION TIME: 30 MINUTES + 20
MINUTES REFRIGERATION

Blanch the green cabbage in boiling water for a few seconds. Blanch the white cabbage too, if you prefer. Drain well; slice.

Peel and slice the pear and apple, sprinkle with a little salt, and pour the citrus juices over them. Chop the dried fig.

Make the dressing by combining the vinegar and the orange and lemon juices drained from the fruit. Add the *crème fraîche* and whisk to a smooth blend. Still whisking, pour in the oil in a thin trickle. Add salt and pepper to taste. Cut up the herbs and mix them into the dressing.

Arrange the cabbage and fruit on a plate; pour on the dressing; chill.

172

RED CABBAGE AND DRIED FRUIT WINTER SALAD
Salade de chou rouge aux fruits secs

7 oz (about 1 cup) pickled red cabbage
10 dried apple rings
2 dried peach halves
6 prunes
1 very small stalk of celery
a few leaves of field lettuce, radicchio
or watercress
1 slice of smoked ham or *poitrine
roulée*★
6 shelled walnuts
1 teaspoon golden raisins
fines herbes★
1 orange
a few green grapes or almonds
(optional)

For the dressing:
1 hard-cooked egg yolk from a large
egg
tiny pinch of mustard powder
1 teaspoon grated horseradish
salt and freshly ground black pepper
2 tablespoons *crème fraîche*★
1 teaspoon peanut oil

SERVES 4
PREPARATION TIME: 20 MINUTES

First make the dressing by
mashing the egg yolk with the
mustard, horseradish, and salt and
pepper to taste. Dilute with a
trickle of vinegar from the pickled
cabbage. Beat in the cream and
the oil, using a wooden spoon. Do
not add any more vinegar: the
sour taste of the cabbage is
enough. Marinate the dried
apples, peaches and pitted prunes
in this dressing for 30 minutes.

Cut the celery stalk into small
pieces. Make a nest from the salad
leaves on a serving plate and pour
the dried fruit and dressing into
the middle. Cut the ham into thin
strips and add this, together with
the walnuts, raisins, *fines herbes*
and the orange cut into thin slices.

Add the grapes and the almonds
as a garnish, if you like. Sunflower
or pumpkin seeds are also good
scattered over the top.

TWO-BEAN SALAD
Salade aux deux z'haricots

¼ lb fresh white (navy) beans or lima
beans
3 oz green beans
1 large shallot, or 1 yellow onion and 1
scallion
1 tablespoon mixed fresh herbs, such
as flat-leafed parsley and chervil
2 canned anchovy fillets in oil
2 teaspoons goat's cheese★
1 teaspoon *crème fraîche*★
1 tablespoon corn oil
1 tablespoon red wine vinegar
salt and freshly ground black pepper
1 tomato

SERVES 4
PREPARATION TIME: 30 MINUTES +
TIME TO COOL
COOKING TIME: ABOUT 15 MINUTES

*Manger l'haricot is French slang for
being in prison, just like "doing
porridge" in Britain. If you cannot find
fresh white beans, use dried navy or lima
beans, soaked and boiled.*

Peel the white beans and put to
cook in boiling salted water while
you trim and boil the green beans.
Finely chop the shallot or onions.
Shred the herbs. Mash half an

anchovy fillet with a fork and mix
with the crumbled goat's cheese
and *crème fraîche*. Trickle in the
oil, stirring briskly, then thin the
mixture by stirring in the vinegar.
Add only a little salt and pepper to
taste, and the herbs. When the
green beans are cooked, drain
them over the tomato in a bowl so
that the hot water loosens its skin.
Rinse the beans in cold water,

then drain again. Peel and crush
the tomato.
  Cut up the remaining anchovies.
Arrange the green beans and
tomato on a dish, top with the
anchovies, pour on half the sauce
and refrigerate. When the white
beans are cooked, drain them.
Cool; mix with the rest of the
sauce. Refrigerate until ready to
serve, then add to the salad.

MOROCCAN EGGPLANT AND PICKLED LEMON SALAD
Salade d'aubergines au citron confit

1 sweet red pepper
3 large eggplants
1 tablespoon peanut oil
1 pickled lemon★
1 clove of garlic
1 teaspoon paprika
juice of 1 fresh lemon
1 tablespoon finely chopped parsley

SERVES 6
PREPARATION TIME: 20 MINUTES
COOKING TIME: 10 MINUTES

*A wonderful Moroccan recipe from Perla
Danan (see page 128).*

Broil the sweet pepper briefly to
char the skin, then peel it. Deseed
and cut into small pieces. Thinly
peel the eggplants and cut them
into thin slices. Fry them in the
oil. Remove them from the pan
and drain on paper towels.
  When the eggplants are cold,
put them in a salad bowl. Add the
sweet pepper. Finely dice the
pickled lemon. Mince the garlic.
Add this and the other ingredients
to the bowl. Mix well and serve
cold, but not chilled: as the cold
would kill the delicate flavor.

Pickled lemons: sterilize a
canning jar. Blanch 10 whole
lemons for 3 minutes; plunge into
cold water. Sprinkle 1 teaspoon
salt into the jar. Cut 8 of the
lemons into quarters leaving the
pieces just joined; remove the
seeds. Put 1 teaspoon of salt into
each and pack tightly in the jar.
Top with 1 sliced lemon and pour
on the juice of the last one.
Sprinkle the inside of the squeezed
halves with 1 teaspoon salt; put
them peel side up on the slices.
Press down, put on the lid; leave
in a warm place for 14 to 18 days.

EGGPLANT AND LEMON SALAD ▶

SWEET SAUCES

Chantilly Whipped Cream *178*
Egg Custard (*Crème anglaise* – and variations) *178*
Confectioner's Custard (*Crème pâtissière*) *179*
Chocolate Sauce *179*
Raspberry Purée with Lime Juice (*Raspberry coulis* – and variations) *179*

FOLDING CREME CHANTILLY
INTO CREME ANGLAISE (see page
178)

RASPBERRY PURÉE SERVED
WITH PISTACHIO ICE CREAM (see
pages 179 and 196)

CREAMS

The French term *crème* means not only cream but also what we would call custard. There are three types which are the bases of numerous desserts, including charlottes, mousses, ice creams and many others. These three basic creams are *crème anglaise* (egg custard), *crème pâtissière* (confectioners' custard) and *crème chantilly* (light whipped cream). All these creams should be kept in the refrigerator for no longer than forty-eight hours.

CHANTILLY WHIPPED CREAM
Crème Chantilly

Basic proportions:
2 cups *crème fleurette*
⅓ cup confectioners' sugar
few drops of vanilla extract
port wine or Cognac (optional)
1 egg white (optional)

Crème Chantilly, light frothy whipped cream, is best made from a cream that is not too rich. If necessary, use thick cream and lighten it by adding a little iced water or milk, so that it takes on the consistency of thick milk. It is hard to go wrong as long as you chill both the cream and the bowl thoroughly. Whip gently at first.

In pastry cooking, *crème Chantilly* is slightly sweet. Pastry chefs generally advise adding ⅓ cup confectioners' sugar to 2 cups cream. You can also add a few drops of pure vanilla extract, Cognac or port wine. A *crème Chantilly* that is being served separately, not being used as the base of a dessert, can be made very light and frothy by folding in a little beaten egg white, but only an hour or two before serving without risk of separation.

EGG CUSTARD
Crème anglaise

1 vanilla bean
2 cups milk
heaping ½ cup sugar
8 egg yolks from large eggs

MAKES ABOUT 2½ CUPS
PREPARATION TIME: 10 MINUTES + 15
MINUTES WAIT
COOKING TIME: 10 MINUTES

PHOTOGRAPH ON PAGE 176

All pastry chefs are unanimous – do not skimp on the egg yolks. Use 7 to 9 yolks (depending on the size of the eggs) to 2 cups of milk.

Halve the vanilla bean lengthwise, put it in the milk, heat to the scalding point; remove from the heat and leave to infuse for 15 minutes.

Whisk together the sugar and egg yolks until the mixture is white. Bring the milk back to the scalding point, strain it in and whisk into the egg yolk mixture. Place the mixture over a not too gentle heat (otherwise it will take too long to thicken and your attention might wander!). Stir the mixture with a wooden spoon constantly. As soon as the custard coats the spoon, and before it begins to boil, remove from the heat but continue stirring for a couple of minutes.

Hints and variations
To check whether the custard is cooked: dip a cold spoon in the custard and remove it. Draw a line with your finger. If the two creamy edges do not meet, the custard is cooked; it is thick enough not to run on the spoon.

To remove any small lumps of egg: strain the custard while it is still hot. Always keep a bowl of cold water ready to stop the cooking by dipping the saucepan in it.
Flavorings: alcohols (like kirsch, rum or brandy), orange water and rose water, can be stirred into the cooled custard. For a *crème au chocolat*, melt 4 squares semisweet chocolate in a little of the milk; for a *crème au café*, infuse coffee beans in the milk for 15 to 30 minutes.

CONFECTIONERS' CUSTARD
Crème pâtissière

8 cups milk
½ cup sugar
8 egg yolks
5 tablespoons cornstarch
5 tablespoons flour
3 tablespoons butter
vanilla bean (optional)

This cream is used for filling all sorts of cakes, and in particular the famous choux à la crème, or cream puffs. The traditional recipe is always used as a base for sweet soufflés, and is made without any egg whites. This recipe is from chef Paul Bugat.

Scald the milk. Beat together the sugar and egg yolks. Beat in the cornstarch and flour a little at a time, and then gradually beat in the hot milk and the butter. Bring the mixture to a boil, and boil for 5 minutes, stirring constantly. Flavor in the same way as a *crème anglaise* (opposite).

CHOCOLATE SAUCE
Sauce au chocolat

5 squares semisweet chocolate
⅔ cup milk
2 tablespoons *crème fraîche**
2 tablespoons butter
3 tablespoons sugar

SERVES 6
COOKING TIME: 5 MINUTES

Serve this sauce hot or cold with ice creams, brioches or charlottes. Always use good-quality chocolate and unsalted or semi-salted butter for the best flavor.

Melt the chocolate with the milk. Add the *crème fraîche*, butter and sugar. When it boils, pour into a sauceboat and serve.

RASPBERRY PURÉE WITH LIME JUICE
Coulis de framboises au citron vert

2¼ lb (about 4 cups) fresh or frozen raspberries
2 cups sugar
juice of 1 lime

MAKES ABOUT 5 CUPS
PREPARATION TIME: 5 MINUTES

PHOTOGRAPH ON PAGE 177

Fruit purée will keep for a week in an airtight container in the refrigerator or for two months in the freezer. If using frozen purée, thaw it in the refrigerator for a day and whisk or blend it to restore its smoothness.

Purée the raspberries with the sugar and the lime juice in a blender or food processor. (You can add more or less sugar to the purée, according to taste.) Strain the mixture, pressing it through a fine sieve with the back of a spoon, to remove the seeds, then refrigerate.

You might like to try replacing the raspberries with an equal amount of black fruit – black currants, blackberries, blueberries etc. – for an interestingly dark, full-flavored purée. Another excellent fruit for a purée is red currants. In both cases, omit the lime juice.

Other fruit purées
Kiwi: Peel 9 large or 15 small kiwi fruit and purée with 1½ cups sugar. Add 1½ tablespoons kirsch or white rum and a little water if the purée is too thick. Blend briefly.
Mango: Peel 4½ lb mangoes, slice the flesh carefully off the seed and purée it with 2 cups sugar. Refrigerate in a tightly covered container to keep the delicate fruit from spoiling.
Apricot: Purée 2½ lb canned or freshly poached apricots with their liquid. If they are unsweetened, add sugar to taste.

DESSERTS

SWEET SOUFFLÉ (see page 198)

PRESENTING FRESH FRUIT (see page 182)

PRESENTATION OF FRESH FRUIT
Les fruits frais bien présentés

Fresh fruit can be as attractive and good to look at as it can be good to eat (photograph on page 181). Here are a few suggestions.
Watermelon: the very thick skin keeps it fresh for a long time. Halve the melon and use a knife to cut out the flesh and deseed it. Cut into cubes and put these back into the watermelon with strawberries, plums, pieces of pineapple, halved apricots or other tropical and soft fruit.
Melon: prepare as watermelon, or scoop out little balls. It goes beautifully with red fruits – raspberries, wild or cultivated strawberries and red currants – as well as black currants and figs.
Mangoes: cut the mango in half lengthwise along the seed. Remove the seed, and use the tip of a knife to cut the flesh into squares. Turn back the skin to open it like a flower. Mangoes go well with strawberries.
Papaya: cut the fruit in half, deseed it and squeeze lime juice over it. This delicately flavored fruit is good for the digestion, so it is ideal after a heavy meal.
Peaches: immerse them for 2 seconds in boiling water, rinse under the cold tap, peel and cut in half. Pit and slice them. Squeeze lemon juice over them to prevent discoloration.
Cherries: rinse them thoroughly, then place them in a bowl with water and ice cubes, or simply serve on a bed of crushed ice.
Figs: quarter them and open them like flowers. They are delicious served with raspberries.

FRESH FIGS WITH HONEY, CREAM AND CINNAMON
Figues fraîches au miel et à la cannelle

16 ripe purple figs
¼ cup runny honey
juice of 2 oranges
juice of 2 lemons
2 pinches of ground cinnamon
scant 1 cup Sauternes or other sweet white wine
scant ½ cup fresh cold *crème fleurette**

SERVES 4
PREPARATION TIME: 20 MINUTES
COOKING TIME: ABOUT 10 MINUTES

Michel Trama is one of France's top younger chefs; unusually, he is self-taught, having started his professional life as a lawyer. This is a recipe he devised for home cooks (see also page 134).

Remove the stalks from the figs; carefully peel them. Cut a cross in the bottom of each reaching at least halfway up and spread them out so that they are fully open.

Caramelize 3 tablespoons honey in a saucepan. As soon as it is caramel-colored, add the orange and lemon juices and heat, stirring. Add 1 pinch of cinnamon and reduce by half. Pour in the wine and cook over a gentle heat for 2 minutes. Leave to cool in a bowl at room temperature, then refrigerate. Chill four dessert dishes too. Combine the last tablespoon of honey with the *crème fleurette* and the second pinch of cinnamon. Whip to obtain a light cream. Put four figs in each dish and half fill each fruit with whipped cream. Pour on the caramel and honey sauce.

Serve chilled but not ice cold, which would kill the flavor.

DRIED FRUIT SALAD
Salade de fruits secs

½ lb (about 1⅔ cups) dried apricots
½ lb (about 1⅓ cups) prunes
½ cup golden raisins and currants
1¼ cups tea
juice of 1 lemon
½ cup sugar
1 tablespoon rose water
1 tablespoon orange flower water
a few slivered almonds

SERVES 6
PREPARATION TIME: 15 MINUTES +
SEVERAL HOURS SOAKING

Dried fruit salads, often dismissed because stewed prunes and the like still carry the stigma of invalid food, can be luscious. The long steeping of the fruit allows you to introduce the flavors of spices, fruit juices, different alcohols and teas, which mingle in the juices and improve the fruit as it soaks, and the salad will then continue to improve with keeping.

If you like very soft fruit, bring it to simmering point briefly after soaking in the same juices.

Put the dried fruit in a bowl and soak it in the tea (you can use strained and diluted leftover tea). After 12 hours, or when the fruit is fully softened, add the lemon juice, sugar and rose and orange flower waters. Mix well and refrigerate. Before serving, sprinkle with almonds. You could also add pine nuts.

DRIED FRUIT SALAD ▶

AUTUMN FRUIT COMPÔTE
Confit de fruits d'automne

2 oranges
½ lemon
4 tart-sweet apples
4 pears
1 cup firmly packed brown sugar
1 teaspoon raisins
1 teaspoon currants
small bunch of fresh grapes

SERVES 4
PREPARATION TIME: 15 MINUTES +
TIME TO COOL
COOKING TIME: 20 MINUTES

Sweetening stewed apples or pears after cooling ensures that the fruit will not stick: cooking the fruit with sugar gives a heavier, thickened syrup. Either way, the time the fruit takes to cook will depend on its ripeness and water content.

Wash the oranges and lemon gently (to remove as much as possible of any preservatives), then pare the zest and shred it into julienne strips. Squeeze the fruits and reserve their juices separately.

Peel, core and slice the apples and pears, dabbing the slices into lemon juice to avoid browning.

Cook them in the rest of the lemon juice and the orange juice with the sugar over a high heat, in a tall pan to avoid boiling over, for 10 minutes. Turn the slices over gently twice during this time. Then add the raisins and currants, turn the heat down and cook gently for another 5 minutes,

turning once more.

Test by dropping a little juice onto a chilled plate: it should set slightly while remaining clear. If it does not set, give the fruit another minute or two and test again. When ready, take off the heat, add the grapes, press them down into the liquid, cover and cool.

MIXED FRUIT POACHED IN RED WINE SYRUP
Soupe de fruits au vin rouge

4 lb various fruits – pears, peaches, plums, apricots, strawberries, cherries
1 bottle (750 ml) of good red wine (it is important to choose a quality wine, but there is no need to use a vintage one)
¾ cup sugar
pared zest of 1 lemon*
1 vanilla bean

SERVES 4
PREPARATION TIME: 15 MINUTES +
TIME TO COOL

Fruit soups, poached fruit traditionally served with croutons fried in butter, migrated from provincial kitchens to restaurant menus after they were revived by nouvelle cuisine *chefs. Roland Magne of Le Pactole, on boulevard Saint-Germain in Paris, serves this mixed fruit and red wine soup with a zabaglione whipped with champagne, but it would be good with* crème fraîche *or* crème anglaise *too (see page 178).*

Pit the fruit as necessary.

Heat the wine with the sugar, lemon zest and vanilla bean, and poach the fruit in it for 4 minutes, but only 2 minutes for the apricots and 1 minute for the strawberries. The idea is to poach them lightly, not to cook them.

Remove from the heat. Gently lift out the fruit with a slotted spoon and transfer it to a glass serving bowl. Reduce the cooking liquid to a quarter of the amount; it should become syrupy. Leave it to cool, then strain it over the poached fruit.

Serve cooled but not refrigerated.
Variation: it is possible to make a thicker soup. After poaching, purée half to three-quarters of the fruit, then mix in the remaining whole fruit.

PEARS WITH GINGER SYRUP
Poires au gingembre

6 large pears
¼ cup sugar
pared zest of 1 lime
1 vanilla bean
a piece of fresh gingerroot (or 1 tablespoon ground ginger)

SERVES 6
PREPARATION TIME: 10 MINUTES + 1 DAY
COOKING TIME: 30 MINUTES

Peel the pears and put them in a saucepan. Cover them with water and add the sugar, lime zest, the vanilla bean split in half and the ginger cut into thin slices. Cook over a gentle heat for 30 minutes. Leave to cool, then refrigerate overnight before serving.

This is good served with a *crème anglaise* (see page 178).

Variation: you could make a reasonable extemporized version of this – useful for those on a camping vacation, long boat journey or caught in a three-day snowstorm – with canned pears, cooked briefly and sprinkled with vanilla sugar,★ ground ginger and lemon juice.

PEACHES IN RUM
Pêches au rhum

12 peaches
2½ cups sugar
1 cup water
1 bottle (560 ml) of white rum
1 vanilla bean
1 cinnamon stick
10 cloves

SERVES 12
PREPARATION TIME: 15 MINUTES +
2 WEEKS TO MATURE
COOKING TIME: 15 MINUTES

Blanch the peaches in boiling water, and peel them. Dissolve the sugar in the water in a saucepan then poach the peaches in the syrup for 5 minutes. Remove them and transfer to a sterilized glass jar.

Reduce the syrup until a candy thermometer reads 221°F. Add half the bottle of rum, the vanilla and the spices. Pour the hot syrup and rum mixture over the peaches. Top up the jar with more rum. Cover with an airtight seal, and keep in a cool, dark, dry place for at least 2 weeks before serving.

FRESH FRUIT PURÉE DESSERTS

Fresh fruit purées, or *coulis* (see page 179 for recipes), can provide precisely the concentrated fruitiness you need in a creamy concoction, or they can replace fresh cream or a *crème anglaise* to lighten a traditional dessert. Match them carefully where other fruits are involved. Raspberry *coulis* is good with melons or pears; red currant with fresh peaches and pineapple; black fruit with red berries and currants. Fruit with seeds should always be sieved.

FRUIT PURÉES WITH FLOATING MERINGUE ISLANDS
Île flottante neige au coulis

4 egg whites from extra large eggs
a few drops of lemon or lime juice
5 cups fruit purée (see page 179)
garnishes (see below)

SERVES 6
PREPARATION TIME: 5 MINUTES +
TIME TO MAKE PUREE AND GARNISH
COOKING TIME: ABOUT 10 MINUTES

Beat the egg whites until stiff, adding the lemon or lime juice. Put 1 heaped tablespoon of the beaten egg into a saucepan of simmering water. Cook for 15 seconds. Turn over carefully, with a slotted spoon, and cook for a further 15 seconds. Drain on paper towels. When all the egg white is poached in the same way, float the "islands" on the fruit purée.

Garnishes: the pared and finely shredded zest of 2 limes, oranges or lemons, cooked gently in the juice of 1 lime with ¼ cup sugar for 15 minutes and drained; a few crushed pistachio nuts, or slivered hazelnuts (filberts), or almonds; shredded mint leaves; a sprinkling of vanilla sugar.★
Variation: for sweeter "islands," you can add ¼ cup sugar to the egg white and beat for a few minutes longer. To avoid oversweetening the dish, reduce the amount of sugar in the purée. These sweeter ones are good with the tarter fruit purées.

For a traditional *île flottante*, make a *crème anglaise* (see page 178), cool and use this as the "lake."

STRAWBERRIES WITH MARBLED WHIPPED CREAM AND PURÉE
Fraises à la crème et au coulis

1 lb (about 3 cups) cultivated strawberries
½ lb (about 2 cups) wild strawberries
¼ cup sugar cane syrup★
3 tablespoons kirsch
scant 1 cup *crème fleurette*★
1 tablespoon vanilla sugar★

SERVES 6-8
PREPARATION TIME: I HOUR TO
MARINATE + 15 MINUTES

Good strawberries are excellent served simply with orange juice, perhaps with a little Cointreau added. But for the times when you want something a little more self-indulgent or when the fruit is not good enough to be served very simply, here is a sophisticated coupe.

Place half the strawberries with 2 tablespoons of sugar syrup and the kirsch in a bowl. Cover and marinate in the refrigerator for at least 1 hour.

Purée the rest of the fruit, gradually adding the rest of the syrup. In a separate bowl, whip

the *crème fleurette* with the vanilla sugar. Combine the fruit purée and two-thirds of the whipped cream.

Reserve a few strawberries, and pour the cream mixture over the rest. Decorate with the reserved cream and strawberries. Serve in chilled goblets.

Do not worry if you are unable to find the exquisitely flavored wild strawberries; simply use all cultivated ones.

SPICED FRUIT BAKED IN PAPER PARCELS
Papillotes de fruits aux épices

4 dried figs
2 very ripe pears
2 bananas
4 teaspoons brown sugar
2 oranges
ground cinnamon
grated nutmeg
a few mixed pink, green and black
peppercorns
a little butter
4 scoops of vanilla ice cream

SERVES 4
PREPARATION TIME: 30 MINUTES + 15
MINUTES SOAKING
COOKING TIME: 5 MINUTES

A simple, inexpensive and light recipe from chef Pierre Larapidie (see page 123); the baked fresh and dried fruit is given a twist by mixed peppercorns, which bring out the sweetness.

Soak the figs for 15 minutes in hot water; drain. Peel and core the pears, and cut them into thin slices. Peel the bananas and cut them into matchsticks.

Preheat the oven to 400°F. Cut four heart shapes measuring 6 by 10 inches from baking parchment paper, and fold them in half. At the center of each half heart shape place half a pear, half a banana and 1 dried fig. Sprinkle with 1 teaspoon sugar and the juice of half an orange. Sprinkle with a little cinnamon and nutmeg and add a few peppercorns. Butter the outer edges of the paper, and fold them over several times to seal the parcels well.

Pour a little boiling water into a roasting pan. Put in the parcels and bake for 5 minutes. Serve at once, in the paper. At the table, burst open the parcels and place a scoop of vanilla ice cream in the center of each one.

PINEAPPLE GRATIN WITH PISTACHIOS
Gratin d'ananas aux pistaches

1 cup *crème fraîche**
2 egg yolks from large eggs
¼ cup granulated sugar
1 teaspoon white rum
½ cup shelled pistachio nuts
14 oz ripe pineapple

SERVES 4
PREPARATION TIME: 15 MINUTES
COOKING TIME: ABOUT 20 MINUTES

A wonderful fresh pineapple gratin created by Eric Hausser when he was pastry chef at Les Ambassadeurs, the restaurant in the Hôtel de Crillon.

Preheat the broiler. Whip the *crème fraîche* and refrigerate it. Whisk together the egg yolks, sugar and rum in a bowl over a pan of simmering water, but not touching it, until frothy. Remove from the heat and fold in the whipped cream and the pistachio nuts. Put a little of this mixture in each dish, arrange the pineapple slices in a rosette on top and place under the broiler for a few minutes. Serve as soon as the surface is golden brown.

STUFFED PEACHES
Pêches farcies

9 large yellow peaches
⅓ cup blanched almonds
¾ cup sugar
½ lb (about 12) almond macaroons
2 large eggs
⅓ cup sweet or mellow white wine
(see suggestions on page 191)
a little butter

SERVES 6
PREPARATION TIME: 15 MINUTES
COOKING TIME: 45 MINUTES

A Provençal recipe for stuffed peaches from a home cook, Anouk Laitier (see page 116). These are as good served at room temperature; chilling them would deaden the flavor.

Preheat the oven to 300°F. Coarsely chop the almonds.

Cut the peaches in half without peeling them. Remove the pits and scoop out some of the flesh to make hollows for stuffing. Put about half the scooped-out flesh in a bowl. Add the sugar, the macaroons reduced to crumbs, the beaten eggs, the almonds and the wine. If the peaches are not very sweet, add more sugar.

Arrange the peach halves in a gratin dish or roasting pan, and fill them with the mixture. Place a pat of butter on top of each peach half. Bake for 45 minutes.

Peeling peaches: for many fruit recipes you need to peel peaches. This is done in the same way as for tomatoes, by immersing them briefly in boiling water to loosen the skin. If the peaches are very ripe, boiling water may not be necessary at all. A peach kernel removed from the pit (with a nutcracker) can be used to give a pleasing tang of bitter almonds to any fruit dish. But use only one kernel, or two at most: that taste is the flavor of cyanide!

STUFFED PEACHES ▶

CLAFOUTIS

A *clafoutis* is a kind of fruit tart with no crust; instead a batter is poured over the fruit. The classic *clafoutis*, a specialty of the Limousin, is made with cherries, but there are many other kinds made with different fruits. In recent years, chefs have taken to replacing the batter with a light custard and to making savory *clafoutis* (page 57). In a tight spot it is possible to get away with well drained canned fruit soaked in some kind of suitable alcohol; like an *eau-de-vie*.★

CHERRY *CLAFOUTIS*
Clafoutis aux griottes

1 lb 2 oz (about 4 cups) fresh or frozen morello or other sour cherries
7 tablespoons butter
2 extra large eggs
½ cup sugar
1 tablespoon vanilla sugar★
1 cup flour
1¾ cups milk
3 tablespoons kirsch (optional)
pinch of salt

SERVES 6
PREPARATION TIME: 5 MINUTES +
TIME TO PIT CHERRIES IF NECESSARY
COOKING TIME: 30 MINUTES

Preheat the oven to 425°F. Use a little of the butter to grease a gratin dish. Melt the rest. Put the pitted fruit into the dish, draining the cherries first. Combine the eggs with the sugar and vanilla sugar, stir in the flour, then the milk, melted butter, kirsch (if used) and salt, and pour the batter over the cherries. Bake for 30 minutes.
Fresh fruit variations: sweet Bing cherries, black currants, plums and blueberries can also be used. The cooking time is the same for thawed frozen fruit. If still frozen, add 5 minutes to the cooking time.
Dried fruit *clafoutis*: for a spiced dried fruit *clafoutis*, use mixed dried raisins, apricots, figs and apples soaked briefly in tea or wine, instead of fresh fruit, and add ground cinnamon, cloves, ginger, and cardamom seeds to the batter. Slivered almonds, toasted skinned hazelnuts (filberts) or whole pine nuts might appeal to you for their crunch.

APPLE *CLAFOUTIS*
Clafoutis aux pommes

6 heaping tablespoons flour
2 tablespoons sugar
pinch of salt
1 heaping teaspoon active dry rapid-rise yeast
2 tablespoons rum
2 extra large eggs
2 cups milk
3 tart-sweet apples, peeled, cored and cut into thin slices (dipped in lemon juice if sliced before making the batter)
2 tablespoons butter
a little sugar, to finish

SERVES 6
PREPARATION TIME: 10 MINUTES + 15 MINUTES WAIT
COOKING TIME: 30 MINUTES

Make a thick batter with the flour, sugar, salt, yeast and rum, mixing in the eggs and milk to obtain a thick batter. Strain and leave for 15 minutes for the yeast to work.
Stir the apple slices into the batter. Put half of the butter into a nonstick or heavy skillet. When it begins to froth, pour in the apples in batter. Use a spatula to spread the batter and make holes in the set layer, tilting the pan to let the liquid batter run around the edges. After 15 minutes, or when there is no (or very little) liquid batter, turn the *clafoutis* over with the help of a plate. Put the rest of the butter in the pan and cook the other side, again for 15 minutes. Unmold onto a dish, and sprinkle with sugar.

COLD MOLDED AND SET DESSERTS

Bavaroises and charlottes can seem unattractively complicated to make because they appear to be so much more than the sum of the parts, but, like most good things in this world, they can be reduced to basics. A *bavaroise* is a custard set with gelatin into which whipped cream is folded; unlike a soufflé, it is not lightened with egg whites. A charlotte is based on a *bavaroise* mixture, but it has egg whites and sometimes whole fruit folded in, and is usually set in an outer casing of whipped cream and cookies.

Mousses, baked custards and gelatins may seem deceptively easy by contrast, but they need to be made with precision for a really good consistency. Here are four recipes with a difference: two mousses made without gelatin; a baked custard with wine and honey replacing the usual milk and sugar; and a red fruit gelatin with a liquid base of light rosé wine.

HONEY, WINE AND CINNAMON CREAM
Crème d'Homère

2 cups sweet white wine, such as Bergerac, Montbazillac, Sauternes, Muscat de Frontignan, or a mellow white wine like Anjou or Vouvray
⅔ cup pale runny honey
pared zest of 1 lemon★
1 cinnamon stick
¼ cup sugar
1½ tablespoons water
8 large eggs

SERVES 4
PREPARATION TIME: 25 MINUTES
COOKING TIME: 45 MINUTES

This recipe was adapted from a recipe in Cuisine Rustique du Languedoc by André Bonnaure. While some chefs use eight whole eggs, others prefer to use only four of the whites. It is a question of individual preference.

In a stainless steel saucepan, bring the wine, honey and lemon zest to a boil. Do not cover the pan, as the wine has to reduce. Simmer for 15 minutes, adding the cinnamon stick 5 minutes before the end. Leave to cool.

Meanwhile, prepare the dish or individual ramekins. Put it or them into hot water to warm. Heat the sugar and water in a small pan until the syrup turns golden (not dark brown). At once remove the dish from the hot water and pour in the syrup – careful, it is very hot indeed – and tilt it so that the inside of the dish is evenly coated. Invert the dish so that excess syrup runs out.

Preheat the oven to 350°F.

Lightly beat the eggs together. Remove the lemon zest and cinnamon from the wine mixture and gradually whisk it into the eggs. Pour the mixture into the dish or ramekins. Put the dish or ramekins in a roasting or baking pan of boiling water, with water reaching halfway up the sides of the dish or ramekins. Bake, keeping the water just simmering, for 30 minutes. Leave to cool in the oven with the door open. Serve warm or chilled.

LIGHT CHOCOLATE AND GINGER MOUSSE
Mousse légère au chocolat et gingembre

7 oz semisweet chocolate
pat of butter
5 egg whites from large eggs
a few drops of lemon juice
1½ oz crystallized ginger

SERVES 6
PREPARATION TIME: 20 MINUTES +
TIME TO COOL AND REFRIGERATE

Contrary to many people's belief, nothing could be easier to make than a chocolate mousse. Here is the proof.

Melt the chocolate over a pan of simmering water. Remove from the heat and stir the butter. Leave until almost cold.

Beat the egg whites with the lemon juice until stiff. Gently fold them into the chocolate. Cut the ginger into thin slivers and add to the mixture. Refrigerate before serving.

You could replace the ginger with strips of blanched orange zest or crushed praline (see page 11).

ROSÉ WINE JELLY
Gelée en vin rosé

2½ cups rosé wine
3 tablespoons sugar
1 tablespoon orange juice
a few fresh or dried green peppercorns
1 heaping teaspoon unflavored gelatin
½ lb (about 2 cups) mixed strawberries, raspberries and red currants

SERVES 4
PREPARATION TIME: 15 MINUTES +
TIME TO COOL AND REFRIGERATE
COOKING TIME: 10 MINUTES

A great favorite with lovers of gelatin desserts, this sparkling dish has fruit set in the gelatin like jewels. You can use white or red wine if you prefer, or fruit syrups or fresh juice instead. With fruit syrups or juices, reduce the amount of sugar or omit it altogether.

Gently heat together the wine, sugar, orange juice and peppercorns in a stainless steel saucepan. As soon as the liquid begins to stir, reduce the heat to minimum. Simmer for 5 minutes.

Remove from the heat, wait a few minutes and add the gelatin. Stir until dissolved. Wash and hull the fruit, and put it into a large bowl or into individual dishes. When the wine mixture is a little cooler, pour it over the fruit. Leave to cool at room temperature, then refrigerate until serving.

WALNUT AND COFFEE MOUSSE WITH CREAM CHEESE
Mousse de fromage blanc aux noix et au café

½ cup *fromage blanc*★
2 tablespoons walnut liqueur★
⅔ cup chopped walnuts
scant ½ cup *crème fraîche*★
2½ tablespoons sugar

For the sauce:
½ cup sugar
about ¼ cup water
⅓ cup strong black coffee

SERVES 4-6
PREPARATION TIME: 30 MINUTES +
TIME TO COOL

A wonderful recipe for a very easy mousse from the menu of Lou Mazouc, the restaurant of Michel Bras (see page 56). The light and airy texture is a pleasant change from heavier mousses set with gelatin; the gentle walnut flavor is played off against a strong coffee sauce.

Combine the *fromage blanc*, the walnut liqueur and the chopped walnuts. Separately whip the *crème fraîche*, then carefully fold it into the walnut mixture with the sugar. Refrigerate.

To make the sauce, caramelize the sugar by gently heating in a dry pan until it is melted and lightly colored. On no account stir the caramel; it prevents the caramelization taking place.
Remove it from the heat, and leave for a couple of minutes to cool. Then add the water and the coffee. Heat gently until the sugar has completely dissolved – do not let it boil – and leave to cool. Serve the mousse with the sauce.

STRAWBERRY *BAVAROISE* WITH BLACK FRUIT SAUCE
Bavaroise aux fraises

3 egg yolks from large eggs
1 tablespoon vanilla sugar★
1 cup scalded milk, cooled to lukewarm
1 heaping teaspoon unflavored gelatin
5 oz (about 1 cup) cultivated strawberries
¾ cup wild strawberries
scant 1 cup *crème fraîche*★
½ lb (about 1½ cups) black fruit (black currants, blackberries, blueberries, etc.)
sugar to taste

SERVES 6
PREPARATION TIME: 30 MINUTES + 2-3
HOURS TO REFRIGERATE
COOKING TIME: 10 MINUTES

This recipe comes from Edouard Carlier of Le Beauvilliers restaurant, Paris.

Whisk the egg yolks and vanilla sugar together and stir in the milk, whisking constantly. Place the mixture in a heavy pan over a gentle heat, and stir continuously until it thickens, without letting it boil. When the custard coats the spoon, remove it from the heat and stir in the gelatin until dissolved. Leave to cool.
Reserve about ½ cup of the best strawberries, and purée the rest. Whip the *crème fraîche* until it is

thick. Fold the fruit purée into the custard, and then the whipped cream. Mix and add the reserved whole fruit. Pour into a mold; refrigerate for 2 to 3 hours until set. Purée the black fruit, and add sugar to taste. Unmold the *bavaroise*, and serve with this sauce.
Variation: you can also make a charlotte. Line the bottom and sides of a charlotte or straight-sided mold with 12 to 15 lady-finger cookies soaked in fruit juice and kirsch. Decorate the dessert with a few reserved fruits; serve with the sauce.

PEAR AND BLACK CURRANT *BAVAROISE*
Bavaroise de poires au cassis

⅔ cup Ceylon tea
6 ripe pears
2½ tablespoons vanilla sugar★
¼ cup white rum
pinch of grated nutmeg
tiny pinch of ground cinnamon
10 madeleines or sponge cake slices
scant 1 cup sugar cane syrup★
1 heaping teaspoon unflavored gelatin
1½ squares semisweet chocolate
1 lb (about 3 cups) black currants
1 cup *crème fraîche*★

For the base:
more melted chocolate

SERVES 6
PREPARATION TIME: 1 HOUR +
4 HOURS TO REFRIGERATE
COOKING TIME: 8 MINUTES

First, make the tea. While it is infusing, peel the pears. Cut four of them into quarters and two into thin slices. Add the vanilla sugar to the strained tea, and poach the pears in it, covered, for 8 minutes over a very gentle heat. Leave to cool.

Pour the rum into a deep dish, and add the nutmeg and cinnamon. Crumble in the madeleines or sponge cake, pour on the sugar cane syrup and leave to soften. Soak the gelatin in a little cold water for 10 minutes.

Meanwhile, set the chocolate to melt slowly over a pan of hot water with 1 tablespoon of the cooking juices from the pears. Purée the black currants, reserving a handful for decoration.

Drain the pears, and dissolve the gelatin in their juice over a very gentle heat. Purée the quartered pears with two-thirds of the gelatin mixture and the *crème fraîche*. Add 2 tablespoons of the madeleine mixture, and lastly the black currant purée.

Lightly butter a mold just large enough to hold all the ingredients. Pour in the black currant mixture, adding a few whole black currants. Tap the mold lightly on the work surface to make sure the mixture settles evenly. Refrigerate.

Now mix the remaining madeleine mixture, the chocolate and the last third of the gelatin mixture. When the first layer has set, place on it the pear slices interspersed with whole black currants. Pour on the chocolate and madeleine mixture, and tap the mold on the work surface to help it settle. Chill for at least 4 hours.

Pour a layer of melted chocolate over the *bavaroise* to make a base. Chill until set. Unmold it carefully.

CHOCOLATE CHARLOTTE
Charlotte au chocolat

ladyfinger cookies to line mold and
cover top
3 tablespoons rum
1 lb 2 oz (18 squares) semisweet
chocolate plus more for decoration
scant 1 cup milk
7 tablespoons softened butter
2 cups *crème fleurette**, chilled
½ cup sugar
4 egg whites
scant ½ cup confectioners' sugar

SERVES 8-10
PREPARATION TIME: 45 MINUTES
COOKING TIME: 10 MINUTES

"You have to go to Vienna to find a chocolate charlotte like that of Jean Moussié," said one appreciative client. *Moussié, chef and owner of Bistro 121 (see page 23) combined family tradition with invention. His wife kindly gave permission for this recipe to be used.*

Line the charlotte mold with the ladyfinger cookies moistened with rum and a little water, and set aside. Break up the chocolate and put it in a saucepan over, but not touching, boiling water. Allow the chocolate to melt. Scald the milk separately and stir it into the melted chocolate to obtain a fairly runny mixture. Remove from the heat when the mixture is warm and stir in the softened butter (do not melt the butter). Stir constantly.

While it cools (do not forget it, stir it carefully from time to time) whip the *crème fleurette*. Add the sugar, whipping constantly. Beat the egg whites and add the confectioners' sugar; continue beating until stiff. Mix the whipped cream and the beaten egg whites, folding them in to keep the mixture light. When the chocolate has cooled and the mixture has almost set, pour it gently into the cream to obtain a chocolate mousse which is both firm and light. Fill the lined charlotte mold with the mixture, cover with more ladyfinger cookies, and chill until set.

Remove from the refrigerator 15 minutes before serving, unmold and decorate with chocolate.

FRESH PINEAPPLE CHARLOTTE
Charlotte à l'ananas

1 pineapple
4 cups water
2½ cups sugar (for syrup)
1 vanilla bean
1 envelope unflavored gelatin
8 egg yolks from large eggs
about 20 ladyfinger cookies
a little kirsch (optional)
crème Chantilly (see page 178), made
with 1½ cups cream and ¼ cup
confectioners' sugar

SERVES 6
PREPARATION TIME: 40 MINUTES +
2 DAYS
COOKING TIME: 30 MINUTES

Fruit charlottes do not have enough body without gelatin. This recipe comes from Jean Millet, a renowned French pâtissier-traiteur who is based in Saint-Germain, Paris.

Poach the pineapple pieces in a syrup made from the water, sugar and vanilla bean. Simmer the syrup for 20 minutes over a low heat, then leave overnight in a cool place.

The next day, put the gelatin to soak in a little water. Remove the pineapple from the syrup, and make a *crème anglaise* (see page 178), using the strained syrup instead of milk. As the syrup is already sweet, only use about ¼ cup more sugar. Use no more than 1 pint of the syrup, or even less. Beat the egg yolks with the sugar to make a mixture that is lemon-colored and light in texture. Taste, and add milk if too sweet. Pour the boiling syrup slowly into the egg mixture, beating all the while. Heat the custard, stirring continuously, and as soon as it coats the spoon, take it off the heat.

Add the soaked gelatin directly to the hot custard. Mix well until dissolved, then pour the custard through a strainer. Stand the bowl in cold water and leave to cool, stirring from time to time. Line the mold with ladyfinger cookies barely moistened with kirsch or a little of the leftover syrup. Place the ladyfingers over the bottom and around the sides, rounded side against the mold. There should be some ladyfingers left over.

Now make a classic *crème Chantilly* (see page 178). When the custard has cooled but has still not thickened, gently fold in the whipped cream with a spatula. Pour a layer into the bottom of the mold. Put in a layer of pineapple pieces, then make another layer of custard, until you have used up all the ingredients, finishing with a layer of custard cream. Press the remaining ladyfingers down into this to make a firm base. Refrigerate until set. To serve, unmold carefully onto a flat dish.

ICE CREAMS AND SHERBETS

Making good ice creams and sherbets is a matter of practice. That includes knowing how quickly your freezer will freeze them, so that you can beat at the right stage to avoid the formation of large crystals. There are a few general points to watch. Always use a metal container; glass is a poor conductor of heat and cold and will cause slow, uneven freezing. If you are adding alcohol, use only a little; too much may act as an antifreeze so that the mixture stays liquid. If using an ice cream making machine, follow the manufacturer's instructions attentively.

PISTACHIO ICE CREAM
Glace à la pistache

8 egg yolks from large eggs
½ cup sugar
2 cups *crème fleurette**
⅔ cup chopped pistachio nuts
½ cup ground almonds
1 cup *crème fraîche**

SERVES 6-8
PREPARATION TIME: 25 MINUTES +
TIME TO COOL + 3 HOURS TO FREEZE

The quality of the nuts is crucial in a good pistachio ice cream. They should be sweet and tender, almost melting in the mouth. Pistachio ice cream is usually sold tinted green with artificial food coloring, but there is no need for this.

Beat together the egg yolks and sugar until the mixture becomes pale. Add the *crème fleurette*. Place in a heavy pan over a gentle heat and stir with a wooden spoon until the mixture thickens. Stir in the chopped pistachio nuts and the almonds. Leave to cool.

Lightly whip the *crème fraîche*, and stir into the mixture. Put in the freezer to set.

Remove from the freezer 10-15 minutes before serving.

LEMON ICE
Sorbet au citron

3 cups water
1¼ cups sugar
juice of 6 lemons
grated zest of 1 lemon*
a few leaves of mint
12 almond cookies, to serve

SERVES 6
PREPARATION TIME: 15 MINUTES OVER
ABOUT 3 HOURS
COOKING TIME: 10 MINUTES

An ice should be made well in advance, preferably the day before. Although it is very simple to make, it requires frequent attention because it has to be whisked twice while it is freezing, and the point at which this has to be done varies according to the temperature of your freezer. But try it, if necessary several times until you get it right – it's worth it. For a real celebration, or somebody you love very much, you could make the butterfly tuiles on page 213.

Bring the water and sugar to a boil. Boil quickly for 5 minutes to reduce, then add the lemon juice and zest and simmer over a low heat for another 5 minutes. Pour into several aluminum icecube trays, without dividers, and leave to cool.

Put the trays in the freezer. As soon as the bottom and sides of the ice have frozen (1 to 2 hours), pull them into the center with a spoon and when the outside has semi-frozen – probably a quarter to half an hour later – pour the ice into a bowl and beat for 5 minutes with an electric beater or whisk. Put the icecube trays back in the freezer and freeze again. When the same stage is reached again, beat a second time.

An hour before serving take the ice out of the freezer and put it on the top shelf of the refrigerator. Serve scooped into goblets or small stemmed glasses, decorated with mint leaves and accompanied by almond cookies. You can also sprinkle it with some *eau-de-vie.**

ICE CREAM, SHERBET AND FRUIT PYRAMID
Pyramide de glaces, de sorbets et de fruits

3¼ lb white peaches
2 mangoes
2¼ lb piece of watermelon
1 medium-sized canteloupe
½ lb fresh litchis
3 quarts mixed ice creams and
sherbets: for example, vanilla, mango,
lime, apple, melon, mint, apricot

SERVES 6-8
PREPARATION TIME: I HOUR +
TIME TO REFRIGERATE

This grand set piece was given to Marie
Claire *by Francois-Xavier Lalanne; her
husband, Claude, is a sculptor. This was
part of a Christmas menu. You must
have a freezer deep enough to hold the
pyramid, and will probably need to
make room in your freezer before you
start. You will also need a half circle of
fine, stiff wire mesh of about 16 inches in
diameter to make a conical base, and a
circular serving dish on which the cone
will fit with plenty of room all round.*

Blanch the peaches in boiling
water, then peel and pit them. Use
a small scoop to make marble-
sized balls from the mangoes,
watermelon and canteloupe; peel
the litchis. Chill the fruit.

Make a cone from the wire
mesh, tying the edges together
firmly. Put the dish and the cone
in the refrigerator or freezer. Use
an ice cream scoop to make balls
of ice cream and sherbet. Keep the
ice cream balls in separate
containers in the freezer.

Build the ice cream balls into a
pyramid around the netting,
pressing them into the mesh a
little to hold them. Fill the spaces
between the ice cream balls with
the mango, melon and litchis,
alternating the colors. Arrange the
peach halves around the base of
the pyramid, then put the whole
thing in the freezer, making sure it
is upright so you do not end up
with a leaning ice-cream tower of
Pisa!

197

HOT SOUFFLÉS

There are two kinds of hot sweet soufflés: those made with flour and those made without flour. In those made with flour, *crème pâtissière* replaces the béchamel that forms the base of a savory soufflé. Some chefs use a third *choux* pastry as an insurance against collapse (this gives a somewhat less unctuous texture); others suggest adding an extra egg yolk, as in the recipe below. Flourless soufflés are very light and creamy and even less stable; they need to be executed with speed. The exact heat of the oven and timing can only be learned by experience.

SWEET SOUFFLÉ
Soufflé sucré

6 large eggs
½ cup sugar
2½ tablespoons flour
2½ tablespoons cornstarch
2 cups milk
1 egg yolk from a large egg
fruit liqueur★
a little butter and sugar to coat the dish

SERVES 4-6
PREPARATION TIME: 20 MINUTES +
TIME TO COOL
COOKING TIME: 20-25 MINUTES

PHOTOGRAPH PAGE 180

Here is a recipe for a well risen, firm and reliable soufflé from chef Gérard Vié of Les Trois Marches in Versailles.

Preheat the oven to 400°. Separate the eggs. Put the sugar in a bowl and add 6 egg yolks. Beat to the "ribbon" stage, that is until the mixture is light in texture and runs in a broad ribbon from the spoon, then add the flour and cornstarch. Pour in the scalded milk, mix well and pour into a saucepan. Cook gently for 10 minutes, stirring constantly, then leave the custard to cool.

Add the extra egg yolk; it helps the soufflé hold. Beat the egg whites in two stages: steadily until they foam, then rapidly, using your wrist and revolving the bowl with your other hand, until stiff. Add the fruit liqueur or other flavoring to the custard, then fold in the whites. Pour into a buttered, sugared 7-inch diameter soufflé dish. Bake for 20 to 25 minutes. Serve at once, straight from the oven.
Flavorings: sweet soufflés have only a small proportion of flavoring ingredients, so a few tricks are necessary to achieve a full flavor. Vanilla, coffee or cocoa beans can be infused in the milk. For orange or lemon flavor, rub a lump of sugar on the rind to extract the oil, then crush it.

FLOURLESS LIME SOUFFLÉ
Soufflé au citron vert sans farine

6 large eggs
6 tablespoons sugar
juice of 3 limes plus a little grated zest
a little butter and sugar to coat the dish

SERVES 4
PREPARATION TIME: 15 MINUTES
COOKING TIME: 15-17 MINUTES

Bernard L'Oiseau of La Côte d'Or (see page 34) gave this recipe to "Âllo-Cuisine;" an article with recipes and advice from chefs in response to readers' queries.

Preheat the oven to 400°F. Separate the eggs. Beat the egg yolks and sugar together to the "ribbon" stage (see above), then add the lime juice and grated zest. Fold in the stiffly beaten egg whites: start by folding a little of the yolk mixture into the whites, and then fold the rest of the whites into the yolk mixture.

Generously butter and sugar two 7-inch soufflé dishes, and pour in the mixture. Bake for 15 to 17 minutes. Serve immediately.

SWEET CRÊPES

DESSERT CRÊPES
Crêpes sucrées

1⅔ cups flour
1 cup sugar
pinch of fine salt
⅓ cup beer
2 large eggs
1 cup cold milk
1 tablespoon neutral flavored oil (such as peanut or sunflower) + more for frying
flavoring to taste: Grand Marnier, Cognac or rum, etc.
butter for frying
sugar or other topping (see variation)

SERVES 4-6
PREPARATION TIME: 10 MINUTES + 2 HOURS TO REST
COOKING TIME: ABOUT 20 MINUTES FOR BASIC RECIPE

Mix the flour and sugar in a large bowl and make a well in the center. Dissolve the salt in the milk in another bowl. Break the eggs into another bowl and add them to the salted beer. Mix well, then pour into the flour and gradually beat the flour into the liquid. When the mixture is smooth, trickle in the milk and beat to combine it. Continue beating until there are no lumps. Stir in the oil and the flavoring. Beat well again, cover and leave to rest for at least 2 hours.

Choose a medium-sized, heavy-bottomed, perfectly smooth crêpe pan. Heat the pan and put in a little pat of butter and a tablespoon of oil. Stir the batter well. Take a sparing tablespoonful of it and pour it into the pan. There should be just enough batter to cover the bottom of the pan in a layer no more than 1/10 inch thick. Let the bottom of the crêpe set, without disturbing it, then shake the pan to loosen it.

Turn it over quickly, using a spatula if you like, and cook the other side for a slightly shorter time, being careful not to let it get dry.

Slide it onto a heated plate, sprinkle with sugar or another topping, and keep warm in a low oven or by putting the plate, covered with a cloth or another plate, over a pan of barely simmering water. Make the rest of the batter into crêpes in the same way. Stack each one on the others as it is made.

Filled sweet crêpes: spread each one with jam, stewed fruit or just cream and sugar, as you prefer. Preheat the oven to 450°F, or heat the broiler to maximum.

Roll up the crêpes and arrange them side by side in a rectangular ovenproof dish. Sprinkle with a mixture of brown sugar and ground almonds and put the dish in the oven or under the broiler for 1 minute to brown the top.

"MERRY WIDOW" CRÊPES
Crêpes "veuve joyeuse"

For the crêpes:
½ cup flour
1 tablespoon sugar
a pinch of salt
2 large eggs
1 cup milk
2½ tablespoons butter

For the soufflé:
3 lemons
1 vanilla bean
1 cup milk
1 cup sugar
yolks of 3 eggs + whites of 5, all large eggs
3½ tablespoons flour

SERVES 6
PREPARATION TIME: 90 MINUTES
COOKING TIME: 30 MINUTES

This recipe is from Maxim's restaurant.

In a bowl, mix together the flour, sugar, salt and eggs. Gradually add the hot milk, beating with a spoon to obtain a smooth batter with no lumps. Gently melt the butter and add to the batter. Leave to rest for at least 1 hour.

Meanwhile, wash and dry the lemons thoroughly and squeeze the juice. Marinate the zests in the juice for 15 minutes.

Make a *crème pâtissière* (see page 179): put the vanilla bean in the milk to infuse. Beat the sugar and egg yolks together until the mixture is pale. Reserve the egg

whites. Sift in the flour, and add the milk and the drained lemon zest. Heat the mixture and boil it for a few minutes. Cool, stirring.

In a heavy pan of 6-inch diameter, make 12 very thin crêpes. Keep them hot. Preheat the oven to 400°F . Whisk the 8 egg whites until stiff, and carefully fold into the cooled *crème pâtissière*, removing the vanilla bean first. Lightly butter an ovenproof dish.

Fill the crêpes with the mixture, fold them in half and cook for 6 to 8 minutes. The soufflé will rise and hold the crêpes open.

PATISSERIE, CAKES AND BREADS

MAKING INDIVIDUAL APPLE
TARTS (see page 207)

STRAWBERRY TART (see page 207)

PASTRIES

Pâte brisée is the ideal base for cooked fruit – including juicy fruits such as peaches, pears and rhubarb – and for all fillings based on custard and cream because it is a pastry which resists sogginess well. But for flans filled just before serving, either with a cream or with uncooked fresh fruit like strawberries and raspberries, the crumblier and more fragile sweet biscuit crust called *pâte sablée* can be used instead. Neither of these pastries are difficult to make providing you remember that kneading gives unwanted elasticity – so all the ingredients should be mixed as quickly as possible without trying to blend them too thoroughly.

    Pâte feuilleté, known in France as "the queen of pastries and the terror of cooks," is not really so difficult. A practiced hand helps, but is not essential. Cold hands are certainly a good idea. So is a cool work surface, ideally a slab of marble. Choux pastry is equally accessible; the baking needs as much attention as the making.

FRENCH PIE PASTRY
Pâté brisée

1⅔ cups sifted flour
pinch of salt
1 level tablespoon sugar (for sweet pastry: for savory quiches and pastries omit the sugar)
1 large egg
¾ cup (1½ sticks) softened butter
scant 1 cup cold milk

MAKES ABOUT I LB
PREPARATION TIME: I5 MINUTES + AT LEAST I HOUR WAITING

This rich pie pastry needs to rest for at least an hour before being rolled out. You can also line the tart dish 24 hours in advance and refrigerate it. This is the easiest of all pastries provided you never use less butter than half the weight of flour.

In a bowl mix the flour with the salt and sugar, then turn out onto the work surface and make a well in the center.

    Break the egg into this well and add the butter in bits. Mix in with the fingertips of one hand, drawing in more flour from the sides of the well with the other hand to make coarse crumbs.

    Then continue mixing and blending, using both hands and adding the cold milk a little at a time, until the dough is nice and smooth. Then comes the *fraisage*. Make sure the work surface is well floured and press the dough down onto it with the heel of your hand. When the dough is flattened, roll it into a ball and wrap it in a sheet of plastic wrap; or place it in a plastic bag, and leave it in the bottom of the refrigerator to rest for at least one hour before using it.

SWEET BUTTERY PIE PASTRY FOR FLANS
Pâte sablée sucrée

scant 1 cup sifted flour
pinch of salt
6 tablespoons sugar
¾ cup (1½ sticks) thoroughly softened butter
1 extra large egg

MAKES ABOUT 1 LB
PREPARATION TIME: 20 MINUTES

Many chefs think it is better to avoid using a rolling pin on this delicate pastry. Instead they recommend gently flattening it and pressing it into a tart or pie pan with your fingertips. Cool your fingers under cold water first, drying them well, before handling the pastry.

Mix the flour, salt and sugar on the work surface and form into a heap, making a well in the center. Put in the butter cut into small pieces and the egg. Mix in exactly as for French pie pastry but more gently and quickly. As soon as the ingredients are smoothly blended and the dough is supple but still has a bread crumb texture, roll it into a ball, flatten slightly and wrap in a plastic bag. Refrigerate overnight.
Variation: an amandine pastry is enriched with about 1 cup ground almonds.

PUFF PASTRY
Pâte feuilletée

3½ cups flour
2½ teaspoons salt
scant 1 cup ice water
1 lb 2 oz (2¼ cups or 4½ sticks) cold butter
extra flour, for rolling

MAKES 2 LB 10 OZ
PREPARATION TIME: 1½ HOURS,
INCLUDING RESTS

Spread the flour into a ring on a cool work surface, and put the salt and the water in the center. Use one hand to mix the flour into the liquid, pushing it in from around the inside of the ring. Work quickly and do not knead. Use a spatula to scrape the mixture together into a ball. Slash it several times with a knife to let air penetrate; this helps to reduce elasticity. Refrigerate for 20 minutes. This mixture is known as the *détrempe* (something tempered).

Put the whole block of butter between two large sheets of plastic wrap. Bang it with the rolling pin, which will make it supple but still firm, and flatten it into a rectangle 1 inch thick.

Quickly, using your fist, flatten the *détrempe* into a rectangle just over twice as long and wide as the rectangle of butter. Peel one sheet of plastic off the butter, lift it up by the other sheet, turn it over and put it in the center of the *détrempe*. Peel off the other sheet. Then fold in the four corners of the *détrempe* so that they meet in the middle and cover the butter.

Flour the work surface lightly, and put the pastry on the floured area, leaving plenty of space for it to spread both away from you and toward you. Flour the rolling pin lightly and put it in the middle of the rectangle. Roll the far half of the pastry away from you with a single pass of the rolling pin to reduce the thickness of the pastry by half; then roll the near half toward you from the same starting point.

Fold one-third of the strip over from the end, so that it covers the central third. Then fold the other end of the strip over the top; the pastry is folded exactly into three.

Reflour the rolling pin and work surface. Give the folded pastry a quarter turn on the work surface and roll it out again, so that it is being stretched at right angles to the first stretching. Again, reduce to ¾ inch thick. Fold the strip into three as before, then cover with a damp cloth to prevent drying, and refrigerate for 20 minutes. The French term for this rolling and folding is *donner un tour*, "giving a turn."

After the pastry has rested, give it another two "turns" at right angles to each other, exactly as before. Refrigerate it for another 20 minutes, then give it a final two turns. The pastry is ready for immediate use. It now consists of 730 layers of *détrempe* enclosing 729 layers of butter!

CHOUX PASTRY
Pâte à choux

1 cup water
pinch of salt
1 teaspoon sugar (for a sweet pastry;
optional)
4 tablespoons butter
scant 1 cup flour
4 large eggs

MAKES ABOUT ¼ LB
PREPARATION TIME: 10 MINUTES
COOKING TIME: 5 MINUTES

Put the water in a saucepan and add the salt, sugar (if used) and the butter cut into little lumps. Bring to a boil. When the butter is melted, add the flour all at once. Keeping the pan on the heat, stir with a wooden spoon to make the flour take up the water. After a minute the mixture will begin to come away from the sides of the pan. Take it off the heat. Use the spatula to work in the eggs one by one until you have a smooth, sticky pastry. Now it is ready to be used.

FRUIT TARTS

The French make a bewildering variety of fruit tarts, of every conceivable form. The earliest fruit tarts were made from scraps of bread dough left over on baking day. Later, a yeast pastry was used, and from this was developed the large range of delicate pastries which the French use in tarts.

In Alsace, the tarts are often topped with a sweet custard and resemble a quiche: they are made with rhubarb, black currants and, most characteristically, damson plums. The pear tart with a frangipane topping is especially typical of Normandy, while the unusual sweet Swiss chard pie with rum and apples comes from Nice. The apple tarts à la mode, also known as tartes fines, are quite different in origin – a creation of recent years – although they keep the traditional catherine wheel of apple slices and jelly glaze of the older country tarts.

ALSACE PLUM TART
Tarte Alsacienne aux quetsches

about ¾ recipe quantity French pie
pastry (page 202)
2¼ lb damsons or other plums
½ cup brown sugar
½ teaspoon ground cinnamon

SERVES 6-8
PREPARATION TIME: 40 MINUTES (NOT
INCLUDING MAKING PASTRY)
COOKING TIME: 30 MINUTES

Preheat the oven to 425°F. Line the tart pan or dish with the pastry and refrigerate while preparing the plums.

Peel, halve and pit the plums. Combine the sugar and cinnamon and sprinkle half the mixture over the bottom of the pastry case. Arrange the plum halves over the bottom, rounded side down. Pack them tightly together and sprinkle with the rest of the cinnamon sugar.

Bake for 15 minutes, then turn down the temperature to 400°F and bake for another 15 minutes. Serve warm with whipped or pouring cream.

Variation: after baking for 15 minutes at 425°F, you can cover the fruit with a mixture made from 1 whole egg and 1 yolk, scant 1 cup crème fleurette and 3 tablespoons brown sugar beaten well together. Bake for another 15 to 20 minutes at 425°F. This makes a delectably creamier tart.

ALSACE PLUM TART ▶

PEAR TART "AMANDINE"
Tarte amandine aux poires

1 recipe quantity amandine pie pastry
(page 203)
1 can pears in syrup
generous ½ cup (1¼ sticks) softened
butter
3¼ cups sugar
2⅓ cups ground almonds
3 large eggs
2 tablespoons flour
1 tablespoon *eau-de-vie*★ Poire
Williams or other pear spirit
⅔ cup slivered almonds
confectioners' sugar, to finish

SERVES 6-8
PREPARATION TIME: 50 MINUTES +
I DAY
COOKING TIME: 30 MINUTES

This recipe was contributed by Dominique Leborgne, while he was chef-pâtissier for the Hôtel Intercontinental, Paris. He is now at the Willard Intercontinental in Washington, D.C.

Make the amandine pastry dough the day before. Roll it into a ball, wrap in plastic wrap and refrigerate.

The next day, drain the pears and cut into thin slices. Prepare the almond cream: work the butter until very soft and gradually cream in half the sugar and ground almonds. Then beat in the eggs one at a time. Then gradually cream in the rest of the sugar and ground almonds, and lastly the flour. Finally add the brandy. Preheat the oven to 400°F.

Roll out the dough or flatten it with your fingers to a thickness of about ¹⁄₁₀ inch and use to line a buttered tart pan or dish, pressing out the sides.

Arrange the pear slices on the bottom and cover with the almond cream. Scatter with almond slivers and bake for about 30 minutes. Serve sprinkled with confectioners' sugar sifted over the top.

SWISS CHARD PIE
Tourte de blettes

For the pastry:
2 large eggs
3½ cups flour
scant 1 cup (1¾ sticks) softened butter
¾ cup sugar
pinch of salt

For the filling:
a bunch of Swiss chard leaves (only
the green part)
½ cup grated Parmesan cheese
2 large eggs
⅔ cup raisins soaked in rum
1 cup pine nuts
scant ½ cup *marc*★
¾ cup firmly packed brown sugar
1 tablespoon olive oil
pinch of pepper
4 tart-sweet apples
a little confectioners' sugar

SERVES 6
PREPARATION TIME: IO MINUTES + I
HOUR WAITING + 20 MINUTES
COOKING TIME: APPROX. I5 MINUTES

Make the pastry, following the method on page 202.

To make the filling, roll up the Swiss chard leaves and cut them into strips. Rinse thoroughly, 2 or 3 times, and drain carefully. In a bowl combine all the other ingredients for the filling except for the apples. Add the Swiss chard and mix well. Preheat the oven to 425°F.

Divide the dough in two. Roll out one half and line a large, fairly deep baking pan with a removable base. Put in the filling, and pack well down. Cut the apples into thin slivers and arrange them on top of the Swiss chard mixture. Roll out the other piece of dough. Fold it into fourths. Use a spatula to place it on top of the pie. Unfold it and seal the edges with moistened fingertips. Prick with a fork and bake in the oven until golden brown. Leave to cool and sift over with confectioners' sugar.

STRAWBERRY TART
Croûte de fraises

½ lb ready-made frozen or homemade
puff pastry (see page 203)
a little beaten egg yolk (optional)
1 lb (about 3 cups) strawberries
3 tablespoons apricot jam
scant 1 cup *crème fleurette★*, chilled
1 tablespoon confectioners' sugar

SERVES 4
PREPARATION TIME: 25 MINUTES +
20-30 MINUTES TO REST
COOKING TIME: 25 MINUTES

PHOTOGRAPH PAGE 201

Roll out the pastry into a 10-inch square, and fold in a narrow strip around the edge to make a double-thickness rim. Place on a baking sheet. Leave to rest for 20 to 30 minutes. Meanwhile, preheat the oven to 400°F.

Bake the crust for 25 minutes until it is golden brown. A little egg yolk brushed on a few minutes before the end will give it a lovely shine. Leave to cool on a wire rack.

Hull the strawberries. Gently melt the apricot jam and sieve it. Whip the *crème fleurette*, which should be nice and chilled, with the confectioners' sugar until thick. Spread two-thirds of the apricot jam on the bottom of the pastry case and spread the cream on top of it, using a pastry bag or a spoon. Arrange the strawberries on top, and brush them lightly with the apricot jam.

INDIVIDUAL APPLE TARTS
Tartes à la mode

2 lb apples (for variety, see recipe
introduction right)
juice of 1 lemon
about ½ cup sugar
1 tablespoon butter
¼ teaspoon ground cinnamon
(optional)
1 teaspoon Calvados (optional)
1 lb 2 oz homemade puff pastry (see
page 203) or ready-made
¼ cup apricot jam

SERVES 6
PREPARATION TIME: 25 MINUTES
COOKING TIME: ABOUT 40 MINUTES

PHOTOGRAPH PAGE 200

Individual apple or pear tarts are a great favorite with top French chefs these days. A number of them, including Alain Senderens, Pierre Troisgros and Gaston Lenôtre, use puff pastry but in an unusual way. They are more interested in its lightness than its flakiness. They "flatten" it with a rolling pin, making it as thin as possible, never thicker than ¹/₁₀ inch, so that it does not rise.

They also slice the apples very thinly. Golden Delicious stay in neat slices but are rather bland, needing extra sugar and flavoring. The French would prefer Reinette or Boscop, for which Northern Spy, Baldwin or Granny Smith are excellent equivalents, and which disintegrate slightly but taste much better. The tarts are cooked in two stages: a very hot oven, then a moderately hot oven.

Peel and core the apples. Cut a quarter of them into neat, thin slices and toss in lemon juice with a little of the sugar. Slice the rest roughly and make into an apple sauce with the butter (reserve a little to grease the baking sheet), the rest of the sugar and, if you like, the cinnamon and/or Calvados.

Preheat the oven to 500°F of its maximum.

Roll out the pastry dough as thinly as possible without folding

it any more. Cut six rounds of dough, each about the size of a saucer. Lay them on a lightly greased baking sheet (unless it is very big, you will need to use two). Spread with the apple sauce. Arrange the apple slices on top, overlapping and in neat circles.

Bake for 15 minutes; then turn the oven down to 415°F and bake for a further 8 to 10 minutes. If you are using two baking sheets, exchange shelves when you turn the oven down. Warm the apricot jam, sieve it and use it to glaze the tops of the tartlets as soon as you take them from the oven. Serve at once.

CAKES

MADELEINES
Madeleines

2 eggs
¾ cup sugar
1 cup flour
½ cup (1 stick) butter
pinch of salt

MAKES 12 MADELEINES
PREPARATION TIME: 15 MINUTES
COOKING TIME: 10-15 MINUTES

Thanks to Marcel Proust, madeleines are are as much part of French literature as cooking. They do not have to be made in the familiar shell-shape molds; in fact in the last century, there were all kinds of differently shaped madeleines.

Prepare these just before serving. Preheat the oven to 450°F. Beat together the eggs and sugar. When the mixture becomes white add the flour, the melted butter and the salt. Pour the mixture into floured and buttered madeleine molds (or muffin tins) and bake for 10-15 minutes.

QUICK LIME AND YOGURT CAKE
Gâteau léger au citron vert

grated zest of 1 lime
1 tablespoon white rum (optional)
2 teaspoons baking powder
1 large egg
scant ¾ cup plain yogurt
1¼ cups sugar
2½ cups flour
⅓ cup peanut oil
⅓ cup sweet white wine

SERVES 6
PREPARATION TIME: 10 MINUTES
COOKING TIME: 30 MINUTES

An ingeniously simple, economical and tasty lime cake that can be made in a trice with an electric mixer. You can substitute orange or grapefruit for the lime. The French would serve this with jam, fruit purée, fromage blanc★ or whipped cream.

Preheat the oven to 425°F. Mix all the ingredients in a blender, then pour the mixture into a 10-inch layer-cake pan. Bake for 30 minutes. Unmold onto a wire rack and leave to cool.

YEASTED APRICOT CAKE
Pastis aux abricots

3½ cups flour
2 packages active dry yeast
scant ½ cup lukewarm water
scant ½ cup lukewarm milk
1¼ cups sugar
4 large eggs
pinch of salt
grated zest of 1 lemon★
2 tablespoons orange flower water
1⅔ cups (1¼ sticks) softened butter
1 lb 2 oz pitted apricots
a little milk or beaten egg

SERVES 6
PREPARATION TIME: 40 MINUTES +
2 HOURS 10 MINUTES TO RISE
COOKING TIME: ABOUT 40 MINUTES

"Pastis" here has nothing to do with the aniseed flavored drink of that name. A pastis is also the name given to a yeasted cake, a specialty of southwestern France.

Mix together the flour, yeast, water and milk in a bowl. Knead for 5 minutes, then add the sugar, eggs, salt, lemon zest, orange flower water and butter. Mix thoroughly and knead for 15 minutes until the dough comes away from the sides of the bowl and makes a ball. Cover with a cloth, and leave to rise for 1 hour in a warm place.

Knead the dough for a further 5 minutes, and put half in a buttered layer-cake pan. Arrange half the apricots on top. Cover with the rest of the dough and press the remaining apricots into it. Leave the dough to rise for another 1¼ hours in a warm room. Preheat the oven to 425°F. Brush the surface with a little milk or beaten egg and bake for about 40 minutes.

YEASTED APRICOT CAKE ▶

GÂTEAUX

An elaborate gâteau forms an impressive end to a special French dinner. Actually the two recipes here only look elaborate. They are made up by combining several fairly simple elements, none of which is beyond the ability of an average cook.

GENOISE SPONGE CAKE
Genoise

4 extra large eggs
heaped ½ cup sugar
scant ⅔ cup flour, or ½ cup flour and
2½ tablespoons potato starch
4 tablespoons butter for the cake pan

MAKES A 10-INCH DIAMETER CAKE
PREPARATION TIME: 15 MINUTES +
TIME TO COOL
COOKING TIME: 30 MINUTES

Whisk the eggs and sugar in a bowl over, but not touching, a pan of boiling water until the mixture becomes white and frothy. Leave to cool.

Preheat the oven to 375°F. Sift the flours into the egg mixture and fold in gently. Pour into a buttered and floured 10-inch cake pan, and bake for 30 minutes.

To tell if the sponge cake is cooked, press it gently. If it is ready, it will "sing" – make a whispering sound.
Variation: you can replace 2½ tablespoons of the flour with the same amount of ground almonds.

RHINEGOLD LAYER CAKE
L'or du Rhin

1 cup flour
5 tablespoons cornstarch
½ cup cocoa powder
5 tablespoons butter
8 large eggs
1¼ cup sugar
2 tablespoons brandy
sheets of gold leaf (optional
decoration)

For the *ganache:*
½ lb (8 squares) semisweet chocolate
¼ cup milk
3½ tablespoons *crème fraîche*★
4½ tablespoons butter

SERVES 8
PREPARATION TIME: 30 MINUTES +
TIME TO COOL
COOKING TIME: 40 MINUTES

There are only two essential elements to this sleek cake. Neither is difficult to make and both are useful separately. The cake is a chocolate genoise dampened with brandy; the filling is ganache, a basic cream used in many different desserts, which is also the perfect truffle mixture. It is best to use semisweet chocolate rather than unsweetened chocolate, as it is then unnecessary to sweeten the ganache. The theatrical, almost decadent decoration is gold leaf, which really is edible and can be bought at Indian grocers or shops selling artists' materials. This recipe is from Paul Mauduit, a celebrated Parisian pâtissier.

Preheat the oven to 350°F. Sift the flour, cornstarch and cocoa powder into a bowl. Gently melt the butter, taking care not to cook it.

Place a bowl over, but not touching, a pan of warm water at blood heat or just above, and whisk the eggs and sugar together until the mixture is frothy and slightly warm. Remove from the heat, and continue whisking while the mixture cools. Then carefully combine the melted butter with the flour mixture, and fold this into the egg mixture.

Pour into a lightly buttered and floured 11 by 7 inch cake pan and bake for 40 minutes. Unmold out onto a wire rack and leave to cool.

Meanwhile, make the *ganache*. Break up the chocolate into large chunks and put in a bowl. Separately scald the milk and the *crème fraîche*, then mix them and pour them over the chocolate, whisking to make a smooth mixture. Beat the butter until creamy, and combine with the chocolate mixture once cooled.

Slice the cooled sponge cake into 4 layers and moisten with the brandy. Spread the *ganache* between the layers, and finish by pouring *ganache* over the top.

Over this smooth surface, you can lay sheets of gold leaf. Serve at a cool room temperature.

RHINEGOLD LAYER CAKE ▶

ICED CHESTNUT GÂTEAU WITH BUTTERFLY TUILES
Gâteau glacé des marrons avec tuiles papillons

1 *Genoise* sponge cake, at least 10 inches in diameter, homemade (see page 210) or purchased
⅔ cup *crème fleurette*★
2 envelopes unflavored gelatin
13 oz canned sweetened chestnut purée★
6 *marrons glacés*
1 tablespoon walnut liqueur★

For the *crème anglaise:*
scant ½ cup milk
3 egg yolks from large eggs
1 tablespoon sugar

For the *sauce anglaise:*
scant ½ cup milk
5 egg yolks from large eggs
scant ¾ cup sugar
1 vanilla bean, or a few drops of pure vanilla extract
2 tablespoons walnut liqueur★
scant 1 cup *crème fleurette*★

Decoration:
marrons glacés
a few walnut halves
a few split almonds
sugar to make caramel and spun sugar
butterfly cookies (see opposite)
silver balls

SERVES 6
PREPARATION TIME: 1 HOUR + SEVERAL PAUSES TO REFRIGERATE
COOKING TIME: ABOUT 20 MINUTES

PHOTOGRAPH ON OPPOSITE PAGE

This recipe is from the Hôtel de Crillon, Paris. The cake should be prepared 12 hours in advance. Sauce anglaise is a lighter version of crème anglaise, *and is made in the same way (see page 178).*

Use a round, deep nonstick cake pan, 10 inches in diameter, or of equivalent size in another shape. Cut a round out of the sponge cake the same diameter as the pan to fit into this exactly, and a good ½ inch thick. Put the *crème fleurette* into a bowl and refrigerate.

Put some water and ice cubes in a large bowl. Prepare a *crème anglaise* (see page 178). Put the bowl of *crème anglaise* in the bowl of iced water and turn for a few seconds to cool.

Dissolve the gelatin in a minimum of water. Stir the gelatin into the cooled *crème anglaise*. Add the chestnut purée, stir again and refrigerate.

Take the *crème fleurette* out of the refrigerator, and whip it with a crushed ice cube until it is stiff. Take out the chestnut cream, which should have begun to set. Whisk vigorously, then carefully fold in the whipped *crème fleurette*.

Swirl some water around in the cake pan and tip it out, leaving a few beads of moisture. Pour in half the chestnut mixture. Put in a few *marrons glacés*, and fill to within ¼ inch of the rim with the rest of the chestnut mixture. Tap

the pan on the work surface to make it settle.

Pour the walnut liqueur over the sponge round and place it on top of the mixture. Cover with wax paper, and refrigerate.

Prepare a *sauce anglaise* (in the same way as a *crème anglaise*, page 178), adding the split vanilla bean (remove it later) or vanilla extract. Remove the sauce from the heat, strain it and add the walnut liqueur. Mix, then add the *crème fleurette*, stirring well to make a smooth blend. Refrigerate.

Unmold the cake just before serving and decorate with a circle of *marrons glacés*, alternating with walnuts and almonds dipped in caramel, butterfly cookies (see opposite) and silver balls.

If you really want to go to town and you are confident playing with a sugar thermometer and caramel, you can also decorate it with golden thread made from spun sugar. To make caramel, heat sugar with a little water until it turns pale gold. To make spun sugar, cook the sugar in the same way but only to the soft crack stage (280°F on a candy thermometer). Turn it out onto an oiled marble slab, fold it over and over with a knife until it becomes viscous, oil your hands and pull it out into thin strands. Good luck!

CHOUX PUFFS
Choux

Choux puffs tend to come in one of two sizes: large, the kind in which you can almost bury your face, or small, those neat mouthfuls usually known as profiteroles in English.
Choux pastry triples or quadruples its size when it is cooked. So for small puffs, pipe or spoon small

nuts of paste onto buttered baking sheets for large ones allow a golf ball per puff. Bake in a preheated oven at 420°F until firm and golden – about 20 minutes for small or 30 minutes for larger ones. Turn over the puffs; return to the oven briefly to cook the underside. Cool, cut open and

scrape out any uncooked pastry with a teaspoon.

Fillings may be *crème Chantilly* or *crème pâtissière* – plain or flavored (see page 179). The puffs may be served with sifted confectioners' sugar, caramel or glacé icing.

BUTTERFLY COOKIES
Tuiles papillons

2 tablespoons butter
thinly pared zest of 1 orange
1 cup sugar
pinch of salt
⅔ cup sifted flour
1 large egg + 4 whites from large eggs
1⅓ cups slivered almonds
dash of orange juice, Grand Marnier
or other orange liqueur (optional)

MAKES 24 SMALL OR 6 LARGE COOKIES
PREPARATION TIME: 3 MINUTES + 1
HOUR WAITING
COOKING TIME: 7-9 MINUTES

Leave the butter to soften at room temperature, but do not let it melt. Cut the orange zest into strips no thicker than ½₅ inch and blanch briefly in boiling water. Drain and reserve.

Cream the butter with a wooden spoon until smooth. Add first the sugar then the pinch of salt. Mix well. Add the flour, the whole egg and then the whites. Beat thoroughly to obtain a smooth blend. Add the orange zest then the almonds and, if you like, a dash of orange juice or Grand Marnier liqueur to flavor. Mix carefully. Let the mixture stand for 1 hour at room temperature.

Preheat the oven to 425°F. Drop a spoonful of the mixture for small butterflies, or a small ladleful for large ones, onto a buttered baking sheet. Use a fork dipped into cold water to spread the mixture to a 2½-inch, or a 5-inch, round. Make rounds in staggered rows, depending size, and leave a little space between each round, as they spread during cooking.

Put in the oven and bake for 7 to 9 minutes, until they turn golden brown. When you take them out of the oven, slide a spatula underneath each one to remove it from the baking sheet, hold it in the center and twist to make a butterfly shape.

ICED CHESTNUT GÂTEAU

MERINGUES

8 chilled egg whites from large eggs
1¼ cups superfine (powdered) sugar
2 cups confectioners' sugar

MAKES ABOUT 15 LARGE MERINGUES
PREPARATION TIME: 15 MINUTES
COOKING TIME: 2 HOURS

A foolproof recipe from Yves Thuriés of Gaillac, winner in 1976 of the French award for the best pastry, dessert and sherbet chef. All pastry chefs agree that whites from eggs that are not quite new-laid are best. The eggs should be refrigerated for a full day before using them. Such is the fame of these meringues that Thuriés' restaurant in Cordes is named after them.

Preheat the oven to 225°F.

Beat the whites at medium, then at high speed. When they begin to stiffen, gradually add the superfine sugar and continue beating until stiff. Sift in the confectioners' sugar, and fold in with a spatula.

Use two spoons, or a pastry bag and tube, to make little heaps of meringue on a buttered and floured baking sheet. Dry out in a very low oven for 2 hours.

For colored meringues, add a few drops of food coloring or coffee extract.

AUVERGNE ORANGE BRIOCHE
Fouace d'Emilienne

2 packages active dry yeast
scant ½ cup lukewarm sugary water
3½ cups bread flour
¾ cup sugar
pinch of salt
4 large eggs
1⅔ (1¼ sticks) butter
2 tablespoons orange flower water
a little candied lemon zest
1 egg white from a large egg
a little coarse sugar

SERVES 6
PREPARATION TIME: 45 MINUTES +
OVERNIGHT
COOKING TIME: 35 MINUTES

Brioche dough is used as a basis of hundreds of French recipes. It is made into variously flavored sweet cakes, some of them flat rather than "brioche-shaped," as well as being used to enclose savory fillings. A specialty of Lyon is saucisson en brioche, *a sort of sublime pig-in-a-blanket.*

Fouace is a specialty from the Auvergne region. This version is quite like what is known as gâche *in the Vendée region: a sweet fruit-flavored bread.*

Dissolve the yeast in the sugary water. Add about ¾ cup flour and leave to rise in a warm place.

Combine the rest of the flour with the sugar, salt, eggs, melted butter, orange flower water and candied lemon rind. Add the yeast mixture. Knead the dough for about 30 minutes, then leave overnight in a warm place.

Preheat the oven to 425°F. Punch down the dough, then make into a loaf shape on a floured baking sheet; and cut slits on the top. Brush the surface with a whisked egg white, and sprinkle with coarse sugar. Bake for about 35 minutes.

BRIOCHE WITH APPLE AND PEAR FILLING
Brioche Dauphinoise aux pommes et poires

2 packages active dry yeast
scant ½ cup lukewarm milk
¾ cup sugar
1¾ cups flour
2 large eggs
pinch of salt
¾ cup (1½ sticks) butter
3 tablespoons *crème fraîche**
4 large apples
1 teaspoon ground cinnamon
(optional)
4 ripe pears

SERVES 4
PREPARATION TIME: 30 MINUTES +
3¾ HOURS WAIT
COOKING TIME: ABOUT 1¼ HOURS

In the fall this cake can also be made with quinces, either on their own or added to the apples and pears.

Dissolve the yeast in the warm milk with ¼ cup sugar. Leave to rise in a warm place for 15 minutes.

Make the dough from the flour, 1 egg, the salt, 5 tablespoons softened butter, the *crème fraîche* and the yeast mixture. Make into a ball and leave to rise in a warm place for about 3 hours.

Meanwhile, peel and quarter the apples. Sauté them in a skillet with the remaining butter.

Sprinkle with the rest of the sugar and cinnamon, and add the peeled and quartered pears. Leave to cool. Once the dough has risen, punch it down. Roll out two-thirds of it and put it in a buttered layer-cake pan; allowing it to hang over the rim a little. Pour the apples and pears into the center. Roll out the rest of the dough and place it over the top. Seal the edges. Leave to rise in a warm place for 30 minutes.

Preheat the oven to 400°F. Brush with beaten egg and bake for 1 hour.

FRENCH GINGERBREAD
Pain d'épices ménagère

4 cups wholewheat flour or 3 cups whole wheat flour and 1½ cups rye flour
1½ cups clear acacia honey
4 teaspoons ground aniseed
1 teaspoon ground cinnamon
½ teaspoon ground cloves
1 tablespoon baking powder
⅓ cup roughly chopped almonds
1 tablespoon chopped candied orange or lemon peel

2 tablespoons slightly salted butter
2 tablespoons sweetened condensed milk, or corn syrup diluted until runny

SERVES 8
PREPARATION TIME: 25 MINUTES + 1¼
HOURS TO REST
COOKING TIME: ABOUT 40 MINUTES

French pain d'épices, *like the gingerbreads of many European countries, has its roots in the distant past. In the Middle Ages, all gingerbread was made with stale bread rather than with flour. It was heavy, hard and rich. The only place where such a gingerbread survives is Siena, where it is called* panforte *("strong bread"). Here is a recipe for a lighter gingerbread more suited to modern tastes.* ▷

◁ Put the flour(s) in a mixing bowl. Bring the honey to a boil in a saucepan and skim it. Take it off the heat and pour it into the flour, stirring with a wooden spoon until the mixture is a smooth, rather stiff dough that you can lift out of the bowl in a single lump. Form the dough into a ball, cover with a cloth and leave to rest in a cool place for at least 1 hour.

Mix the spices in a small bowl. Make a hole in the dough, tip in the baking powder and knead hard to combine it. Re-form the dough into a ball. Press it down lightly and sprinkle with spices. Knead again thoroughly to distribute them equally, then knead in the almonds and candied peel. Form the dough into a ball again and leave it to rest while you preheat the oven to 425°F and thickly butter a large loaf pan, taking care to cover the corners. Put the pan in a cool place for 5 minutes to stiffen the butter.

Spread the dough into the pan and smooth the surface flat. Bake for 30 minutes.

Turn off the oven. Take out the gingerbread and brush the top with condensed milk or diluted syrup, then put it back in the oven for 4 minutes. Then brush it again and give it a final 4 minutes in the oven. Let it cool slightly before turning it out onto a wire cake rack.

A SELECTION OF FRENCH BREADS

DRINKS

CIDER AND CALVADOS
COCKTAIL (see page 218)

SPARKLING WHITE WINE
MARQUISE (see page 218)

SPARKLING WHITE WINE *MARQUISE*
Marquise au vin blanc pétillant

2 kiwi fruit
¼ lb (about 1 cup) red fruit (such as raspberries or red currants)
slices of lime
½ cup sugar cane syrup★
dash of Angostura bitters
juice of 1 lemon
1 bottle (750 ml) sparkling white wine

MAKES SCANT I QUART
PREPARATION TIME: IO MINUTES + I HOUR CHILLING

Peel and dice the kiwi fruit. Mix all the ingredients, except the wine, and refrigerate for at least 1 hour. Add the chilled wine just before serving in large wine glasses.

For this you could choose any sparkling wine, such as a Crémant de Bourgogne or Loire, for example. Make sure it is well chilled first.

CIDER AND CALVADOS COCKTAIL
Cocktail de cidre et Calvados

4 cups (1 quart) dry hard cider
¾ cup Calvados
¼ cup of raspberry (or strawberry or black currant) liqueur
slices of orange
ice cubes

MAKES ABOUT 5 CUPS
PREPARATION TIME: IO MINUTES

Cider is a popular drink in Normandy and Brittany. It is also distilled into Calvados, a delightful but rather hangover-inducing spirit. Farmers are allowed to distill a limited quantity themselves, and to sell it. Use only a good hard dry, still cider for cooking.

Combine all the ingredients and serve chilled in frosted tall glasses, with an ice cube and a slice of orange in each.

RED FRUIT PUNCH
Punch aux fruits rouges

1¾ lb mixed red fruit (cherries, strawberries, raspberries, red currants)
3 cups dark rum
⅔ cup lemon juice
1¼ cups sugar cane syrup★
4 cups (1 quart) soda water

MAKES ABOUT 2½ QUARTS
PREPARATION TIME: 5 MINUTES + 2 HOURS MARINATING

Both these punches were inspired by recipes from a book on cocktails and alcoholic drinks by Ninette Lyon.

Clean all the fruit and put it in a bowl. Pour on the rum, lemon juice and syrup, and leave to marinate in a cool place for 2 hours.

Before serving, put a large block of ice in the punch bowl and pour in the punch. Add the soda water. Ladle into tall glasses and drink with straws.

ISLAND PUNCH
Punch des îles

1¼ cups white rum
4 cups (1 quart) fruit juice
sugar cane syrup, to taste
4-5 tablespoons grenadine syrup
cubes of fruit to match the fruit juice
banana slices

MAKES ABOUT 1½ QUARTS
PREPARATION TIME: 5 MINUTES + 2 HOURS CHILLING

In the Caribbean, no festive occasion is complete without a punch presented in the most attractive way. To make Caribbean-style punch, you will need a young white sugar-cane rum, dry but full-flavored. Serve a large bowl of fruit juice or lemonade and some extra ice cubes beside the punch for those who don't want to drink it too strong.

Mix the liquid ingredients. Chill for several hours and serve in a bowl with the fruit. Ladle into tall glasses (but not too big, as the drink is quite strong) and serve with straws.

The fruit juice can be pineapple, grapefruit, lemon or lime.

MIMOSA COCKTAIL

REAL LEMONADE

FRESH MINT COOLER

BLUE GEM
Clip bleu

5 parts grapefruit juice
4 parts Cointreau
1 part lime-flavored Perrier
dash blue Curaçao
ice cubes

PREPARATION TIME: 10 MINUTES

Put all the ingredients in a cocktail shaker and mix. Serve in cocktail glasses.

MIMOSA COCKTAIL
Le mimosa

juice of 1 orange
1 teaspoon Campari
½ cup dry sparkling white wine

MAKES ¾ CUP
PREPARATION TIME: 5 MINUTES

Pour the orange juice into a white wine glass and add the Campari. Top up with the wine.

REAL LEMONADE
Agua-limon

2¼ lb lemons
8 cups (2 quarts) water
2½ cups sugar
few drops of vanilla extract

MAKES ABOUT 3 QUARTS
PREPARATION TIME: 30 MINUTES + 12
HOURS MARINATING
PHOTOGRAPH PAGE 216

Squeeze the juice from the lemons and chop the rind. Marinate the chopped rind overnight in half the water. Strain.
  Mix the sugar with the rest of the water, and add the vanilla, the lemon juice, and the soaking water. Serve in large glasses.

FRESH MINT COOLER
Menthe fraîche

¾ cup leaves of mint
6 sugar cubes
lemon slices

MAKES SCANT 1 QUART
PREPARATION TIME: 10 MINUTES + 3
HOURS CHILLING

Put the mint leaves in a teapot and pour on boiling water. Add the sugar and lemon slices. Chill. Strain and serve very cold in tall glasses.

WATERMELON COOLER
Boisson à la pastèque

½ watermelon
few drops of lemon juice
fresh leaves of mint

MAKES ABOUT 2½-4 CUPS
PREPARATION TIME: 10 MINUTES + 30
MINUTES CHILLING

Remove the seeds from the watermelon, discard the rind and cut the flesh into chunks. Put it in the blender with the lemon juice and a few mint leaves and blend until smooth. Serve chilled in tall glasses.

INDEX

NB Asterisks (*) in the recipes refer readers to The French Larder

INDEX

NB Asterisks (*) in the recipes refer readers to The French Larder

NB Asterisks (*) in the recipes refer readers to The French Larder

BIBLIOGRAPHY

Fernande Allard, *La Cuisine de Chez Allard*, Nicholas de Rabaudy, J.C. Lattès, Paris, 1982

Fettouma Benkirane, *La Nouvelle Cuisine Marocaine*, J.P. Taillandier/Sochepress, Paris, 1986

Louise Bertholle, *Secrets of the Great French Restaurants*, Weidenfeld and Nicolson, 1974; Papermac 1982, 1987; first published as *Les Recettes Secrètes des Meilleurs Restaurants de France*, Guide Michelin Paris, 1985; reissued Guide Michelin, 1985

Adrienne Biasin, *La Table d'Adrienne*, (Olivier) Orban, Paris, 1983

Paul Bocuse, *Paul Bocuse in Your Kitchen*, Pantheon, New York, 1982; published as *New Cuisine of Paul Bocuse*, Grafton, London, 1985; first published as *Bocuse dans vôtre Cuisine*, Flammarion, Paris, 1982

André Bonnard, *Cuisine Rustique de Languedoc*, Morell, Paris, 1970

Anne-Marie Carrière, *200 Recettes des meilleures Cuisinières de France*, Albin Michel, Paris, 1977

James de Coquet, *Lettre aux gourmets, aux gourmands, aux gastronomes*, J-C Simoën, Paris, 1978

Robert J. Courtine, *Le Grand Jeu de la Cuisine*, Larousse, Paris, 1980

Cuisine du Terroir: The Lost Domain of French Cooking, ed. by Sue Lorman and Simon Mallet, Blenheim House Books, London, 1987; first published as *Les Recettes du Terroir, les maîtres Cuisiniers de France*, Robert Laffont, Paris, 1984

Alan and Jane Davidson (eds.), *Dumas on Food: selections from 'Le grand dictionnaire de cuisine'*, Michael Joseph, London, 1979; O.U.P. 1987

Fredy Giradet, *Cuisine Spontanée*, Macmillan, London, 1985; Papermac, London, 1986; published as *The Cuisine of Fredy Giradet*, Morrow, New York, 1985, first published as *La Cuisine Spontanée*, Robert Laffont, Paris, 1982

Michel Guérard, *Cuisine Gourmande*, ed. by Caroline Conran, Papermac, London, 1978; Morrow, New York, 1979; first published as *La Cuisine Gourmande*, Robert Laffont, Paris, 1970
Cuisine Minceur, ed. by Caroline Conran, Pan, London, 1977; Morrow, New York, 1986; first published as *La Grande Cuisine Minceur*, Robert Laffont, Paris, 1976

Zette Guinaudeau Franc, *Les Secrètes des Cuisines en Terre Marocaine*, Jean-Pierre Taillandier, Paris, 1981

Jacques Manière, *Le Grand Livre de la Cuisine à Vapeur*, DeNoël, Paris, 1985

Jacques Médecin, *La Cuisine du Comté de Nice*, Juillard, Paris, 1981

Paul et Jean Minchelli, *Le Duc, toute la cuisine de la mer*, Olivier Orsan, Paris, 1986

Vivianne et Nina Moryoussef, *La Cuisine Marocaine*, J.P. Taillandier/Sochepress, Paris, 1983

Raymond Oliver, *Cuisine pour mes amis*, Albin Michel, Paris, 1976

R.O. and Dr. Michel Chast, *Les Régimes Gourmands*, Albin Michel, Paris, 1978

Ferdinand Point, *Ma Gastronomie*, Flammarion, Paris, 1974 and 1987; Lyceum-Wilton, Connecticut, 1979

Edouard de Pomiane, *Cooking in Ten Minutes*, Faber, London, 1985; also published as *La Cuisine en dix minutes*, Calmann-Levy, Paris, 1969 *Cooking with Pomiane*, ed. by Peggie Benton, Cassirer, Oxford, 1962 and Faber & Faber 1969

Alain Senderens, *La Grande Cuisine à petits prix*, Robert Laffont, Paris, 1984 *The Cuisine of Alain Senderens*, ed. by Caroline Conran, Macmillan, London, 1982; published as *The Three-Star Recipes of Alain Senderens*, Morrow, New York, 1982; first published as *La Cuisine Réussie, les 200 meilleures recettes de l'Archestrate*, Jean-Claude Lattès, Paris, 1981

Raymond Thuillier, *La Cuisine de Baumanière*, Stock, Paris, 1980

Yves Thuries, *Le Livre des Recettes d'un Compagnon du Tour de France*, Sociète Édital, Paris, 1972-86 (seven volumes)

Jean et Paul Troisgros, *The Nouvelle Cuisine of Jean and Paul Troisgros*, Morrow, New York, 1978; paperback, Morrow, New York, 1985; Macmillan, London, 1980; Papermac, London, 1982; first published as *Cuisiniers à Roanne: Les Recettes Originales de Jean et Paul Troisgros*, Robert Laffont, Paris, 1977
Les Petits Plats de Troisgros, Robert Laffont, Paris, 1985

Celine Vance and R.J. Courtine, *Les Grands Recettes du Temps Jadis*, Bordas, Paris, 1979

Pierre Vedel, *Recettes pour les Amis*, Robert Laffont, Paris, 1984

F. Werner, *Grandes Cuisines Rhônes Alpes*, Glénat, Paris, 1985 (A collection of recipes from chefs such as Troisgros, Bocuse etc.)

PHOTOGRAPHIC ACKNOWLEDGMENTS

1 Marcel Duffas
2 Jean-Louis Bloch-Lainé
4 Claude Ferrand
5 Jean-Louis Bloch-Lainé
8-11 Marcel Duffas
12 Jean-Louis Bloch-Lainé
13 Hervé Amiard
14 Jean-Louis Bloch-Lainé
16-19 Peter Knaup
23 Jean-Louis Bloch-Lainé
24 André Martin
27-28 Jean-Louis Bloch-Lainé
29-36 André Martin
38 Peter Knaup
41 André Martin
42 Claude Ferrand
43 Jean-Louis Bloch-Lainé
44-46 Sacha
49 Jean-Louis Bloch-Lainé
51 Claude Ferrand
53 Peter Knaup
54 Sacha
56 Alex Mclean
58 Marcel Duffas
60-61 André Martin

65-69 Jean-Louis Bloch-Lainé
71 Marcel Duffas
73 André Martin
74 Beni Truttman
76 Jean-Louis Bloch-Lainé
77-79 Alex Mclean
80 Peter Knaup
83-85 Jean-Louis Bloch-Lainé
87 André Martin
88 Claude Ferrand
91 Beni Truttmann
92 André Martin
93 Marcel Duffas
96 Sacha
97 Jean-Louis Bloch-Lainé
98 Claude Ferrand
99-101 Marcel Duffas
102-113 Jean-Louis Bloch-Lainé
114 André Martin
117 Claude Ferrand
120 André Martin
121 Jean-Louis Bloch-Lainé
122 Claude Ferrand
125 André Martin
126 Marcel Duffas

127 André Martin
130 Peter Knaup
131-131 Jean-Louis Bloch-Lainé
133 Sacha
134 Peter Knaup
136 Marcel Duffas
139 André Martin
143 Peter Knaup
145 Jean-Louis Bloch-Lainé
148 Claude Ferrand
150 Jean-Louis Bloch-Lainé
151 Guillaume Lieurey
153-154 Jean-Louis Bloch-Lainé
156 Claude Ferrand
157 Jean-Louis Bloch-Lainé
158 Hervé Amiard
159 André Martin
151 Jean-Louis Bloch-Lainé
165 Maurice Smith
166 Claude Ferrand
167 André Martin
169 Hervé Amiard
171 Jean-Louis Bloch-Lainé
172 Christian Moser
173 Daniel Fauchon

174 Christian Moser
175-176 Jean-Louis Bloch-Lainé
177 Claude Ferrand
180 Daniel Fauchon
181 André Martin
183-184 Claude Ferrand
185 *above* Michel Certain
185 *below* Claude Ferrand
186 Michel Certain
187 Claude Ferrand
188 André Martin
189-190 Marcel Duffas
193-195 Jean-Louis Bloch-Lainé
197 Peter Knapp
200-205 André Martin
206 Marcel Duffas
207 André Martin
208 Peter Knapp
209 Sacha
211-213 Jean-Louis Bloch-Lainé
215 Marcel Duffas
216 D. Macaire
217 André Martin
219 D. Macaire

All photographs have been styled by Jacqueline Saulnier except the following:
Nathalie Le Foll 4, 8-11, 16, 19, 42, 44, 46, 51, 54, 56, 77, 79, 88, 96, 101, 117, 122, 126, 130, 133, 136, 156, 165, 167, 181, 185-190, 206, 208, 209, 215, 216, 219. Marianne Comolli 180.